ALL FOR ONE: TERRORISM, NATO AND THE UNITED STATES

For those lost in New York, Pennsylvania and Washington

All for One: Terrorism, NATO and the United States

TOM LANSFORD
The University of Southern Mississippi
Gulf Coast

Ashgate

© Tom Lansford 2002

Published by
Ashgate Publishing Limited
Gower House
Croft Road
Aldershot
Hamphire GU11 3HR
England

Ashgate Publishing Company
131 Main Street
Burlington, VT 05401-5600 USA

Ashgate website: http://www.ashgate.com

British Library Cataloguing in Publication Data
Lansford, Tom
   All for one : terrorism, NATO and the United States
   1. North Atlantic Treaty Organization 2. Terrorism
   3. Terrorism - Prevention - International cooperation
   4. Afghanistan - History - 1989 -
   I. Title
   355'.031

Library of Congress Cataloging-in-Publication Data
Lansford, Tom, 1967-
   All for one: terrorism, NATO and the United States / Tom Lansford.
     p. cm.
   Includes bibliographical references and index.
   ISBN 0-7546-3045-5
   1. North Atlantic Treaty Organization--Military policy. 2. September 11 Terrorist
Attacks, 2001. 3. War on Terrorism, 2001- I. Title.

D860 .L355 2002
973.931--dc21   2002024893

ISBN 0 7546 3045 5
Printed and bound by Athenaeum Press, Ltd.,
Gateshead, Tyne & Wear.

Contents

List of Abbreviations

ABM	Anti-Ballistic Missile
ARRC	Allied Rapid Reaction Corps
CFSP	Common Foreign and Security Policy
CJTF	Combined and Joint Task Force
CSCE	Conference for Security and Cooperation in Europe
DCI	Defense Capabilities Initiative
DGP	Senior Defense Group on Proliferation
DTSI	Defense Trade Security Initiative
EADRCC	Euro-Atlantic Disaster Response Coordination Center
EAPC	Euro-Atlantic Partnership Council
ECSC	European Coal and Steel Community
EDC	European Defense Community
ERRF	European Rapid Reaction Force
ESDI/ESDP	European Security and Defense Identity/Policy
EU	European Union
IFOR	Implementation Force
ITAR	International Trafficking In Arms
KFOR	Kosovo Force
KLA	Kosovo Liberation Army
MAP	Membership Action Plan
MCG	Mediterranean Cooperation Group
NAC	North Atlantic Council
NACC	North Atlantic Cooperation Council
NAEWF	NATO Airborne Early Warning Force
NMD	National Missile Defense
OSCE	Organization for Security and Cooperation in Europe
PARP	Planning and Review Process
PfP	Partnership-for-Peace
PJC	Permanent Joint Council
RRF	Rapid Reaction Facility
SACEUR	Supreme Allied Commander, Europe
SACLANT	Supreme Allied Commander, Atlantic
SFOR	Stabilization Force
SGP	Senior Politico-Military Group on Proliferation
SHAPE	Supreme Headquarters Allied Powers Europe
STANAVFORLANT	Standing Naval Force Atlantic
STANAVFORMED	Standing Naval Force Mediterranean
WEU	Western European Union
WMD	Weapons of Mass Destruction
WTC	World Trade Center
WTO	World Trade Organization

Acknowledgments

This work would not have been possible without the assistance and support of a variety of people. I would like to thank Ms. Kirstin Howgate for her role in bringing this project to fruition. I would also like to thank Ms. Maureen Mansell-Ward and Ms. Amber Parker for their aid in editing the manuscript. My friend and colleague Patrick Hayden provided valuable insights and assistance in the book's preparation. I wish to thank Mr. James D. Buffett for help in finishing the manuscript. I am also grateful to Dr. Denise von Herrmann for her support during the completion of the book. This project would not have been possible without assistance from NATO's Public Affairs Office and I express my gratitude to the staff. I also want to thank Kyle Bromwell, Drew Lucas and Mike Pappas. Finally, as always, I would like to thank Amber for putting up with me.

Introduction

The First Test of
Article 5

September 11

On 11 September 2001 at 8:45 am (Eastern Standard Time), hijacked American Airlines Flight 11 flew directly into the north tower of the World Trade Center (WTC) complex in New York City. The impact created an enormous explosion and set the skyscraper on fire. Approximately 18 minutes later, a second airliner, United Flight 175, crashed into the south tower of the complex. At 9:43, a third jet flew into the Pentagon, outside of Washington, D.C. In little over an hour, the south tower of the WTC collapsed, followed shortly by the north tower. Meanwhile, after they realized the motives of their captors, a group of passengers aboard a fourth hijacked airliner, United Airlines Flight 83, launched an attack against their hijackers which led the flight to crash in Somerset County, Pennsylvania. The crash occurred well short of its suspected target in Washington, D.C.

The events of 11 September, dramatically altered the notions of security in the United States and most of the world. The attacks led the administration of George W. Bush to reconfigure the nation's security policies and recalculate relations with a number of nations. Nationstates such as Pakistan which had U.S.-sponsored sanctions in place against them and nations such as Russia which had strained relations with the United States found themselves transformed into vital partners in the global campaign against terrorism.[1] In addition, policies which limited American arms sales and transfers were also abrogated in order to provide the administration with the tools to provide rewards for cooperation with the United States.

Yet while the United States had to reevaluate its foreign and security policy toward many areas of the globe, the nation's closet allies, its partners in the North Atlantic Treaty Organization (NATO), immediately rallied behind the Bush administration. Following the attacks, NATO began to work in close collaboration with the Bush administration to develop policies and strategies to maximize the assets of the Alliance and to support the efforts of the United States. NATO's political and military support demonstrated the broad utility of the Alliance to American security policy and served as a partial repayment for America's underwriting of European security in the post-World War II era.

The genesis behind NATO's 1949 formation was centered around American concerns over the ability of the West Europeans to protect themselves from both an overt Soviet attack and from military pressure from the former superpower. As an enticement to join the organization, NATO members were bound together by the so-called "Three Musketeer" or "all for one" covenant of Article 5 of the North Atlantic Treaty (commonly known as the Washington Treaty) which stated that "an armed attack against one or more of them [NATO members] in Europe or North America shall be considered against them all; and . . . each of them . . . will assist the Party or Parties so attacked."[2]   This single Article was the main strength of NATO for it provided concrete American security guarantees for the West European states and assured that if any of the small or medium-sized nations were attacked, they could count on American military support.   Ironically, the first invocation of Article 5 would be in response to an attack on the United States. After NATO's highest political body, the North Atlantic Council, confirmed that the attacks on 11 September were initiated from outside the United States it invoked Article 5 on 2 October 2001.

This work examines NATO's historic first "all for one" operation from the political machinations behind the decision to designate the attacks an Article 5 event to the Alliance's subsequent military and intelligence support for the American-led campaign against Al-Qaeda and the Taliban.   This analysis proceeds along two tracks.   To begin with, the importance of NATO as the embodiment of the norms and principles which underlie the transatlantic security regime will be assessed in light of the changed concepts of national and international security following the attacks of 11 September.   Furthermore, the specific capabilities and assets of NATO will be evaluated against the tactical and strategic needs of the American-led campaign against international terrorism.   The work concludes with an assessment of the Alliance's role in the effort against those substate groups that continue to pose a security threat to NATO's memberstates and its future relations with coalition partners such as Russia.

NATO and Collective Security

Lord Ismay, the first Secretary General of NATO once wryly remarked that the Alliance was created in order to "keep the Russians out [of Europe], the Americans in and the Germans down."   This now-famous quip quite accurately described the main missions of NATO during the Cold War period from the European perspective.   The major Western European nations, led by France and Great Britain, sought to pool their military resources and ensure American participation in continental security in order to counter the perceived threat from the Soviet Union. In addition, the Europeans were quite straightforward in their determination that the new security organization would serve to protect them from any future threat posed by a resurgent Germany.[3] Even German inclusion in NATO was perceived mainly as a means to encage the nation in the emerging institutional framework of Western Europe. Concurrently, NATO also served to both formalize and institutionalize the American security commitment to Western Europe.

From the American perspective, NATO served as a means to foster military cooperation among the former wartime enemies and hence alleviate massive U.S. expenditures in order to guarantee European security and prevent a third world war from originating in the region. In addition, NATO served as a vehicle to promote the post-World War II ideals of American foreign policy, including democracy and collective security. While institutions such as the United Nations failed to achieve the goals of collective security as envisioned at their formation, NATO exceeded the goals set out by the major powers involved in its creation. It continues to be the primary security institution in the Transatlantic region and the embodiment of the area's security regime. As such, NATO's endorsement of and support of the American-led operations became a critical effort in both the political and military campaign against international terrorism, including the Taliban, the Al-Qaeda network and other substate or state-sponsored actors involved in international terrorism directed against the United States and its principal allies.

Methodology

Critical to an analysis of the NATO response to the attacks of 11 September is an examination of the role of regimes in international security. NATO provides the institutional framework for the transatlantic security regime and has been the main source for the development of the high degree of security interdependence between the Alliance partners. During the Cold War era, there were unequal levels of security cooperation between the United States and its NATO partners. Indeed, one of the principal attractions of NATO membership to the European states was the preponderance of military capabilities the United States brought to the Alliance. This served to counter Soviet military capabilities which from 1945 through 1989 were perceived to be the main security threat to Western Europe.

With the end of the Cold War, direct military threats to the transatlantic states seemed to dissipate. However, the decade of the 1990s witnessed a variety of ethnic and regional conflicts on the periphery of Europe which led to the deployment of NATO forces outside of the geographic borders of the Alliance for the first time in the organization's history. This included operations in the Balkans, such as those in Bosnia, Kosovo and Macedonia. NATO involvement in peace enforcement and humanitarian missions marked a transition in the main missions of the Alliance and a recognition of the growing importance of security threats that were minimized during the bipolar superpower conflict. These threats have lessened the overall importance of the American nuclear guarantee and elevated the importance of multilateral operations, especially in an era of declining defense outlays. This in turn has reinforced the importance of security interdependence and necessitated an increased American reliance on NATO's joint and combined assets. NATO's involvement in the anti-terrorist operations is demonstrative of this trend.

Organization

The first chapters of this work present the development and role of the transatlantic security regime in the context of the growing body of literature on regime formation and its relationship to interdependence. The first chapter begins with an overview of regime theory and the growth of interdependence in the global system. While the realist school of international relations emphasizes the role and importance of the nationstate as the primary actor in global affairs, liberal institutionalists assert that the growing number of international organizations and institutions have eroded the traditional high degree of sovereignty of nationstates. Not that the growth of these bodies has been detrimental to all nationstates. Instead, many nations have been able to augment their capabilities by pooling their resources in international institutions such as NATO. For instance, nations often engage in tactics such as coalition-building and bandwagoning with more powerful or more capable states.[4] Concurrently, even hegemonic states can bolster their power through coalitions. Central to the proliferation of international regimes and institutions has been the growth in the degree of economic and security interdependence. Building upon a number of seminal works this chapter seeks to answer questions related to the expansion of security interdependence in the context of international relations theory.

NATO began its institutional existence as a hybrid which combined the main components of a traditional defensive alliance and a collective security system. Defensive alliances direct their efforts toward deterrence of or the defeat of an external threat. A collective security system seeks to "hold members [of the system] accountable for the maintenance of an internal security norm."[5]   The second chapter examines the broad concepts of collective security, including efforts to develop the internal norms which became the basis for the transatlantic security regime. The chapter examines the internalization of the regime's norms and the subsequent efforts to export these ideals and principles in order to broaden the geographic boundaries encompassed by the regime. It addresses questions over the degree of security interdependence between the United States and its NATO partners and those concerning the degree of primacy held by the United States in the context of the Alliance. Past NATO operations, including those in the Balkans are assessed in order to isolate the main decision-making procedures and operational approaches utilized by the Alliance. The 1999 expansion of NATO, which included the admission of the Czech Republic, Hungary and Poland, is also detailed. Specifically, the chapter identifies the relationships between the Alliance's structures and functions and the broad norms of interdependence and collective security.

The next two chapters of the work overview NATO's structure and its political response to the attacks on 11 September. Many scholars assert that the end of the super conflict diminished the cohesion of the Alliance, yet its post-Cold War history demonstrates an ability to rise to meet a variety of political and military challenges. While NATO is a military organization, it also epitomizes civilian control in civil-military relations. The Alliance's highest body is the North Atlantic Council which is composed of civilian representatives from each of the nineteen memberstates. Any decision becomes the result of intense political discourse and reflects the agendas of the individual members. As such, the internalization of the norms and principles of the regime becomes critically important as NATO's political bodies endeavor to develop a consensus to undertake military operations.

The third chapter examines the political decision among the Alliance partners to invoke Article 5. This analysis includes an overview of NATO as an organization and an assessment of the leadership provided by the Alliance's Secretary General, Lord Robertson. It also details the formation of coalitions within NATO over the optimum response to the attacks and the initial reluctance by some of the Alliance members to invoke Article 5. The principal blocs were the Atlanticists which favored quick military action and the Europeanists which emphasized diplomatic efforts and attempts to use the United Nations to bolster any Alliance actions. The Atlanticist bloc was led by the United States and the United Kingdom and the Europeanist bloc was led by Germany. The chapter concludes with a survey of the evidence supplied by the United States in order to convince the partners that the terrorist attack was initiated by an outside power.

Once the decision was made to invoke Article 5, it then became necessary for the leadership organs of NATO to determine the size and scope of the Alliance's response. The fourth chapter of the work examines the intricacies involved in operationalizing a response once the decision was made to designate the attacks an Article 5 violation of the Washington Treaty. Article 5 was envisioned as a means to bring together the military forces of the organization to respond to a massive attack by the Soviet Union and its Warsaw Pact satellites. However, the nature of both the attack and the enemy identified by the United States did not necessitate the deployment of substantial military units. Instead the United States requested permission to utilize air bases and flight paths and asked for very specific assets that would essentially free identical American capabilities to be used for operations in

Afghanistan. This reflected the development of a series of coalitions, including internal coalitions within the Alliance. The request for only narrow assets and assistance allowed the United States to accomplish two goals. First, the Bush administration could establish a military coalition which utilized those forces with the highest level of interoperability with American troops (namely, the forces of the United Kingdom). Second, the administration could utilize those assets from each of the partners that were most necessary to the mission.

The final chapters of the work examine NATO's role in the American-led operations against the Taliban and the Al Qaeda network. These three chapters endeavor to answer the central question: does the United States *need* its NATO partners to undertake a broad campaign against the substate and state actors involved in international terrorism? If so, what tangible and intangible assets do the Alliance partners contribute to the American-led effort? If not, what is the continuing value of the Transatlantic Alliance?

The fifth chapter examines the military support NATO provided for the American-led operations in Afghanistan. It begins with a chronology of the military action in Afghanistan and then presents a survey of the Alliance assets tasked to participate in the Article 5 mission. These capabilities include both intelligence resources and the national conventional forces deployed in support of Operation Enduring Freedom. The chapter concentrates on deployments, such as that of the NATO Airborne Early Warning Force (NAEWF) and the substitution of NATO forces for American units involved in ongoing missions in the Balkans. It also overviews the contributions of non-NATO allies, including Australia and Japan.

The sixth chapter analyzes the variety of support that the Alliance provided for the United States outside of direct participation in the military operations in Afghanistan. This included planning and involvement in the post-combat humanitarian operations and counter proliferation of WMD efforts. It also overviews the efforts to improve relations with Russia and establish closer institutional relations between the Alliance and Russia. In addition, the chapter explores the broader issues of burdensharing as they relate to Alliance participation in the ongoing broad campaign against international terrorism.

The role of NATO in future operations against global terrorist networks forms the central theme of the conclusion to the study. It concentrates on the issues involved in deepening and widening the Alliance. The final chapter also explores the growing relationship between NATO and the EU, especially as the Union endeavors to develop its own autonomous military capabilities. The attacks on 11 September 2001 confirmed the need for a recalculation of national security policy. The attacks demonstrated that the geographic isolation of the United States no longer served as its main protection from attack. However, the record of the Alliance demonstrated the utility of cooperation and collaboration in defense matters. Although the changed security environment has reduced the need for large conventional armies, it has confirmed the need for specialized military units and increased intelligence assets. It has also affirmed the importance of shared assets. Fortunately, the policies of cooperation that were instrumental in the evolution of NATO are the same policies that are optimal in confronting the new security threats faced by the West.

Notes

1. Sanctions were put in place against India and Pakistan following the nuclear tests of both nations in 1998. These sanctions were lifted in the wake of the attacks. Concurrently, relations between the United States and Russia were strained over a variety of issues, including the U.S.-led military operations in Kosovo in 2000, and President Bush's plans to develop a national ballistic missile defense system.
2. Article 5 specifically states "That the parties agree that an armed attack against one or more of them in Europe or North American shall be considered an attack against them all; and consequently they agree that, if such an attack occurs, each of them, in exercise of the right of individual or collective self-defense recognized by Article 51 of the Charter of the United Nations, will assist the Party or Parties so attacked by taking forthwith, individually and in concert with other Parties, such action as it deems necessary, including the use of armed force, to restore and maintain the security of the North Atlantic area. Any such armed attack and all measures taken as a result thereof shall immediately be reported to the Security Council. Such measures shall be terminated when the Security Council has taken the measures necessary to restore and maintain international peace and security;" *The North Atlantic Treaty* (Washington, D.C.: 4 April 1949).
3. In fact, the forerunner of NATO, the Brussels Treaty, was essentially an anti-German alliance among the main Allied powers of Western Europe.
4. On this theme, see Stephen M. Walt, "Alliance Formation and the Balance of World Power," *International Security* 9, no. 4 (Spring 1985): 225-41.
5. George W. Downs, "Beyond the Debate on Collective Security," in George W. Downs, ed., *Collective Security Beyond the Cold War* (Ann Arbor: University of Michigan, 1994), 2.

Chapter 1

Regime Formation and the Formation of NATO

Introduction

The attacks on the WTC and the Pentagon on 11 September 2001 and the subsequent anthrax incidents which began in October of the same year represented the greatest test of American security policy since the Cuban Missile Crisis of 1962. The nature of the attack and the enormous loss of civilian life combined to dramatically test the conventional security dictums which had been in place since the end of the Cold War. The myth of American security invincibility was shattered and the episode demonstrated the vulnerability of the United States to the same type of substate and state-sponsored terrorist groups that have operated in other areas of the world since the 1960s. Other attacks, including the 1993 bombing of the WTC, failed to significantly impact national policy and were, for the most part, treated as isolated criminal acts which did not rise to the level of a direct threat to national security.

One main component of American security policy which continued to play a significant role in the Bush administration's plans to combat the groups responsible for the September attacks was the emphasis on multilateralism and collective action. Since the end of the Second World War, American security policy has been grounded in the principles of multilateralism and collective security. Whenever possible, successive administrations have sought to develop coalitions and alliances during military operations. For instance, the United States created a series of security institutions to promote the core foundations of American foreign policy. These values included free trade, democracy and collective defense.[1] Examples of these security organizations included NATO, the South-East Asia Treaty Organization (SEATO) and the Central Treaty Organization (CENTO). The most successful of these international institutions was the collective security organization, NATO.

In order to understand the importance of multilateralism to American security policy, it is necessary to examine the principles which underlie international security organizations in general and NATO in particular. This section traces the phenomenon of the rise of international institutions during the post-World War II era in the context of international relations theory. This initial chapter sets the theoretical framework for the remainder of the study. Specifically, the chapter begins with an overview of the role and place of international institutions in global affairs by examining the divergent views of the utility of these organizations. The chapter also surveys the main theoretical tenets upon which regime theory is based, including cooperation in an anarchical world and interdependence. It concludes with an analysis of the impact of regimes and their representative institutions on states and on the international system.

International Relations Theory: Realism and Institutionalism

In the modern era, international relations theory has been dominated by two contending approaches, each seeking to establish itself as the dominant paradigm of the field. The older of the two schools is realism which has its roots in the fourth century BC work of Thucydides who asserted that every state with the power to do so would become "expansionist."[2] At its most basic level political realism is based on three broad assumptions: "1) states (or city-states) are the key units of action; 2) they seek power, either as an end in itself or as a means to other ends; and 3) they behave in ways that are, by and large, rational, and therefore comprehensible to outsiders in rational terms."[3] To this foundation, later scholars such as Hans J. Morgenthau and Kenneth Waltz would further define and refine realist theory.[4]

Contemporary realists view the world as an anarchical "self-help" system in which states must rely on their resources and power to ensure their survival since there is no effective governmental body above that of the individual nationstate.[5] As such, states must constantly seek power.[6] This serves as their optimum protection against rivals because all states will "drive for universal domination" of the world or at least of their region.[7] The presence of anarchy in the international system is a key principle of realism "for no central authority imposes limits on the pursuit of sovereign interests."[8] Hence, external state action is constrained only by other countries and the powerful nationstate can overcome those restraints on unilateral action.

Cooperation among nationstates exists only when there is some tangible benefit to be gained or under the auspices of a hegemonic power which has the resources and power to enforce such cooperation. Here a hegemon can be envisioned as a state:

> powerful enough to maintain the essential rules governing interstate relations, and willing to do so. In addition to its role in maintaining a regime, such a state can abrogate existing rules, prevent the adoption of rules that it opposes, or play the dominant role in constructing new rules. In a hegemonal system, therefore, the preponderant state has both positive and negative power.[9]

In fact Robert O. Keohane's work on hegemonic stability theory suggests that a hegemon is necessary to both set and administer the rules of the international system and "hegemonic structures of power, dominated by a single country, are most conducive to the development of strong international regimes, whose rules are relatively precise and well-obeyed."[10]

Because of the primacy of the individual state and the constant drive to gain relative power, realists contend that international institutions cannot acquire significant capabilities or set universal rules. If international organizations or regimes do exist, they merely reflect the preferences of the dominant states in the global arena. As such, they exist only to bolster or protect the power and resources of the hegemon or primary powers. To realist scholars, "institutions are merely an intervening variable" in the process of international relations which does not significantly impact state behavior or outcomes.[11] Some of the most respected scholars in the field have even judged the study of regimes and international institutions a "fad" and "one of those shifts in fashion not too difficult to explain as a temporary reaction to events in the real world but in itself making little in the way of long-term contribution to knowledge."[12]

In contrast to the realist school of international relations is the liberal or idealist school. Idealism can be described as the broad attempt to apply legal or moral standards to state conduct. Among the early proponents of this field was Immanuel Kant who endeavored to promote international law. In many respects Kant personified the idealist tradition and is "said to have given hopeful priority to the way the world *ought to be* [italics in original] over the way it *actually is*."[13] In the twentieth century, Woodrow Wilson is usually presented, sometimes disparagingly and sometimes in honor, as one of the most ardent supporters of the idealist tradition in international relations.

The proliferation of international organizations and regimes in the post-World War II era revived the idealist school as scholars sought to explain the increasing number and power of these institutions. This new generation of "institutionalists" or neoliberal institutionalists contends that there should be a recalculation of the notion of power and that some international organizations have eclipsed nationstates as the most significant actors in world politics.[14] Institutionalists refute the realist definition of power which they assert is too narrow. Instead, the scholars from the liberal institutionalist school define power in a much broader fashion:

> power is more than military strength. It depends at least as much on economic strength, the attractiveness of one's ideas and economic system, and one's willingness to spend resources on foreign policy. For many purposes – securing cooperation from other advanced societies, ensuring growth in the world economy, cleaning the global environment – military strength is not very important at all.[15]

Institutionalists also contend that even if the world is anarchical, cooperation can occur without the leadership of a hegemon. Under their interpretation, cooperation is defined as "goal-directed behavior that entails mutual policy adjustments so that all sides end up better off than they would otherwise be."[16] Under this interpretation, states engage in collaborative or cooperative behavior in order to partake in systemic gains in resources or power. The key to facilitating such cooperation is the evolution of international institutions and regimes.[17]

In many respects, neoliberal institutionalism is a hybrid between traditional realism and idealism. Institutionalist theory accepts many of the main contentions of the realist school. For instance, states are recognized to be the primary actors in international relations. In addition, the presence of systemic anarchy is also acknowledged. Furthermore, most institutionalists accept that states are rational actors which engage in cost-benefit analysis in decision-making.[18]

One of the main areas of disagreement between the two schools is over the issue of gains by a state. Realists tend to view international relations as a zero-sum game. In other words, one state's gain is another state's loss. For instance, if one nationstate is growing in military power, it is doing so at the expense of its neighbors who are growing weaker in relation to the country in ascension. However, institutionalist theory holds that international politics is not a zero-sum game. The gains of one state might actually benefit another. Robert O. Keohane argues that states' "utility functions are independent of one another: they do not gain or lose utility simply because of the gains or losses of others."[19] This is particularly true in the economic sphere. There is opportunity for mutual gain from one state's rising economy, especially in a globalized market where a nation undergoing a period of economic growth can positively benefit another state in recession through trade.[20] In addition, a nation's security gains can also benefit its neighbors by strengthening regional security or stability.[21]

The second main area of dispute between realism and institutionalism concerns the utility of international regimes. Institutionalists assert that there has been the development of a broad system of international norms which have the capability to regulate or moderate state behavior. The regimes which make up this global system are not hierarchical, that is imposed from above by a hegemonic power such as the United States, but instead have developed a degree of independence and autonomy which has in turn led them to evolve in ways unforeseen when they were created.

The Components of International Regimes

In international relations theory, institutions and organizations have their basis in the regimes which serve as the foundation for cooperation in a given sphere. Regimes can be defined as the "sets of implicit or explicit principles, norms, rules, and decision-making procedures around which actors' expectations converge in a given area of international relations."[22] Regimes represent the accepted ideals which serve as the foundation for international bodies. They also encompass the common ideologies and beliefs which link together the people, institutions and policies of international interaction. Each of these four components - principles, norms, rules and decision-making procedures - are critically important in determining the potential success or failure or the regime.

The first main component of a regime is the principles which serve as its foundation. Stephen Krasner defines principles as "beliefs of fact, causation, and rectitude."[23] They are those:

> prevailing beliefs that underlie states' policy orientations to a variety of issue areas . . . Principles do not constitute specific legal or policy guidelines in an issue area. They underlie, and may provide explanations for, states' acceptance of behavioral prescriptions and proscriptions in an area of international relations, but they are not part of a regulatory framework per se.[24]

The most significant principle which is common to almost all international regimes is that of "reciprocation" which is the "belief that if one helps others or fails to hurt them, even at some opportunity cost to oneself, they will reciprocate when the tables are turned."[25] This principle can serve as the essence of the framework necessary so that regimes are self-regulating and do not require a hegemonic power to enforce the rules and norms.

Norms are the second main component of regimes. While principles represent ideals, norms are focused on behavior.[26] Norms impact behavior since they are "collective beliefs that regulate the behavior and identity of actors."[27] Specifically, norms are the "standards of behavior defined in terms of rights and obligations"[28] and contemporary examples of accepted international norms include sovereignty and free trade.[29] The relationship between regimes and norms is critically important since these constructs form the basis for national political identity and international behavior. Thomas Risse-Kappen defines identity as predicated on:

> norms firmly embedded in the political culture of . . . states and norms shape the identity of political actors through the processes of socialization, communication, and enactment. . . . Collectively held identities not only define who "we" are, but they also delineate the boundaries against "them," the "other." Identities then prescribe norms of appropriate behavior.[30]

Hence for norms to be effective, they must be accepted and internalized by the states encompassed by the regime. As Ann Florini points out: "the most important characteristic of a norm is that it is considered a *legitimate* [italics in original] behavioral claim. No matter how a norm arises, it must take on an aura of legitimacy before it can be considered a norm. Norms are obeyed not because they are enforced, but because they are seen as legitimate."[31]

International norms can be classified in two broad categories. The first category is known as sovereignty norms and is comprised of norms that been developed from the "traditional structure" of international relations.[32] In some cases, the historical development of these norms has taken centuries. As the name implies, sovereignty norms are rooted in the now-accepted international concepts of national sovereignty. For instance, sovereignty norms not only demarcate a state's territory, but they also allow for the establishment of buffer zones and other forms of spheres of influence.[33] Sovereignty norms also grant recognized states sole political authority within their borders, except under extreme circumstances. Indeed, modern state sovereignty rests on the established norm of "the recognition by both internal and external actors that the state has the exclusive authority to intervene coercively in activities within its territory."[34] One salient feature of sovereignty norms is that they enjoy much higher levels of acceptance than do those of the second major norm category, interdependence norms.

Interdependence norms include those norms that arise "from international interdependencies in particular issue areas that incline states to maximize welfare through collaboration."[35] Interdependence norms most commonly develop in the economic sphere. For instance, the globalization of industry, capital and labor has increasingly led states to seek relative gains, as opposed to absolute gains, in markets in order to preserve the economic well-being of trade partners. Examples of this type of normative behavior include adherence to agreed-upon exchange rates or to the most-favored nation trades status concept. Robert W. Cox labels this norm "policy harmonization" (the attempt to harmonize economic policies so as not to negatively impact trading partners).[36] In the security sphere, efforts to harmonize security policy in order to maximize benefits are present in organizations such as NATO.[37]

Norms are critically important to the functions of international regimes. For instance, norms serve to dissuade nations from "cheating" on or violating global agreements by specifically detailing the conditions under which other actors are prepared to act.[38] Contemporary examples of this would include the Nuclear Non-proliferation Treaty (NPT). Nationstates are constrained by the widespread acceptance of settled norms in international relations. Settled norms require special justification to violate. For example, Gregory A. Raymond cites the economic norms, "contracts ought to be kept," and "debts ought to be paid," as settled norms.[39] In addition, norms can serve to detail the specific procedures related to international transactions. This manifestation of norms is most apparent in the global economic sphere. International treaties such as the agreement which serves as the basis for the World Trade Organization (WTO) have significantly reduced the cost of business transactions for individual nations. One of the most prominent contemporary international norms is that of multilateral action. Unilateral action, especially in security matters, has been increasingly abandoned in favor of military action by broad coalitions. Examples of this sort of normative behavior include United Nations peace-enforcement operations or the American-led coalition during the Persian Gulf War. This norm on collective action provides the basis for many global regimes to engage in group implementation of treaties and agreements.[40]

Rules are the third major component of international regimes. While norms tend to be broad-based, rules are grounded in specificity. In international relations, rules are the application of individual norms to specific circumstances. Again, Krasner describes them as "specific prescriptions or proscriptions for action."[41] Robert Gilpin points out that rules predate regimes and are a basic component of every human society:

> The need for rules and rights arises from the basic human condition of scarcity of material resources and the need for order and predictability in human affairs. In order to minimize conflict over the distribution of scarce goods and to facilitate fruitful cooperation among individuals, every social system creates rules and laws for governing behavior. This is as true for international systems as for domestic political systems.[42]

Rules are often the most tangible aspects of a regime. Jack A. Finlayson and Mark W. Zacher note that "rules are generally codified and activities to implement them can usually be observed."[43] Rules have their basis in either custom or international agreement.

In general, rules in the international system fit into three broad categories. First, rules establish the broad standards and customs which govern diplomatic and other political dealings between sovereign states. An example of this type of rule would be the accepted principle of diplomatic immunity. Second, rules also cover military interaction between countries. In the modern sense, these rules have developed in areas such as treatment of prisoners and the rights and responsibilities of neutral states during conflict. Third, and finally, rules have evolved to cover economic interaction. In fact the economic sphere contains the most highly developed system of rules in international politics. These rules are designed to protect both the individual merchant or company and the economic well-being of the individual state.[44]

A rule's effectiveness is directly proportional to the enforcement mechanisms necessary to ensure compliance (either passively or under duress). Hedley Bull observed that "a rule, in order to be effective in society, must be obeyed to some degree, and must be reckoned as a factor in the calculations of those to whom it applies, even those who elect to violate it."[45]   Within a state, a rule is usually enforced by government which has the sole sovereign authority for the legitimate use or delegation of force within its borders.[46] However, in the international arena, enforcement is not as straightforward. Individual states may act alone or in concert to enforce rules, however compliance may also be administered by international organizations or institutions. Hence, Bosnian-Serb violations of the specific rules of international agreements prompted NATO military action to enforce compliance in Bosnia-Herzegovina.

The fourth and final component of international regimes are the decision-making procedures. These patterns are key to both the enforcement capabilities of the regime and its adaptability (and therefore its long-term survival). In order to be effective, conclusions reached within the regime cannot be based on independent decision-making capabilities. In other words, the regime must impose constraints on the ability of individual actors to make choices. Regimes cannot exist when actors' choices are not circumscribed by the rules, principles and norms which form the regime.[47] Instead regimes are comprised of actors who "forego independent decision-making in order to deal with the dilemmas of common interests and common aversions."[48]

A regime's decision-making procedures are based on the normative principles which underlie the regime. These norms direct states' behavior and provide the framework for decisions and can be divided into two general categories. Substantive norms are the written or unwritten codes of behavior which detail the individual actions taken in response to specific actions. Procedural norms outline the standards employed when regimes develop and utilize decision-making structures or guidelines. For instance, procedural norms determine which actors are involved in establishing the rules for decision-making and which actors are necessary to approve decisions. These norms also dictate who is necessary to implement decisions. Taken together, these norms form the "decision-making framework" of a particular regime.[49]

Institutions and Regimes

Since regimes are the combination of norms, principles, rules and decision-making procedures, they do not have the capability to enforce compliance.[50] Instead, regimes must rely on formal structures, known as institutions, to conduct enforcement measures.[51] Hence, institutions are essentially formalized versions of regimes.[52] International institutions can also be defined more narrowly as "persistent and connected sets of rules and principles that prescribe behavioral roles, constrain activity, and shape expectations."[53] For instance, Western Europe has developed a complex free trade regime that is guided by both tacit and explicit rules. Enforcement of these rules is coordinated through institutions such as the European Union which formalizes the norms and rules. These institutions also employ multilateral decision-making processes.[54]

Hedley Bull formulated eight functions that regimes and representative institutions must perform in order for its rules to be successful. First, the rules must be "made" or promulgated. In short, they must be clearly understood to be tied to the regime. Second, the rules and principles must be "communicated" so that they are fully understood by all actors involved. Third, the rules should be "administered" or enforced by the requisite institutions. Fourth, there should be clear mechanisms so that the rules or principles are "interpreted" if uncertainty arises and so that there are readily available procedures to improve understanding. Fifth, the rules have to be "enforced." Institutions cannot allow multiple or excessive violations to a regime without seriously undermining the very existence of that regime. Sixth, the rules must be "legitimized" and accepted as valid by the actors involved in the regime. Otherwise, there is little incentive to enforce the rules. Seventh, rules need to be "capable of adaption" so that they can evolve to take into account changes in the regime or the global system. Eighth, and finally, the institutions of the regime must be "protected" from developments which would weaken them or decrease their effectiveness.[55]

Ernst B. Haas further expounds on the relationship between regimes and institutions by asserting that a regime encompasses the "norms, rules and procedures agreed to in order to regulate an issue area" and that involves "institutional collaboration on topics and issues characterized by complex interdependence – not all kinds of collaboration or even multinational arrangements."[56] In other words, Haas correctly concentrates on the necessity to understand that not all cooperation is the manifestation of an international regime and cooperative behavior does not lead to regime formation in and of itself. Instead, building upon the work of Bull and Haas, regimes must be understood to involve a degree of complexity and utility that extends beyond the traditional zero-sum calculations of the benefits of cooperation to individual states.

On a broad level, membership in an international institution benefits states in a variety of practical and easily identifiable ways. First, institutions allow states greater access to collective or public goods. Public goods are those benefits in which there is nonrivalry in consumption (consumption of the benefit or resource by one actor does not impair the ability of another actor to gain the same benefit) and nonexcludability (actors cannot be denied access to the goods or resources). For instance, within the framework of NATO, security can be considered a public good. The United Kingdom does not "consume" more security than Germany or the Netherlands. In addition, all members are granted access to the same security framework regardless of population or geographic size.

Second, institutions allow states to pool their resources and therefore expand their power potential. For example, even a hegemonic power such as the United States can augment its power. For example, the U.S. provides more than 50 percent of NATO's annual operating budget, but because of the principle of public goods, it receives 100 percent of the Alliance's security guarantees. This principle has been the underlying feature of alliances and coalitions throughout the history of international relations since states are limited in their ability to improve their own resource potential and power projection capabilities. When internal efforts to improve security are not enough or are not practical, states turn to alliances and coalitions. Robert I. Rotberrg and Theodore K. Rabb describe the motives behind alliance formation thus: "In international politics, success leads to failure. The excessive accumulation of power by one state or coalition of states elicits the opposition of others."[57] In international relations theory, such efforts are known as "balancing" and usually result in alliance formation or the strengthening of existing alliances. Concurrently, balancing can bolster the norms or rules of existing regimes and their institutions by reenforcing the commitment of states to the institution.

In addition to expanding the power potential of states through collective action, institutions can also lower individual costs. Institutions provide internal cost savings, especially in security matters. Not only does collective defense, whether in the form of an alliance or a security organization such as NATO, allow states to reduce military expenditures because of enhanced security, these systems promote arms control within the security system.[58] This phenomenon serves the related function of reducing internal tensions between memberstates.

Third, institutions alleviate problems associated with burdensharing. In most traditional alliances and coalitions, there is often an unequal division of tasks and relative inequities in the related costs of maintaining the balancing instrument. Simply put, some members do not do their "share" in maintaining the alliance or coalition. This condition is commonly referred to as the "free-rider" problem and is one of the main realist criticisms of liberal institutionalism. Realists contend that since states are rational actors, they will either attempt to free-ride at every opportunity, thus undermining any international organization since all members would be consistently seeking opportunities to cheat, or they would simply not join and seek to gain the rewards of public goods without any costs. Michael Hechter summarizes the realist critique in the following manner:

> Rational self-interest actors will not join large organizations to pursue collective goods when they can reap the benefit of other people's activity to pursue those ends. This means that the rational actor in the utilitarian model will always be a free rider whenever given the opportunity. Thus, according to utilitarian behavioral premises, social

organization is unlikely to arise even among those individuals who have strong personal interest in reaping the benefits that such an organization provides.[59]

However, the rules and decision-making procedures of institutions may be fashioned to overcome the free-rider problem. Rules can be developed to ensure equity in effort (or at least to ensure relative equality of burden). These institutional rules provide a disincentive to "undercontribute."[60] Furthermore, states engaged in an attempt to free-ride often find themselves shut out of the decision-making process and thus unable to influence the goals or actions of the institution if they remain outside (here the incentive for power augmentation comes into play). The relationship between France and NATO is a prime example of the free-rider problem. France withdrew from NATO's integrated military structures in 1966.[61] However, France gradually restored relations during the 1990s so that it could influence Alliance decisions on expansion and the out-of-area debate.[62]

Fourth, regimes aid the transfer of information between states. Institutions provide a forum to exchange information on both domestic policies and foreign affairs. In a broad sense this fosters cooperation and discourages states from acting unilaterally, thus helping maintain stability in the international system. The openness cultivated by international institutions and organizations helps ameliorate one of the most persistent problems in international security – the security dilemma. The security dilemma occurs when a state's endeavor to increase its own security prompts other states to respond with reciprocal efforts.[63] The result is often arms races and heightened tensions which leave the original state with an overall loss in security.[64] The security dilemma occurs because neighboring states cannot distinguish between defensive and offensive military preparations.[65] Therefore, the security dilemma may be worsened dramatically if increases in defensive capabilities upset the offensive-defensive balance military balance between states.[66]

Fifth, institutions provide a forum for states to develop and implement linkage strategies. Linkage strategies allow actors within a regime to use cooperative behavior in one issue area in order to gain concessions or approval in a different area. Linkage strategies are most effective in the cases of actors whose interests are bound together in a variety of regimes or institutions. For instance, the nationstates of the transatlantic region Europe are joined together in an institutional framework that includes organizations devoted to security, economics and regional politics. Hence cooperation in one regime can lead to like behavior in others. These linkages could be in the form of an immediate quid pro quo, likewise they could be in anticipation of, or as an incentive for, future cooperation. An example of linkage strategy would be France's assent to German rearmament and entry into NATO in 1955 in exchange for German cooperation in the economic sphere (which manifested itself after the establishment of the European Coal and Steel Community, or ECSC, in 1952 and was followed by the 1957 Rome Treaty which established the European Economic Community or EEC).[67]

Conversely, institutions also provide a means to limit linkage strategies. In this case, institutions can enforce uniform rules and procedures which prevent overlap on varied interests. One significant manifestation of this ability is the capability of institutions to impose discipline on democracies. Through participation in a regime and its representative institutions, national government can prevent domestic constraints from exerting undue influences.[68] In addition, the prospect of joining international organizations can prompt national governments to engage in efforts to harmonize their laws and foreign policies with those of the regime. This phenomenon is known as "anticipatory adaption."[69] By promoting the adoption of similar rules, principles and norms in international affairs, international institutions and regimes facilitate the formation of broad, transnational coalitions over issues such as free trade or democratization.

Sixth and finally, regimes encourage cooperation between nationstates that extends beyond the original mandate of the organization and beyond short term linkage strategies. Institutions are able to facilitate patterns of cooperation and collaboration among their memberstates and these habits can expedite further bargaining both within and outside of the auspices of the institution or organization. These patterns of cooperation mean that states have less incentive to attempt to "cheat,"[70] or gain unlawful advantages because of the "shadow of the future" – that is knowledge that nations will have to interact with other states within the regime time and again.[71] Consequently, institutions promote cooperation among members and discourage unilateral action (including cheating within the regime) because, as Arthur A. Stein points out, that "institution may be required again in the future, and destroying them because of short-term changes may be very costly in the long run. Institutional maintenance is not, then, a function of a waiving calculation; it becomes a factor in the decision calculus that keeps short-term calculations from becoming decisive."[72]

Hegemons and Interdependence

One of the main determinants of the success or failure of international regimes and their respective institutions is the degree of support given to them by primary powers. Oran R. Young contends that one of the main factors in regime formation is the establishment of "imposed orders" which "are deliberately established by dominant actors who succeed in getting others to conform to the requirements of these orders through some combination of coercion, cooption, and the manipulation of incentives."[73] Primary or hegemonic powers can play a significant role in the creation of regimes by initially providing both the leadership and the enforcement mechanisms necessary to ensure the success of the resultant international institutions or organizations.[74] However, these regimes reflect the interests of these great powers and often become a means for the powerful states to expand or reinforce their influence and global presence. For instance, John Gerard Ruggie asserts that the proliferation of multilateral institutions in the post-World War II era, was the result of American preferences for "world order."[75] Robert O. Keohane summarizes this view of the relationship between powerful states and international regimes as: "the view that concentration of power in one dominant state facilitates the development of strong regimes, and that fragmentation of power is associated with regime collapse."[76]

Published in 1984, *After Hegemony: Cooperation and Discord in the World Political Economy* by Robert O. Keohane is the seminal work on the relationship between hegemonic powers and international regimes and institutions. The study examines first the impact that hegemons have on the formation of international bodies in the world's political economy and then analyzes the means by which the norms, principles and rules of these organizations are internalized by the global system. Keohane's work is centered around the experiences of the United States which was the world's last, undisputed hegemonic power in the immediate aftermath of World War II.[77] Although from different theoretical perspectives, Keohane's work, which predates that of Ruggie, foreshadows the latter's contentions on the relationship between the proliferation of international regimes and institutions and American preferences for the post-World War II era.

After Hegemony concludes with an assertion that cooperation can take place even without a hegemon. This is possible when institutions and regimes are able to step in and fill the role of the declining hegemon in maintaining the patterns of cooperation and collaboration.[78] Hence, Keohane contends that as regimes and institutions become increasingly strengthened, hegemonic states will be less important in promoting cooperation and providing stability in the world. *After Hegemony* also serves as a analytical vehicle to reconcile realist and liberal institutionalist arguments over the strength and viability of international institutions in an otherwise anarchical world.

Significantly, Keohane, in a collaboration with Joseph S. Nye, demonstrates that in the aftermath of the Cold War, when the Soviet threat can no longer be validated as the main factor in holding the transatlantic institutions together, institutional cohesion actually expanded (both geographically and in power terms) rather than eroded. This runs counter to realist assertions about external threats being the basis for alliance formation and the "glue" which holds together international security institutions.[79] Keohane and Nye write that:

In short, institutions are the shadows of the past that shape visions and choices about the future. Without institutional signposts . . . it would have been much more difficult to maintain steady and common positions during periods of revolutionary change [the end of the Cold War] in the structure of the international system. The existence and invention of international institutions provided critical signposts to define the national interest as well as useful instruments to implement it. While the institutions did not themselves determine the national strategy, in a period of rapid change strategy might have evolved quite differently without them.[80]

Hence, again counter to realist principles, international institutions gained a degree of influence and prominence in world affairs which made their importance equal to that of sovereign states.[81] Key to the analysis of Keohane and Nye is the principle of interdependence. These two scholars define interdependence as "mutual dependence" with dependence being explained as "state of being determined or significantly affected by external forces."[82] This theme of interdependence forms the basis for another collaboration between Keohane and Nye, *Power and Interdependence*.[83] The authors trace the ability of states to utilize linkage strategies within the institutional forums to set their own agendas and form coalitions.[84] Interdependence prompts states to seek nonconfrontational solutions to problems. In this fashion it reinforces international norms on negotiation and diplomacy.

Hence, institutions became a means of facilitating cooperation, even without hegemonic leadership. Hegemons may be necessary for *initiating* cooperation, but not for continuing cooperation. The hegemon maybe initially needed to set international "rules" and reward or punish states by those rules. In the early life of a regime the hegemon distributes public goods such as security or free trade. But, cooperation can survive and even strengthen as a hegemon declines. Indeed, once formalized in a regime or institution, patterns of cooperation may compel compliance even by great powers. As Keohane notes: "interdependence means that even great powers cannot act effectively on their own. To regain some influence over events, governments and firms have to collaborate with one another; they have to sacrifice their unilateral freedom of action for some degree of mastery. over transnational flows of goods, capital, technology, ideas, and people."[85]

Furthermore, complex interdependence constrains the economic component of a state's external sovereignty. States with a high degree of interdependence "recognize that the attempt to provide every service and fulfill every function of statehood on an independent and autonomous basis is extremely inefficient, and they prefer a situation which provides for specialization and divisions of labor among nations."[86] The main consequence of this deepening division of labor among states is an increase in dependency. Over time, these patterns of cooperation and dependency lead to the development of long-term reciprocity as "governments

All for One

develop reputations for compliance, not just to the letter of the law but to the spirit as well."[87] The impact of reputation within a regime tends to dampen unilateralism and prompt both internal and external conformity with the norms and rules, if not the principles, of regimes. All of these factors combine to reinforce state preferences for cooperation. State preferences for cooperation, in turn, reinforce and propagate interdependence, so that the system moves closer to integration.

Over the past few years, an impressive body of literature has surfaced which challenges the realist notion that states are unitary actors. These works assert that domestic considerations affect foreign policy decisions, and that the two are often intertwined. Thus, there is an intersection between the manifestation of internal and external sovereignty.[88] Peter Katzenstein asserts that "the main purpose of all strategies of foreign economic policy is to make domestic policy compatible with the international political economy."[89] David A. Baldwin contends that "economic statecraft" or "foreign economic policy" has superseded the traditional emphasis on national security policy.[90]

The result of these factors is that national governments do not formulate policy in a vacuum. Instead, interdependence and "economic ties generate societal-based economic concerns that affect the capacities state leaders of status quo powers have to mobilize economic resources and political support . . . . In this way, economic ties influence the preferences status quo powers have for making . . . commitments.[91] Policymakers have also had to balance the potential costs of security policies and programs in regards to national economies and social spending.[92] As a result, actions which may appear irrational will occur because endeavors which are rational at the international level may be "impolitic" at the domestic level, and thus may not be taken.[93]

Conclusion

Realism and liberal institutionalism are the dominant, but competing, schools of international relations. Realism emphasizes the primacy of the state as the main actor in global affairs and the presence of anarchy in the international system. However, in the aftermath of World War II, there has been a proliferation of institutions and regimes which have become increasingly important in global politics. Liberal institutionalism incorporates many of the basic premises of realism, including anarchy and the importance of individual states, but it emphasizes the importance of international institutions and regimes in the current world system.

The spread of regimes and institutions has reflected American preferences for the international system. The norms, rules, principles and decision-making procedures which form the basis for international regimes in both the economic and security spheres have reinforced core American foreign policy goals, a trend well documented in the work of John G. Ruggie.[94]

In the post-war period, international regimes and institutions have demonstrated a variety of membership benefits to individual states. For the United States, these regimes and their representative institutions have provided a means to husband resources and to promote internalization of the regimes' norms and principles by the memberstates. The regimes also facilitate cooperation by increasing the relative gains for actors participating in the institutions, all the while promoting current cooperation as states seek to participate in future gains and reducing transactions costs. Institutions create a broad framework for implementing or maintaining international rules and norms, since these principles do not apply to a specific case, or a specific country, but are employed over a number of cases and a number of states. Both global economic regimes, including the WTO, and security regimes, such as NATO, have not only augmented the assets of the United States, their decision-making procedures have allowed the United States to pursue linkage strategies and to build coalitions in other issue areas.

Regimes can reinforce individual state strategy in a period of increased multinational actors. The international bodies can legitimize domestic policies that comply with international norms and rules. They can also internationalize domestic priorities, including security efforts. In the global arena, international organizations can legitimize the status quo even as states pursue idiosyncratic goals as the bodies serve as a means for reconciling divergent interests. Hence, the gains provided by international institutions provide incentives for continued cooperation and interdependence that create a self-perpetuating international system in which nationstates learn that participation in such organizations and collaboration with other states augments potential gains while reinforcing the power of individual states.

The American response to the attacks on 11 September 2001 demonstrates the importance of cooperation and multilateralism to U.S. national security policy. Instead of undertaking unilateral action, the Bush administration immediately embarked on a variety of initiatives designed both to utilize existing international institutions and to develop diplomatic and military coalitions. In fact, the main focus of the administration's security policy has been the effort to secure both overt and tacit military support. Central to this policy priority was the endeavor to convince NATO to invoke Article 5 and to secure the greatest levels of support from the Alliance partners. In order to understand the importance of the Alliance to American security policy, it is necessary to survey the role that NATO has played in the development of the transatlantic security regime. This theme is examined at length in the next chapter.

Notes

1. On this theme see John Gerard Ruggie, "Third Try at World Order?" *Political Science Quarterly* (Fall 1994): 553-70 or Tony Smith, *America's Mission: The United States and the Worldwide Struggle for Democracy in the Twentieth Century* (Princeton: Princeton University, 1994).

2. Thucydides' writings on the Peloponnesian War, especially in light of his emphasis on the role of power in relations between the Greek city states, are generally considered to lay the foundation for modern realism; Steven Forde, "International Realism and the Science of Politics: Thucydides, Machiavelli, and Neorealism," *International Studies Quarterly* 39, no. 2 (June 1995), 147.

3. Robert O. Keohane, "Realism, Neorealism and the Study of World Politics," in Robert O. Keohane, ed., *Neorealism and its Critics* (New York: Columbia, 1986), 7.

4. Morgenthau and his contemporaries E.H.Carr and Raymond Aron, examined the rise and fall of great powers as a result of the competition for power and global dominance; see E.H. Carr, *The Twenty Years Crisis, 1919-1939: An Introduction to the Study of International Relations* (London: MacMillan, 1939; reprint London: MacMillan, 1946); Hans J. Morgenthau, *Politics Among Nations: The Struggle for Power and Peace* (New York: Knopf, 1948); and Raymond Aron, *Peace and War: A Theory of International Relations* (Malabar: Robert E. Krieger, 1966). Waltz elaborated on traditional realism through the development of what would come to be known as neorealism or structuralism realism. This offshoot of traditional realism emphasized the structure of the international system and the distribution of power as the main determinants of state behavior; see Kenneth N. Waltz, *Man, the State and War: A Theoretical Analysis* (New York: Columbia University, 1959); and Kenneth N. Waltz, *The Theory of International Politics* (Reading, MA: Addison Wesley, 1979).

5. Paul Viotti and Mark Kauppi, eds., *International Relations Theory: Realism, Pluralism, Globalism* (New York: MacMillan, 1993), 48.

6. Here power can be broadly defined "as the ability of an actor to get others to do something they otherwise would not do (and at an acceptable cost to the actor); Robert O. Keohane and Joseph S. Nye, *Power and Interdependence*, 2ⁿᵈ ed. (New York: HarperCollins, 1989), 11.

7. Kenneth N. Waltz, "Anarchic Orders and Balances of Power," in Keohane, *Neorealism and its Critics*, 117.

8. Kenneth A. Oye, "Explaining Cooperation Under Anarchy: Hypotheses and Strategies," in Kenneth A. Oye, ed., *Cooperation Under Anarchy* (Princeton: Princeton University, 1986), 1.

9. Keohane and Nye, *Power and Interdependence*, 44.

10. See Robert O. Keohane, "The Theory of Hegemonic Stability and Changes in International Economic Regimes, 1967-1977," in Ole Holsti, Randolph Siverson and Alexander L. George, eds., *Change in the International System* (Boulder: Westview, 1980).

11. Michael E. Brown, Sean M. Lynn-Jones and Steven E. Miller, eds., *The Perils of Anarchy: Contemporary Realism and International Security* (Cambridge: MIT, 1995), 340.

12. Susan Strange, "*Cave! hic Dragones:* A Critique of Regime Analysis," in Stephen Krasner, ed., *International Regimes* (Ithaca: Cornell, 1983; reprint 1993), 337.

13. Jean Bartelson, "The Trial of Judgement: A Note on Kant and the Paradoxes of Internationalism," *International Studies Quarterly* 39, no. 2 (June 1995), 263.
14. On the decline of the nationstate in relation to international organizations, see Ernst B. Haas, *Beyond the Nation-State: Functionalism and International Organization* (Stanford: Stanford University, 1964).
15. Robert O. Keohane, "The Diplomacy of Structural Change: Multilateral Institutions and State Strategies," in Helga Haftendorn and Christian Tuschhoff, eds., *America and Europe in an Era of Change* (Boulder: Westview, 1993), 44-45.
16. Helen Milner, "International Theories of Cooperation Among Nations: Strengths and Weaknesses," *World Politics* 44, no. 3 (April 1992): 468.
17. See David Baldwin, ed., *Neorealism and Neoliberalism: The Contemporary Debate* (New York: Columbia University, 1993).
18. A growing number of scholars, especially game theorists, contend that domestic groups can cause states to engage in policies that appear irrational. For instance, Robert Putnam asserts that all nations engage in a "two-level" game when it comes to foreign policy: "The politics of many international negotiations can usefully be conceived as a two level game. At the national level, domestic groups pursue their interests by pressuring the government to adopt favorable policies, and politicians seek power by constructing coalitions among those groups. At the international level, national governments seek to maximize their own ability to satisfy domestic pressures, while minimizing the adverse consequences of foreign developments. Neither of the two games can be ignored by central decision makers, so long as their countries remain interdependent, yet sovereign;" Robert Putnam, "Diplomacy and Domestic Politics: The Logic of Two-Level Games," *International Organization* 42 (Summer 1988), 434.
19. Robert O. Keohane, *After Hegemony: Cooperation and Discord in the World Political Economy* (Princeton: Princeton University, 1984), 27.
20. Richard Rosecrance, "International Relations Theory Revisited," *International Organization* 35, no. 4 (Autumn 1981), 705-6.
21. The most oft-cited example of this is the heightened security gained by Canada and Mexico in the Cold War era because of their proximity to the United States.
22. Stephen Krasner, "Structural Causes and Regime Consequences: Regimes as Intervening Variables," in Stephen Krasner, ed., *International Regimes* (Ithaca: Cornell University, 1983), 2.
23. Ibid.
24. Jack A. Finlayson and Mark W. Zacher, "The GATT and the Regulation of Trade Barriers: Regime Dynamics and Functions," in Krasner, *International Regimes*, 276.
25. Robert O. Keohane, "The Demand for International Regimes," in Krasner, *International Regimes*, 158.
26. Ann Florini, "The Evolution of International Norms," *International Studies Quarterly* 40, no. 3 (September, 1996): 364.
27. Robert Herman, "Identity, Norms, and National Security," in Peter J. Katzenstein, ed., *The Culture of National Security: Norms and Identity in World Politics* (New York: Columbia University, 1996), 274.
28. Krasner, "Structural Causes," 2.

29. Andrew P. Cortell and James W. Davis, Jr., "How Do International Institutions Matter? The Domestic Impact of International Rules and Norms," *International Studies Quarterly* 40, no. 4 (December 1996): 452.
30. Thomas Risse-Kappen, "Collective Identity in a Democratic Community," in Katzenstein, 366-67.
31. Florini, 365.
32. Finlayson and Zacher, 276.
33. Gregory A. Raymond, "Problems and Prospects in the Study of International Norms," *Mershon International Studies Review* 41, no. 2 (November 1997): 214.
34. Janice E. Thomson, "State Sovereignty in International Relations: Bridging the Gap Between Theory and Empirical Research," *International Studies Quarterly* 39, no. 2 (June 1995), 219.
35. Finlayson and Zacher, 276.
36. Robert W. Cox, "Social Forces, States and World Orders: Beyond International Relations Theory," in *Neorealism and its Critics*, ed. Robert O. Keohane (New York: Columbia University, 1986), 231.
37. In NATO, these efforts would include coordination on issues such as defense spending, weapons production and procurement, and troop deployment.
38. As an example, norms can determine prearranged courses of action for transgressions of international agreements: if state A violates agreement B, then the other signatories to B pledge that C course of action will result.
39. Raymond, "Problems and Prospects," 224.
40. For examples of this type of behavior see Axelrod and Keohane.
41. Krasner, "Structural Causes," 2.
42. Robert Gilpin, *War and Change in World Politics* (Cambridge: Cambridge University, 1981), 34-35. Gilpin's work is based on that of Hedley Bull. See Hedley Bull, *The Anarchical Society: A Study of Order in World Politics* (New York: Columbia University, 1977), especially pages 46-51.
43. Finlayson and Zacher, 277.
44. Gilpin, *War and Change*, 35.
45. Bull, 56.
46. Ibid., 57.
47. Arthur A. Stein, "Coordination and Collaboration: Regimes in an Anarchic World," in Krasner, *International Regimes*, 116-17.
48. Ibid., 127.
49. Finlayson and Zacher, 276.
50. Andreas Hansenclever, Peter Mayer, and Volker Rittberger, "Interests, Power, Knowledge: The Study of International Regimes," *Mershon International Studies Review* 40, no. 2 (October 1996): 179.
51. Robert O. Keohane combines principles, norms and rules into a single category with his definition of regimes: "institutions with explicit rules, agreed upon by governments, that pertain to particular sets of issues in international relations;" Robert O. Keohane, "Neoliberal Institutionalism: A Perspective on World Politics," in *International Institutions and State Power: Essays in International Relations Theory*, ed. Robert O. Keohane (Boulder: Westview, 1989), 4.

52. Charles A. Kupchan, "The Case for Collective Security," in Downs, *Collective Security*, 48.
53. Robert O. Keohane, Peter Haas, and Marc Levy, eds., *Institutions for the Earth: Sources of Effective International Environmental Protection* (Cambridge: MIT, 1993), 4-5.
54. Furthermore, this regime has reinforced the drive for relative gains whereby all memberstates can benefit from economic increases accrued by one member; Randall L. Schweller, "Neorealism's Status-Quo Bias: What Security Dilemma?" *Security Studies*, Special Issue, Realism: Restatements and Renewal, 5, no. 3 (Spring 1996), 92.
55. Bull, 56-7.
56. See Ernst B. Haas, "Why Collaborate? Issue Linkages and International Regimes," *World Politics* 3 (1980): 357-405.
57. Robert I. Rotberrg and Theodore K. Rabb, eds., *The Origin and Prevention of Major Wars* (Cambridge: Cambridge University, 1989), 49.
58. Downs and Iida, 30.
59. Michael Hechter, "Karl Polanyi's Social Theory: A Critique," *Politics and Society* 10, no. 4 (Winter: 1981), 403.
60. Charles Lipson, "Is the Future of Collective Security Like the Past?" in Downs, *Collective Security*, 115.
61. For a detailed overview of the circumstances surrounding the French withdrawal, see Michael M. Harrison and Mark G. McDonough, *Negotiations on the French Withdrawal From NATO: FPI Case Studies, No. 5* (Washington, D.C.: Johns Hopkins, 1987).
62. France's actions led Robert J. Art to note that "France has gone in four short years from NATO's denigrator to its supporter," Robert J. Art, "Why Western Europe Needs the United States and NATO," *Political Science Quarterly* 111, no. 1 (Spring 1996), 34.
63. One of the original, and best, definitions of the security dilemma is that of John Herz, who asserted that actors must be "concerned about their security from being attacked, subjected, dominated, or annihilated by other groups and individuals. Striving to attain security from such attack, they are driven to acquire more and more power in order to escape the impact of the power of others. This, in turn, renders the others more insecure and compels them to prepare for the worst. Since none can ever feel entirely secure in such a world of competing units, power competition ensues, and the vicious circle of security and power accumulation is on;" John Herz, "Idealist Internationalism and the Security Dilemma," *World Politics*, 2 (1950): 157.
64. This circumstance was first noted by John Herz, who termed the phenomenon "the security and power dilemma;" John Herz, *Political Realism and Political Idealism* (Chicago: University of Chicago, 1951).
65. This phenomenon, usually known as offense-defense distinguishability, is examined at length in George Quester, *Offense and Defense in the International System* (New York: JohnWiley & Sons, 1977). Quester points out that an actor needs far more significant offensive capabilities to overcome a defensive position (usually a ratio of assets of three-to-one in favor of the offensive forces). Hence, improvements in defensive capabilities require a corresponding increase three times as great in offensive capabilities in order to maintain equilibrium.

66. Robert Jervis, "Cooperation Under the Security Dilemma," *World Politics*, 30, no. 2 (January 1978), 188.

67. For an overview of the linkages between French security and economic policy in regard to the Federal Republic of Germany, see Edward Furdson, *The European Defense Community: A History* (London: Macmillan, 1980).

68. Keohane and Nye, *Power and Interdependence*, 271-72.

69. Kalypso Nicolaidis, "East European Trade in the Aftermath of 1989: Did International Institutions Matter?," in Robert O. Keohane, Joseph S. Nye and Stanley Hoffman, eds., *After the Cold War: International Institutions and State Strategies in Europe, 1989-1991* (Cambridge: Harvard University, 1993), 197.

70. Cheating implies either observed or unobserved non-compliance with a regime's norms or rules; it can thus be considered a "breach of promise." In most institutionalist literature, defection is the term used to describe cheating; John J. Mearsheimer, "The False Promise of International Institutions," *International Security* 19, no. 3 (Winter 1994): 5-49.

71. Kenneth Oye, "Explaining Cooperation Under Anarchy," in *Cooperation Under Anarchy*, ed. Kenneth A. Oye (Princeton: Princeton University, 1986), 14-15.

72. Arthur A. Stein, *Why Nations Cooperate: Circumstance and Choice in International Relations* (London: Cornell University, 1990), 52.

73. Oran R. Young, "Regime Dynamics: The Rise and Fall of International Regimes" in Krasner, *International Regimes*, 100.

74. On this notion of "leadership theory," see David A. Lake, "Leadership, Hegemony, and the International Economy: Naked Emperor or Tattered Monarch with Potential?" *International Studies Quarterly* 37, no. 4 (December 1993): 459-89.

75. See Ruggie, "Third Try," 553-570.

76. Keohane, "The Demand for International Regimes," 142.

77. America's status as a hegemon is confirmed by its command of the global economy in the aftermath of the Second World War and its short-term monopoly on nuclear weapons.

78. Keohane, *After Hegemony*, 24, 39.

79. Stephen M. Walt asserts writes that "Alliances are most commonly viewed as a response to threats," Walt, 209.

80. Robert O. Keohane and Joseph S. Nye, "The United States and International Institutions in Europe After the Cold War," in Keohane, Nye and Hoffman, 125.

81. The continuing importance of international institutions in the post-Cold War era is also examined in Miles Kahler, *Regional Futures and Transatlantic Economic Relations* (New York: Council on Foreign Relations, 1995).

82. Keohane and Nye, *Power and Interdependence*, 8.

83. The authors distinguish between interdependence and interconnectedness where there are simple reciprocal trade patterns or security arrangements. They also distinguish between interdependence and relationships that are simply "mutually beneficial." Interdependence is tied to close, though not always equal, levels of symmetry and relationships that involve costly transaction effects; Ibid., 9. For instance, the United States and Europe are interdependent in economic terms because of the volume of trade, whereas the United States would not be economically interdependent with newly-developing nations in Africa, even if they supplied a necessary commodity such as diamonds, because of the asymmetry of trade.

84. Ibid., 35-36.

85. Keohane, "Diplomacy," 48.
86. Richard Rosecrance, *Rise of the Trading State: Commerce and Conquest in the Modern World* (New York: Basic Books, 1986), 24.
87. Keohane and Nye, *Power and Interdependence*, 276.
88. Arthur A. Stein cites the internal actors and governmental dynamics of a state as the most widespread form of regime. This model of domestic regimes is applicable to international systems and demonstrates the interconnectedness between internal and external sovereignty: "A regime exists when the interaction between the parties is not unconstrained or is not based on independent decision-making. Domestic society constitutes the most common regime. Even the freest and most open societies do not allow individualism and market forces full play; people are not free to choose from among every conceivable option – their choice set is constrained. . . . Domestic society, characterized by the agreement of individuals to eschew the use of force in settling disputes, constitutes a regime precisely because it constrains the behavior of its citizens;" Stein, *Why Nations Cooperate*, 117.
89. See Peter J. Katzenstein, ed., *Between Power and Plenty: Foreign Economic Policy and Advanced Industrial States* (Madison: University of Wisconsin, 1978), 4.
90. David Baldwin, *Economic Statecraft* (Princeton: Princeton University, 1985), 29-50.
91. Paul A. Papyoanou, "Economic Interdependence and the Balance of Power," *International Studies Quarterly* 41, no. 1 (March 1997), 114.
92. Ibid., 117.
93. Putnam, "Two-Level Games," 436.
94. Again, see Ruggie, "Third Try."

Chapter 2

NATO's Role in the Transatlantic Security Regime

Introduction

In the aftermath of World War II, the administration of Harry S. Truman sought to avoid the mistakes made following World War I and prevent a return to isolationism in American foreign policy. One of the most significant demonstrations of the administration's commitment to global engagement was the formation of NATO, the nation's first peacetime military alliance. NATO provided concrete American security guarantees for its Western European allies and verified the commitment of the United States to continued opposition to the Soviet Union both regionally and globally.

NATO ultimately became one of the most successful peacetime military organizations in history and the centerpiece of the security policies of the United States and the major West European powers. Unlike most other military alliances, NATO was formed not simply as a defensive or offensive coalition, but as an institution which could both defend against external threats and which could regulate conduct between its memberstates. The success of NATO was directly tied to its utility to defend against the Soviet Union and to provide an institutional framework to rearm Germany without creating security dilemmas for its European neighbors. As such NATO evolved as both a defensive military alliance and a collective security organization. It served to protect the external borders of the transatlantic region and regulate the conduct of memberstates within the Alliance.

Throughout the course of its history, NATO has served both political and military purposes. It has combined the strengths of a military alliance and a collective security system. The transatlantic alliance has also demonstrated an ability to adapt to new missions and to evolve to meet changing global circumstances. This was nowhere more apparent than at the end of the Cold War when the organization embraced former enemy states and adjusted to new missions. It also undertook a revised role in Europe's security architecture. At the dawn of the new millennium NATO has been called upon to undertake military operations outside of its territory and increasingly act as the main guarantor of all of Europe's peace and stability.

Security Regimes

International organizations temper global anarchy by constraining individual states' unilateral pursuit of policy.[1] Security regimes provide the foundation for multilateral military institutions and establish the rules and norms of the multilateral bodies. They provide incentives for cooperation and collaboration and they diminish the harmful impact of any potential security dilemma.

Security cooperation occurs when states seek to cooperate in order to overcome deficiencies in security matters. Hence security regimes and other forms of military collaboration:

> are mechanisms for aggregating the capabilities of states in situations in which individually the states have inadequate capability to deal with threats that confront them. In fact, the scale required to generate the capability to assure survival often exceeds that of anyone state, so that cooperation becomes necessary.[2]

As Edward Gulick stated, "States A and B might each be smaller and weaker than C, but allied they might well be equal to, or greater than, C."[3]

The nature of military preparedness means that nations often find it difficult to distinguish between offensive and defensive security improvements. Any military build-up may be perceived as threatening the status quo because of the uncertainty present in international affairs. For instance, Robert Jervis contends that "the primacy of security, its competitive nature, the unforgiving nature of the arena, and the uncertainty of how much security the state needs and has, all compound the prisoners' dilemma and make it sharper than the problems that arise in most other areas."[4]

Hence, even defensive preparations and upgrades may lead to reciprocal efforts by other nations and result in the net loss of security at the heart of the security dilemma. This condition is worsened by the technological innovations of the worldwide military revolution which have reinforced the importance of a preemptive or first strike.[5]

Of all of the possible international regimes, security regimes are often the most difficult to establish and maintain. There are four principle reasons for this:

> First, security matters comprise a much higher level of competitiveness than do other areas, including economics. In the economic realm, one state's gains do not necessarily translate into another state's losses. In fact, economic gains by one state can prove beneficial to others. In security matters, however, one state's gains usually come at the expense of another's, whether it be in terms of direct territorial loss or through losses in relative security. Second, as pointed out, the inability to effectively distinguish between offensive and defensive motives leads states to respond to both types of behavior in the same manner. Third, small errors in security matters can have much larger consequences than minor errors in economic or geopolitical terms. Fourth, in the security realm,

measuring one's own security and detecting what others are doing is difficult. This leads to a much greater sense of uncertainty in the security realm.[6]

Successful security regimes are often short-lived affairs and dissipate after the main threat to the coalition or alliance is defeated or diminished. Like other regimes, a hegemonic power is usually at the root of the creation of the regime, but the hegemon may either be the instigator or the stimulus for the formation of the regime. In other words, a hegemon may actively seek to establish the regime or the regime may form in opposition to the hegemon in an effort to prevent universal domination.[7] Consequently, states tend to either bandwagon with a hegemon or balance against it.[8] During the life of a security regime, states will join or defect depending upon what they perceive to be in their best interests and in response to the power and control of hegemonic states.[9]

The success of a security regime is dependent upon a variety of variables. Historically, those regimes with the support and involvement of the great powers of the day have had the best chance for success since these powers can agree to and enforce the rules and norms of the organization.[10] Also, exclusion of any major power tends to lead to the creation of rival coalitions in an effort to balance against the original regime. Memberstates within the region must agree that their security is not best assured through territorial expansion at the expense of other memberstates. This is a key precondition to prevent internal conflict. Concurrently, memberstates must internalize the norms implicit in security cooperation and collaboration – mainly that the security gains of one memberstate do not threaten other memberstates and may, in fact, boost the overall security of all of the allies or partners.[11] States must also perceive that the individual pursuit of security is more costly than efforts to develop multilateral security capabilities. Cooperation must be seen as a utilitarian policy which frees resources for either greater security augmentation or for non-security uses, including economic or social programs.[12]

The more integrated a state becomes within a security regime or organization, the less autonomy that state enjoys in security matters. A deep degree of integration results in "bindingness" – the overt curtailment of sovereignty in return for a stronger institutional framework and, therefore, greater access to resources and capabilities.[13] States become "bound" to the regime as the costs of leaving or defecting from the regime increase.[14]

Security regimes have varying degrees of bindingness depending upon their internal dynamics and their type. In general, coalitions are the least binding, followed by alliances, collective security systems and confederations. An example of a coalition would be the allied powers which supported the United States during its military campaign in the Persian Gulf War. There were only limited costs associated with membership in the coalition and few, if any, real sanctions for leaving. As was the case with the conflict in Persian Gulf, coalitions are often the result of bandwagoning efforts. Alliances have a higher degree of cohesion and structure, but also lack a central decision-making structure. Examples of alliances include the anti-German Triple Entente of 1914 or the 1939 Non-Aggression Pact between Germany and the Soviet Union. Alliances can be the result of balancing or bandwagoning. Often alliances do have a high degree of organization (these are known as formal alliances). Formal alliances usually have decision-making structures and both implicit and explicit rules.

Since they are centered around the maintenance of internal security norms among member states, collective security systems generally have a high degree of organization and explicit rules and norms. Charles Lipson cites the Concert of Europe as one of the most successful historical examples of a collective security system (albeit one that could not be replicated today).[15] The most rigid and highly developed form of security regime is the confederation. These organizations involve "a deliberate banding together of states to create a central, permanent, statelike political structure that is capable of acting like a state, yet is not a single state but a union of states."[16] An illustration of a confederation would be the failed European Defense Community (EDC) of the 1950s. The range of security regimes is a continuum with coalitions and alliances at one extreme, formal alliances and collective security systems in the middle, and confederations at the other extreme.[17]

Because they facilitate the exchange of information and improve transparency, even in the security sphere, regimes provide a means to overcome security threats. They also offer states, even major powers, enhanced capabilities and resources. The success of NATO is tied to the internalization of the norms and rules of the organization and the institutionalization of the patterns of security cooperation at the core of the transatlantic organization. As such, it embodies the main characteristics of the two major types of security regime: the traditional military alliance; and the collective security system.

Alliances and Coalitions

The oldest and most common form of security regime is the alliance or coalition. Alliances may be simply defined as "a formal or informal arrangement for security cooperation between two or more sovereign states."[18] Glenn Snyder proposes a more formal definition of alliances as "formal associations of states for the use (or non-use) of military force, intended for either the security aggrandizement of their members, against specific other states."[19] The formal differences between alliances and coalitions (although the terms are often used interchangeably) center on the degree of formality and cohesiveness of the security arrangements. Alliances are usually much more formal, with memberstates bound together through treaties or international agreements. In contrast, coalitions tend to be less defined with few overt or tacit rules and norms. Because of their lack of demarcation, coalitions tend to be more short-lived than alliances. Nonetheless, the basic principles of the two are closely linked. Both types of security arrangements may be formed to either balance against threats or as a means of bandwagoning.

In addition, both alliances and coalitions are almost exclusively formed in opposition to an external threat to the memberstates that form the core of the arrangement. Hence, they are dependent on external threats or dangers to provide cohesiveness. These exterior factors are the key variable in both the development and maintenance of the alliance or coalition.

The sum total of the security threat arrayed against the alliance or coalition is termed the "threat quotient."[20] This phrase encompasses the total resources and capabilities faced by the memberstates. The strength and durability of the alliance is directly proportional to the level of the threat quotient. A high threat quotient usually leads to a high degree of cohesiveness and stability within the alliance. Conversely, alliances that face a low threat quotient are much more likely to be subject to internal rivalries and to undergo diplomatic revolutions which either end the arrangement or dramatically alter the character of the alliance.[21]

The main advantage of membership in alliance and coalitions is the ability to prevent regional or global hegemony. As such, through collaboration, small- and medium-sized states may prevent major powers from gaining security ascendency or hegemony.[22] Even though these security arrangements are often developed in response to direct military action, cooperation usually continues after the conflicts as members seek to ensure that hegemonic powers do not reassert themselves.[23] States gain a variety of benefits from participation in alliances and coalitions besides the obvious security advantages. For instance, cooperation in the security sphere can lead to cooperation in other areas. Robert Jervis contends that:

> Common goals give each state a stake in the well-being of the others: to the extent that they expect to cooperate in the future, they want all to be strong, especially if they think they may again have to contain the former enemy. Far from states' values being negatively interdependent (as is often the case in world politics), they are positively linked: each gains if the other is satisfied, and willing and able to carry out its international obligations.[24]

As patterns of cooperation are established and linkages develop, institutional frameworks are put in place to regulate interaction. This lowers transaction costs and improves transparency.[25] In addition, decisionmakers develop formal and informal relationships with their counterparts. This is especially true in the case of the formal alliance. These relationships have the effect of further facilitating future cooperation and lessening uncertainty in the security sphere.

At one level, NATO was established in 1949 as a formal alliance. From its very outset, the organization has had highly developed rules, norms and formal decision-making structures and procedures. The impetus behind its creation was the perceived external threat posed by the Soviet Union. Yet, the presence of a primary power, the United States, meant that NATO was a case of both bandwagoning (with the United States) and balancing (against the Soviet Union). Nevertheless, just as NATO was designed to counter an outside threat, it was also designed to regulate the security interaction of its memberstates in the manner of a collective security organization.

Collective Security Systems

Security alliances and coalitions are developed in response to external threats. These systems endeavor to promote collective responses to such threats, but maintain the security autonomy of memberstates within the system. When the external threat is defeated or dissipates, the cohesiveness of the system is challenged. The result is usually the demise of the security arrangement. States may decide to make their own hegemonal bid.[26] In addition, states may attempt to take preemptive measures if they perceive that an alliance partner is going to defect or if the future costs of security cooperation may outweigh the benefits. This would lead the alliance partner to defect.[27] For instance, the defeat of Germany in World War I eroded the alliance that had been arrayed against the Central Powers and resulted in the essential withdrawal of the United States from European security until World War II.

Unlike alliances and coalitions, collective security arrangements focus almost exclusively on the internal dimensions of security and promote long range cooperation even without a current threat. Consequently, collective security systems are more adaptable and flexible. These systems are "the collective commitment of a group to hold its members accountable for the maintenance of an internal security norm."[28] The central essence of a collective security system is its emphasis on self-regulation and collective punishment. In practice such a system would ideally encompass "a group of states attempts to reduce security threats by agreeing to collectively punish any member state that violates the system's norms."[29] The system rests on the "Three Musketeers" principle of all-for-one. It deters both internal and external threats by ensuring that states which violate the regime's norms and rules are punished by a coalition of "preponderant" force.[30] In order to maintain stability among its memberstates, collective security systems usually have norms which ensure a degree of parity in military capabilities and which promote transparency in order to reduce uncertainty.[31]

The failed League of Nations was the most ambitious collective security system to date and its inability to prevent or end aggression in the 1920s and 1930s led many scholars and policymakers to label such systems impractical.[32] There are three major criticisms over the utility of collective security organizations.[33] First, many realist critics assert that collective security systems need a relatively equal distribution of power which means that systems cannot have a primary or hegemonic power because it would dominate the system and lead states to balance against it. Second, states have different threat perceptions and will want to pursue divergent policies. As George Downs points out, "What is a vital interest for one state may be of no concern for another."[34] These differences could prevent joint action. Third, and finally, is the free - rider problem. As discussed in the previous chapter, members of organizations often do not pay their "share" of the costs.[35] This leads to internal conflict and provides incentives for states to endeavor to cheat or at least reduce their commitments to the system.

Although critics assert that collective security systems require a diffusion of power, Downs and Iida contend that the presence of a hegemonic or primary power can actually facilitate both the creation and the maintenance of the system in the same manner that a hegemon sets and enforces the rules of any other regime.[36] Primary or hegemonic powers increase the cohesiveness of the system and increase the likelihood that defectors will be punished.[37] Strong leadership can also ameliorate the free rider problem through enforcement of strict rules and procedures. In addition, collective security arrangements reinforce the commonality of interests by promoting similar policies and system-wide stability. For instance, Charles Kupchan contends, "a collective security system, by building on and promoting the political compatibility that makes such an institution possible, may perpetuate and make more durable a peaceful and desirable international setting."[38] States internalize patterns of cooperation because they assume other states will reciprocate.[39] The free rider problem is further alleviated because collective security systems promote long term cooperation which makes it likely that states will fulfill their commitments since patterns of cooperation become internalized.[40] Consequently, regimes may "lock-in cooperation."[41]

Collective security systems have major advantages over other security regimes because they allow for easy identification of threats. Because of the high levels of transparency within the system, potential violators are quickly recognized. Meanwhile, external threats are minimized because of the potential for collective responses. Concurrently, collective security systems provide a means to rehabilitate former adversaries by coopting them into the system. An example of this would be the cooption of the Federal Republic of Germany into the transatlantic alliance after World War II.[42]

NATO and Western Europe's Security Regime

The current security regime in Western Europe has its genesis in alliance that opposed Germany and the Axis powers during World War II. The Allied alliance was recast following the war as the Soviet Union defected in order to pursue its own security policies and new members, including the former wartime foes, were brought into the nascent regime. As the Soviet Union sought to expand and then consolidate its influence on the continent, the regime began to balance against its former ally.

In the aftermath of the Second World War, there were three central issues in Western European security: 1) how to counter the Soviet threat; 2) what was the role and place of Germany, even a divided West Germany, in Europe; and 3) how could the West European states best ensure the continued participation of the United States in continental security. Hence, the leaders of Great Britain, France and the other West European states were faced with a potential external threat, the Soviet Union, a possible internal threat, Germany, and the desire or even need for external security support and leadership.

NATO and the EDC

The institutional framework that codified the region's security regime began with the 1947 Dunkirk Treaty which was an anti-German alliance of the Western European states. The Dunkirk Treaty was followed by the Brussels Treaty of March 1948, which joined Belgium, France, Great Britain, Luxembourg and the Netherlands together in a collective defense arrangement which came to be known as the Western European Union (WEU). The Treaty established a framework for joint security and was seen as the first step toward a wider Atlantic alliance that would include the United States.[43]

For close to a decade, the Europeans proceeded along two tracks, developing separate institutions to deal with the three core issues. First, NATO was formed in order both to counter the Soviet threat and to ensure continued American participation in European defense. The Berlin blockade gave impetus to the 1948 negotiations over the Washington Treaty which established the transatlantic alliance. These negotiations occurred as American and European military planners began close cooperation to develop long-range military plans.[44] The signing of the Washington Treaty on 4 April 1949 confirmed American participation in European security, although the degree of commitment was initially unclear.[45] Second, in order to deal with the internal threat, the European Defense Community (EDC) was developed. The EDC was designed as a means to allow West German rearmament by creating an integrated European army.[46] It was also seen as a means to "rehabilitate" the Federal Republic of Germany by the major powers, including Germany itself.[47] German Chancellor Konrad Adenauer saw the EDC as the first major step in the process of reintegrating his country into the society of states of Western Europe.[48]

Efforts to develop Europe's security architecture were given impetus by the onset of the Korean War which seemed to demonstrate the willingness of the Soviet bloc to engage in conventional wars. The Truman administration initially predicted that by 1952, the Soviets would have the combined nuclear and conventional forces to overwhelm Western Europe, even with American forces stationed there.[49]

Leaders in both Europe and the United States were convinced that only with a rearmed Germany could the Soviet threat be countered. NATO's first Supreme Allied Commander Europe, American General Dwight D. Eisenhower concluded that ". . . even with the maximum potential realized through collective efforts of member nations, there is little hope for the economical long-term attainment of security and stability in Europe unless Germany can be counted on the side of the free nations."[50]

Ultimately, the EDC initiative would fail as the main powers involved in its development, the United States, Great Britain and France pursued divergent policy goals:

> The Americans wanted the Federal Republic rearmed as a means to alleviate the need for massive American ground deployments in Europe at a time when the nation was involved in an Asian war. The British were working to ensure continued American participation in continental defense in the face of a perceived increase in a Soviet threat to European security, all the while limiting their own contributions to continental security. Meanwhile French policymakers wanted to confirm both American and British participation in continental defense and prevent a resurgence in German power.[51]

Nonetheless, the failure of the EDC reaffirmed the centrality and importance of NATO. The WEU, which had existed only on paper until this point, was resurrected as a means to incorporate Germany into the fledgling security regime. The WEU served as the bridge by which the Federal Republic could be integrated into NATO.[52] Under the 1955 Paris Accords, France, Great Britain and the United States ended their occupation of West Germany. In exchange the Federal Republic was invited to join the WEU and was subsequently invited to join NATO. The transatlantic alliance would oversee the "operational aspects" of the German military, while the WEU supervised the political and legal steps necessary for German rearmament.[53] In a concession to the French, the Federal Republic pledged to pursue a peaceful foreign policy and, in particular, never "have recourse to force to achieve the reunification of Germany."[54] By 1955, the central questions about European security were essentially settled, at least for the near-term future. NATO provided a substantive security guarantee against Soviet aggression and ensured American participation in European defense. Meanwhile, Germany was anchored within the growing security institutions of the West.

Security Primacy and Leadership

The entry of Germany into NATO was not the organization's first expansion.[55] In 1952, Greece and Turkey became members of the organization. The entry of these two states demonstrated the importance of American leadership within the alliance.[56]   NATO would have two more rounds of expansion, in 1982 with the entry of Spain and in 1999 with the expansion to the Czech Republic, Hungary and Poland. While institutions such as NATO or the WEU reflected American strategic interests, they also benefited all memberstates by enhancing the public good of security available to all and by providing those advantages common to all regimes. Since the security regime of Western Europe benefited all of its memberstates it made American primacy in security matters more palatable.   For instance, John Ikenberry and Charles Kupchan contend that "rightful rule emerges if the hegemon is able to induce smaller powers to buy into its vision of international order and to accept as their own - in short, to internalize and embrace - the principles and norms espoused by the hegemon."[57] NATO was also attractive since the United States provided the lion's share of the budget and paid for the operational costs of its troop deployments in Europe.[58]   Hence the United States was able to fulfill the leadership role within NATO and the larger European security regime. Nonetheless, throughout the Cold War, France endeavored repeatedly to challenge U.S. security primacy in an effort to expand its influence and further its perceived national interests.[59]

France and NATO

From World War II onward, French security policy has been dichotomous. On one level, successive governments in Paris have worked to ensure an American military presence on the continent to serve as a balancer against both Germany and Russia. Yet, on another level, Paris has consistently worked to promote itself as the leader of Western Europe's security regime, often to the detriment of American strategic interests.

In 1958, French President Charles de Gaulle proposed a reorganization of NATO which would result in a tripartite structure in which the United States, France and Great Britain would assume shared and equal leadership of the alliance.[60] Although the United States made concessions toward France, the Eisenhower administration was unwilling to accept the French proposal. De Gaulle perceived that the United States and Great Britain dominated NATO and with the rejection of his initiative, the French president began to slowly but deliberately limit military relations between France and NATO. De Gaulle staunchly supported the United States during the Cuban Missile Crisis of 1962, but by 1965 it was clear that France intended to withdraw (or defect) from NATO.

Nonetheless, France wished to remain part of the region's security regime and even remain part of NATO's political structure. As such, the French withdrawal from NATO's integrated military command was less a matter of the nation defecting from the regime, and more an effort to maximize the benefits of membership while paying only a minimum of the costs – a classic free-rider problem. De Gaulle understood that France remained a critical component of the transatlantic alliance, and therefore, could use its leverage to extract greater rewards from the regime. In 1966, France officially withdrew from NATO's integrated military structure, but it continued to take part in non-defense activities and to participate in the political structures of the alliance. The impact of the French withdrawal was summarized thus:

> France's withdrawal required the Atlantic Alliance to make numerous changes in its institutional arrangements, conduct of meetings, and relations with French political and military liaison personnel. The aim of the fourteen allies was to maintain the maximum possible degree of allied unity, both in the arenas where France chose to participate as a full member and in those aspects of the Alliance where France preferred to remain at a certain distance. The French aim was to gain whatever benefits the Alliance might provide that would serve France's national interests and security without violating what de Gaulle regarded as key areas of national sovereignty and military independence.[61]

Throughout the crisis, the United States played the role of benevolent hegemon and accepted the French decision without imposing significant sanctions (which paved the way for continued French interaction with NATO). Rather than "punishing" France, the United States patiently "waited-out de Gaulle."[62] France merely exploited the willingness of the United States to allow free-riders. She adopted a "privileged position and an ungrateful stand" under de Gaulle.[63] Even during this period French forces continued to be involved in joint programs with NATO. De Gaulle's successors ultimately returned France, more or less, back into the folds of NATO.[64] One can find numerous other examples in which the United States has allowed nations to work at cross-purposes with American interests if the costs to the United States are relatively minor. The United States has been able to play the benevolent hegemon by acting more as "a senior partner, rather than as an adversary," in international organizations.[65] The United States operates out of the assumption that public goods such as free trade or security are not zero-sum variables.

ESDI

Throughout the institutional history of NATO, France has led the Europeanist bloc of nations that sought greater autonomy and influence for the West European states in the region's security region. This drive peaked in the 1980s, before resurfacing again in the late 1990s. Specifically, the Europeanist states sought greater control of military assets in Europe and greater influence in the decision-making procedures of NATO. The drive for an autonomous security structure outside of NATO came to be known as the European Security and Defense Identity (ESDI). In the 1980s, the French choose the moribund WEU as the vehicle for the development of ESDI, and the organization was reactivated by a French initiative in 1984. The major Europeanist states included France, Belgium, Italy, Germany, and Spain.[66]

The Europeanist states were opposed by a bloc of the European states within NATO known as the Atlanticist countries. The Atlanticists were led by the United Kingdom and included Denmark, the Netherlands, Portugal and Norway. Following negotiations over the revival of the WEU in 1987, it was decided that the organization would be a consultative body with no standing forces.[67] Hence, the WEU would not emerge as a threat to NATO as the central component of Europe's security regime.

The Europeanists had to be contend with the notion that the region's security system would cease to be dominated by NATO and that power and control would be dispersed over a variety of organizations and institutions. At the time, Peter van Ham asserted that:

> Consensus has gradually been built that the "New Europe" will be based on many institutions, of which the EU and NATO are likely to become the main pillars. The WEU, as the organization responsible for defence within the EU, is to function as the bridge between both organizations. Over time, WEU may develop into a fully fledged European defence organization taking responsibility for handling some problems Europeans can no longer expect the United States to solve for them (either directly or working through NATO). Institutions like the United Nations, the CSCE [Conference on Security and Cooperation in Europe, now the Organization for Security and Cooperation in Europe or OSCE] and the Council of Europe will, of course, remain essential frameworks for preserving international peace and security, managing essential European and global problems, and – perhaps most importantly – for developing a regional society based on law which can be monitored and enforced.[68]

Nevertheless, the United States was able to maintain the centrality of NATO during the 1980s and beyond. The success of NATO during the Cold War period was tied to the ability of the organization to prompt memberstates to internalize the rules and norms of the regime that NATO typifies. NATO was also able to increase the confidence among memberstates that others will not defect. Furthermore, the lengthy nature of the relationships among NATO's memberstates also increases the ability of states to form linkage strategies.[69] With the notable exception of France, NATO's memberstates were willing to trade a certain amount of legal freedom of action in security issues in exchange for a greater degree of realistic influence over the polices of partner states.[70] This is important because the stronger, and more complex, the degrees of interdependence that can be forged between nations the less likely that single issues can break those nations apart - even if the single issue was the original reason behind the formation of the alliance. Thus, the longer that NATO survived, the stronger the organization became, and the more likely that it would assume functions outside of its original mandate as separate security issues became increasingly intertwined.

The End of the Cold War

In 1989, the Berlin Wall fell, signaling the beginning of the demise of the Soviet bloc. At the point of its greatest triumph, the defeat of its main external threat – the Soviet Union, NATO also faced its most significant challenges as an institution. The end of the bipolar conflict called into question the utility of NATO and its role in the security regime of Europe.

In many ways NATO was a victim of its own success. The demise of the Soviet Union removed the major external security threat to the nations of Western Europe, at least in terms of a direct large-scale military invasion. In addition, even a reunified Germany no longer posed an internal security threat to its neighbors. Indeed, because of the region's security regime and because of progress on the political and economic spheres, Europe was moving toward the denationalization of borders.[71] Hence, NATO had succeeded as both an alliance and a collective security system. There were even calls on both sides of the Atlantic for the United States to diminish or even end its security presence on the continent.

In an effort to reduce defense expenditures and realize a "peace-dividend" from the end of the Cold War, there were dramatic decreases in troop deployments in Europe. Between 1991 and 1999, the United States reduced its forces stationed in Europe from 350,000 to 100,000 and its NATO partners had total troop reductions of some 500,000. Overall, NATO assets were reduced by almost 40 percent and the Alliance's forces that were ready for combat within 30 days was lowered to 60 percent (during the Cold War, almost 90 percent of NATO forces could be combat-ready within two days). In addition, NATO's nuclear weapons were decreased by 80 percent as the result of arms control agreements between the United States and Russia.[72]

However, before the rubble had even been cleared from the collapse of communism in Europe, new security threats to the region began to emerge. The Persian Gulf War of 1990-1991 demonstrated the potential for events outside of the geographic scope of Western Europe's security regime to impact the region. The conflict also demonstrated the military superiority of the United States in terms of advanced weaponry, command and control assets and strategic lift.[73] Indeed, the conflict demonstrated that no European nation had the "over-the-horizon" capability to deploy large numbers of troops as quickly as the United States could.[74]

New Threats to Europe

The Persian Gulf War was followed by a sequence of events which demonstrated that while the direct military threats to Western Europe had dissipated, there were a number of emerging new threats. These threats included: 1) ethnic and religious conflict in Europe; 2) new threats from the Maghreb and Middle East; and, 3) the proliferation of weapons of mass destruction. Many of these challenges to European security were not "new" but they received new attention after the Cold War ended since they emerged as the most significant risks for Western European peace and stability.

By 1991, all of the former Eastern bloc states had significant minority problems that ranged from outright armed strife as in the case of the former Yugoslav states to questions of citizenship in the Baltic states.[75] The most pressing problems associated with ethnic and religious conflict occurred in the former Yugoslavia. Widespread conflict eventually prompted armed intervention or peace-enforcement deployments in Bosnia, Kosovo and Macedonia. These conflicts threatened European security on a variety of levels. First, the Yugoslav conflicts led to the greatest loss of life since the Second World War and the majority of casualties were unarmed civilians. Furthermore, the brutality of the ethnic conflict was genocidal in nature as various parties sought to "ethnically-cleanse" areas of populations with different religions. Second, the strife created enormous refugee problems. For instance, Germany now accounts for some 3 percent of the world's total asylum seekers mainly because of the Yugoslav conflicts.[76] It is estimated that there are some 7.3 million foreign residents in Germany or approximately 9 percent of the nation's total population.[77] Germany is home to approximately 70 percent of the refugees from the former Yugoslavia and has spent over DM 17 billion on their care.[78] Third, and finally, the conflicts threatened to re-awake centuries-old tensions as the Serbs sought support from Russia, the Croats and Slovenes looked to Germany and Austria, and the Bosnians and Kosovars sought aid from Muslim states.

Instability in the Mediterranean also posed risks for the states of Western Europe.[79] An ongoing civil war in Algeria produced a refugee problem for France and also led to terrorist acts in that nation.[80] There has also been widespread civil unrest, especially in 1997 and 1998.[81] France is home to some 4 million Muslims of whom 800,000 are of Algerian descent. The conflict in Algeria resulted in large numbers of illegal refugees seeking shelter in France.[82] Unemployment among the refugees is approximately 33 percent which places added strains on the French social welfare system. Instability in the Maghreb and Mediterranean region is especially troubling since Europe remains dependent on these areas for the majority of its imported energy supplies.

In addition to direct conflict on its borders, Western Europe also faced potential security threats from the proliferation of weapons of mass destruction (WMD).

Such weapons include chemical, biological and nuclear munitions. Following the collapse of the Soviet Union, there were a number of celebrated incidents involving the attempted smuggling of nuclear materials. One official commented that "even potatoes are probably much better guarded today than radioactive materials" in the immediate post-Soviet period.[83]   During the Cold War, the American nuclear umbrella seemed to preclude the possibility of nuclear attack on Western Europe, but the potential acquisition of nuclear weapons by a rogue or pariah state such as Iraq or the acquisition of an atomic weapon by a substate group proved a much more difficult issue to deal with, especially as a number of states, including Iran, Iraq, Syria and Libya initiated WMD programs. The use of chemical weapons against the Kurds in Iraq by Saddam Hussein and the 1995 Aum Shinri Kyo chemical attack on a Tokyo subway demonstrated the potential for the use of such weapons. Many states in the Middle East acquired the systems necessary to deliver WMDs against the European continent. Such systems included submarines, long-range bombers and ballistic missiles with ranges of more than 1,000 kilometers.[84]

New Challenges to NATO

As policymakers in Western Europe began to recognize the danger of new security threats in the post-Cold War period, the main component of the region's security regime, NATO, itself faced new challenges. Since many of the emerging security threats were outside of the geographic scope of the transatlantic area, policymakers and officials warned that NATO needed to be able to go "out-of-area" in order to address these new risks (within NATO there was a recognized need to go "out-of area or out of business"). In addition, in light of Russian cooperation during the Gulf War and in mediation efforts in the former Yugoslavia, many in Western Europe perceived NATO as a relic of the Cold War whose continued existence would create tensions between the former superpower and Western Europe. This was especially true in light of the desire by the new governments of many former communist nations in Europe to join the institutions of the West. Furthermore, the demise of the Soviet Union renewed the call for ESDI since many perceived that the strong American military presence was no longer needed. Finally, NATO faced pressure from potential rival security organizations such as the revised WEU or the CSCE. This challenge was significant in that the WEU had already demonstrated its ability to undertake operations in Yugoslavia and the Persian Gulf.[85]

However, as early as 1990, the administration of George W. Bush sounded a call for reforms to NATO's basic mission and role. The administration wanted to alter NATO so that it could remain the core element of European security and thereby maintain American influence in Europe.[86]   In order to allow NATO to undertake operations outside of Europe, a rapid reaction force (the Allied Rapid Reaction Corps or ARRC) was established. ARRC could be tasked to undertake humanitarian operations or security operations for organizations such as the United Nations or the European Union.[87]

The formation of ARRC was followed by the promulgation of NATO's "New Strategic Concept" at the 1991 Rome Conference. The "New Strategic Concept" tasked NATO with new missions and created new structures to allow the organization to engage with its former Cold War adversaries. The North Atlantic Cooperation Council (NACC) was established as a forum both for NATO states and members of the former Warsaw Pact to meet and develop security policies. Membership in NACC was enhanced in 1994 with the creation of the Partnership-for-Peace (PfP) program. Membership in PfP allowed non-NATO states to undertake military training exercises with NATO forces. It was also envisioned as a first step toward eventual NATO membership.

Concurrently, NATO sought to diminish the drive for ESDI through the establishment of a new type of operation, the combined and joint task force (CJTF). Under CJTF, coalitions of NATO members, and potentially PfP memberstates, could undertake operations without involving the whole organization. For instance, France, Italy and Germany would be free to initiate a humanitarian operation without American or British participation. CJTF was envisioned as a means to allow the Europeans greater autonomy within NATO, while maintaining some degree of American involvement.[88] CJTF would allow European forces access to NATO resources, even though the operations could be conducted under the auspices of the WEU.[89]

The "New Strategic Concept" was followed by decisions at the 1994 Brussels Summit to increase NATO's efforts to counter the proliferation of WMDs. Again, new working groups were created within the Alliance and tasked to develop policies by which NATO could address concerns over WMDs and establish defenses against these threats.[90] Following the 1999 Washington Summit, NATO created a WMD Center to coordinate between the various committees and national groups working on WMD issues.[91] In 2000, the WMD Center also initiated programs to enhance cooperation with states outside of the Alliance, including members of the EAPC.

The efforts to develop counter-measures and strategies for dealing with WMDs were enhanced by inviting Russian participation in the counter-proliferation efforts. Meanwhile, NATO also began to meet with Russian political and defense officials in a series of conferences known as the 16 + 1 meetings. These meetings were formalized in 1997 with a charter between NATO and Russia. The charter established the NATO-Russia Permanent Joint Council. This body was tasked to study and coordinate efforts on security matters, including joint peacekeeping operations and arms control efforts.[92] The Charter also cleared the way for NATO expansion by pledging that the Alliance would not station nuclear weapons on the territory of any new member that was a former Warsaw Pact state.

In order to enhance NATO interaction with non-memberstates, NACC was superseded by the creation of the Euro-Atlantic Partnership Council (EAPC) in

1997.[93] EAPC was designed to expand the political intercourse between NATO and PfP memberstates and to increase cooperation among the Alliance and its partners to "a qualitatively new level."[94]   Significantly, the EAPC was also tasked to coordinate NATO missions with the other major European security organizations, namely the OSCE and the WEU.

As NATO relations with its former enemies improved, so too did relations with its erstwhile renegade member. As it became clear in the mid-1990s that NATO would remain the cornerstone of European security, France began to reintegrate into the organization in order to exert influence and prevent itself from being marginalized in future decisions over issues such as expansion and in NATO operations. In 1994, France agreed to participate in NATO's anti-WMD efforts.[95] The following year, France announced that it would fully reintegrate into NATO's military structures.

At the Madrid Summit in 1997, three former members of the Warsaw Pact were invited to join NATO. These countries were judged to have made significant progress in democratization, civil-military relations and had established a high degree of interoperability with NATO forces (through PfP exercises and consultations). The Czech Republic, Hungary and Poland formally acceded to the Washington Treaty on 12 March 1999.[96] NATO thus demonstrated its ability to expand and incorporate new members. Another round of enlargement is set to be decided in 2002, with nine potential candidates.[97]

In April of 1999, at NATO's Washington Summit, the Alliance agreed upon a new Strategic Concept which incorporated lessons learned from NATO participation in peace-keeping and peace-enforcement operations in the Balkans. The representatives of the memberstates reaffirmed the centrality of NATO to transatlantic security, but also endorsed a greater role for the European Union in future security operations through the development of a common foreign and security policy (CFSP). The new Strategic Concept specifically states that a CFSP "would be compatible with the common security and defense policy established within the framework of the Washington Treaty."[98] In order to develop ESDI within the existing transatlantic framework, the Summit also called upon the European states to more fully develop their military and security capabilities through the Defense Capabilities Initiative (DCI). DCI is designed to better delineate the needs and capabilities of the alliance partners for future operations and thereby reduce redundancy and repetition of function and production.[99]   The DCI reinforces the Union's own Headline and Capability Goals in that it is designed to establish a clear separation between what the Europeans will contribute to NATO and what resources they will utilize for operations in which NATO as a whole is not involved.[100]

Much of the renewed momentum for ESDI and CFSP developed as a result of the experiences of the Western European states in humanitarian and peace-enforcement operations in the former Yugoslavia. Differences over strategy and tactics, as well as long-range goals, were exacerbated by the almost complete reliance of the European states on the United States for advanced weaponry and rapid deployment assets. Much to the dismay of the Europeanist states, these missions underscored the continued reliance of the European security regime on the military might of the remaining superpower.

NATO's First Shooting Wars

Somewhat ironically, although NATO was formed in 1949 partially as a means to counter the Soviet Union, it was not until after the Cold War ended that NATO undertook combat operations. Operations in the former Yugoslavia demonstrated the centrality of NATO to European security since it was only through the operations of the Alliance that American military resources and credibility could be brought to bear. The missions in Bosnia, Kosovo and Macedonia illustrated the importance of NATO as a security institution that could coordinate the deployment of troops from many different nations and that could assemble the firepower necessary to successfully prosecute both peace-enforcement operations and combat missions.

Bosnia

In the immediate wake of the Cold War, the nations of the EU sought to assert themselves by taking a leading role in the crisis in the former Yugoslavia. Germany was the first nation to recognize the independence of Croatia, and EU support for the break-up of Yugoslavia contrasted with American policy which championed a single Yugoslav Republic. Nonetheless, the administration of George Bush was very willing to allow the Europeans to oversee the resultant series of crises. In this regard the U.S. had an "exaggerated confidence" in the capability of the EU and other multilateral organizations to mediate the growing ethnic conflict in the Balkans.[101]

By the end of 1991, Yugoslavia was on the verge of disintegration as Croatia, Slovenia, Bosnia-Herzegovina and Macedonia declared their independence in rapid succession. The result was a series of bloody ethnic-conflicts which were undertaken to create ethnically homogenous societies. In these conflicts, the Serbian leader Slobodan Milosevic utilized nationalism in an effort to bolster and maintain his political power by drawing Serbs into a series of conflicts whose goals were not the preservation of the former Yugoslavia, but the effort to create "ethnically pure" Serbian communities with allegiance to their "parent nation" of Serbia. The Croats countered with similar efforts to drive out Serbs and create their own cross-border communities.[102] The conflicts created thousands of refugees and prompted atrocities on a scale unseen in Europe since the Second World War.

The inability of the European Union and the Organization for Security and Cooperation in Europe (OSCE) to end ethnic conflict in the former Yugoslav republic of Bosnia demonstrated the continued centrality of NATO to Europe's security regime. Following a declaration of independence from Yugoslavia, the state of Bosnia became engulfed in a brutal ethnic conflict in which some 250,000 people were killed and some 1.3 million people were displaced. The fighting marked the worst violence in Europe since the end of the Second World War. Led by Europeanist states, mainly France and Germany, the European Union sought to manage the crisis without U.S. involvement in order to demonstrate its growing political and diplomatic power.

In 1992, as the European Union sought to diffuse the crisis in Bosnia through cooperation with the UN and the OSCE, it found it necessary to turn to NATO for military support. That year, in conjunction with the WEU, NATO aircraft began enforcing a "no-fly" zone (Operation Deny Flight) over the region and participated in the naval missions to enforce an arms embargo (Operation Sharp Guard). This marked the first time that NATO assets were deployed in an out-of-area mission. On 28 February 1994, NATO engaged in combat for the first time.

Throughout this period, NATO aircraft engaged in support missions for the UN Protection Force (UNPROFOR) in Bosnia. This included airstrikes against Bosnian Serb positions. Following the shelling of Sarajevo by the Bosnian Serbs, on 30 August 1995, NATO launched a 12-day series of strikes on the Serb positions (code-named Operation Deliberate Force). These strikes were instrumental in compelling the Serbs to accept the Dayton Peace Plan in November 1995. Under the auspices of the plan, NATO troops were deployed in a peace-enforcement role. The mission was named the Implementation Force (IFOR) and made up of NATO forces as well as the troops from 18 other nations.[103] IFOR was later replaced by a smaller force, the Stabilization Force or SFOR.[104] IFOR numbered 60,000 troops, while SFOR had been reduced to 21,000 by February 2001. IFOR was responsible for separating the forces of the Federation of Bosnia and Herzegovina and the Republic of Serbska and enforcing the general provisions of the Dayton Peace Accords. SFOR had a more ambitious mandate which includes the development of civilian institutions within the region.

The operations resulted in the return of some 723,000 refugees and open elections. In addition, IFOR/SFOR was responsible for the arrest of 21 indicted war criminals and the removal of 120,000 mines and 11,000 small arms from Bosnia. Most importantly, the IFOR and SFOR operations both involved Russian forces. The former Cold War adversary contributed about 1,200 troops. The twin operations did not officially subordinate Russian troops to NATO, but it did establish a unity of command whereby the Russian contingent served under NATO's area commander of the mission.[105]

The missions in Bosnia demonstrated the importance of NATO as a means to provide military credibility to international peace-operations. IFOR and SFOR also showed that NATO could undertake operations out-of-area and that it had a unique ability to coordinate multinational troops from both sides of the Cold War and provide the capabilities and assets to conduct such operations.

Kosovo

The lessons of Bosnia were reinforced to an even greater degree by NATO's experiences in Kosovo. Ethnic conflict in Kosovo erupted as a result of tensions between the ethnic Serbs and the ethnic Albanian majority in the province.[106] Kosovo had enjoyed autonomous status until 1989 when Serb leader, and later president of Yugoslavia, Slobodan Milosevic arranged to end the special standing. The regime in Belgrade also endeavored to suppress Albanian culture. In response, an indigenous independence movement, the Kosovo Liberation Army (KLA), emerged as the main opposition group and engaged in an armed struggle against the Serbs.

By 1998, ethnic conflict in the province had produced 120,000 internal and external refugees because of the conflict between the KLA and government troops.[107] Beginning in March 1998, Serb paramilitaries and government soldiers initiated a widespread ethnic cleansing campaign that followed the pattern of the Bosnian campaign.[108] By the next year, there were some 2,000 casualties and some 400,000 refugees.

There were a variety of international efforts to mediate the conflict, but these were rebuffed by the regime in Belgrade. A series of well-publicized civilian massacres increased the pressure on Milosevic, including coercion from the Serbs' only major ally, Russia. The UN also passed Resolution 1199 which threatened military action against the Serbs unless they negotiated. As a result, Milosevic agreed to talks at Rambouillet, France in the Spring of 1999. However, the Serbs rejected the resultant accords because the central component included a demand for greater autonomy for Kosovo.

Following the rejection of the Rambouillet Accords, the Serbs engaged in a widespread drive to ethnically cleanse the province of the ethnic Albanians. Within a short period, there were 1.5 million refugees and at least 5,000 civilian casualties. In short, almost 90 percent of the Albanian population had been driven from their homes or killed. NATO responded with a 77-day air campaign which show-cased American military technology. On 3 June 1999, an agreement was reached between a Russian envoy, former Prime Minister Chernomyrdin, EU envoy Finnish President Ahtisaari, and Milosevic. One week later, the Serbs began to withdraw.

NATO troops formed the core of the 50,000-member Kosovo Force (KFOR). KFOR was tasked to facilitate the return of refugees and ensure an end to ethnic conflict in the area. Since KFOR's deployment, some 900,000 refugees have returned to their homes in Kosovo. KFOR has also overseen local elections and cleared some 1.1 million square meters of landmines. NATO troops also patrol the major roadways and are involved in the rebuilding efforts. Since their deployment, NATO forces have also worked with the International Court of Justice to document crimes against humanity.[109]

Although the campaign resulted in an Alliance victory, the operation exposed a number of significant fissures within NATO. Even staunch Atlanticist states such as Great Britain were displeased with the unwillingness of the administration of William J. Clinton to even consider ground troops as an option to end the conflict.[110] Concurrently, the Europeanist states complained that Washington "consistently devalued nonmilitary approaches to security."[111] They also decried the seeming unwillingness of Washington to develop and implement a proactive Balkan security policy in consultation with its NATO allies.[112] Differences over policy with Washington helped propel the drive for a CFSP and helped garner the support of states, such as Great Britain, that had traditionally been the staunchest supporters of the United States.[113]

Meanwhile, there was also dissatisfaction in the United States with the Kosovo campaign. The United States paid $3 billion of the $5 billion costs of the air campaign and incurred annual costs of $3.5 billion to maintain its 7,000-member contribution to KFOR. The costs of the campaign reawakened questions over burdensharing within NATO. Furthermore, many American officials and policymakers were displeased with the tensions the Kosovo crisis created between the United States and Russia.

Macedonia

For the European states, NATO involvement in Macedonia provided a much more practical model for security operations than the military campaign in Kosovo. Following its declaration of independence from Yugoslavia in September of 1991, Macedonia faced both external and internal security threats. Serbia and Greece both refused to recognize the new state and both imposed economic blockades on the fledgling country.[114] Internally, the multiethnic state with its large Albanian population faced the potential for ethnic conflict of the sort seen in Bosnia and later Kosovo.[115]

International efforts to prevent an outbreak of ethnic conflict in Macedonia began with the deployment of a battalion of observers on the border between that nation and Kosovo. In 1993, the troop number grew to 1,000 with the addition of an American battalion. The mission was also placed under the auspices of UNPROFOR, but Macedonia requested that the force be separated. The request was approved by the UN Security Council and the force was renamed UN Preventative Deployment Force (UNPREDEF). UNPREDEF included 540 American troops, 556 troops from the Nordic peacekeeping battalion and 53 other observers.[116]

The early deployment of forces was seen as key to preventing the outbreak of hostilities. As the conflict in Kosovo intensified, NATO asked for and received permission to station troops in Macedonia as a staging point for operations in Kosovo. The presence of international forces in Macedonia led to pressure on the Greek government to end its embargo. In 1995, an accord was signed by the two nations and Greece ultimately became the main trading partner with the new country. In addition, Macedonia joined the Council of Europe, the OSCE and NATO's PfP and the EAPC.

Following the deployment of KFOR to the north, NATO has maintained about 2,500 troops in Macedonia. During Operation Essential Harvest, NATO forces helped enforce a cease-fire agreement between Albanian separatists and the government. NATO forces collected 3,300 small arms and more than 70,000 rounds of ammunition. Alliance troops also provided border security and arrested more than 300 suspected rebels who were endeavoring to cross illegally into Macedonia. In 2001, these forces conducted Operation Amber Fox in order to protect monitors engaged in the effort to end conflict between warring factions in the country.[117]

Lessons From the Cold War and Beyond

NATO's experiences in the former Yugoslavia demonstrated the continued centrality of the Alliance to Europe's security regime. Furthermore, the variety of new missions and new tasks adopted since the end of the Cold War illustrated the Alliance's ability to adapt and internalize the requirements needed to meet the changing global security environment. NATO began its existence as an anti-Soviet alliance whose structure and functions also incorporated the main elements of a collective security system. Hence, on one level, NATO provided security guarantees against an external threat, the Soviet Union, and allowed the nationstates of Western Europe to concentrate on non-military issues, including economics and social welfare, in the post-World War II era. On another level, NATO's security assurances opened the way for the reincorporation of the Federal Republic of Germany into the society of states that formed Western Europe. This further strengthened the ability of states to cooperate and collaborate on issues beyond security through linkage strategies and the establishment of domestic preferences for continued transnational cooperation. The result was the denationalization of borders within Western Europe and the growth of regional political, economic and security integration.

The Cold War success of NATO would be replicated in the post-Cold War era in a similar, albeit alternative, fashion. Because of its history, NATO was the primary security organization that the newly democratizing states of Central and Eastern Europe wanted to join. The entry of the Czech Republic, Hungary and

Poland, showed the capability of the Alliance to expand, and pledges of new rounds of expansion ensured continued interest in membership. For these states, NATO provided the same internal and external security guarantees that had marked its achievements during the bipolar conflict. The Alliance could provide security assurances against a resurgent Russia and provide the mechanism for the former Soviet bloc states to be rehabilitated into the Western community of nations. Hence, the former Soviet bloc states, including Russia, joined the PfP and EAPC or developed even closer means of cooperation through direct accords with the Alliance.

In the former Yugoslavia, NATO also demonstrated its military potential both in concrete terms, in Bosnia and Kosovo, and as a guarantor of security and stability, as in Macedonia. The Alliance also showed itself capable of addressing new security threats such as ethnic conflict and humanitarian peace operations even as it sought to develop the means to deal with issues such as the proliferation of WMDs. Yet, as was the case with the end of the Cold War, the operations in the former Yugoslavia reinforced the drive for an autonomous ESDI and a CFSP for the European Union. Dissatisfaction with American leadership during the Kosovo campaign stirred efforts to establish a reaction force for the Union which could be deployed without American assent or the use of U.S. capabilities. As the political machinations behind the development of independent European ground on, NATO was again called upon to address a different security threat – that of terrorism – in the wake of the attacks on 11 September 2001.

Notes

1. D. Scott Bennett describes security as "the drive for self preservation," and asserts that "true security is obtained by ensuring that the territorial and political boundaries of the homeland and 'vital' territory cannot be changed by others;" D. Scott Bennett, "Security, Bargaining and the End of Interstate Rivalry," *International Studies Quarterly* 40, no. 2 (June 1996): 163.
2. Katja Weber, "Hierarchy Amidst Anarchy: A Transaction Costs Approach to International Security Cooperation," *International Studies Quarterly* 41, no. 2 (June 1997): 326.
3. Gulick, 61.
4. Robert Jervis, "Security Regimes," in *International Regimes*, ed. Stephen Krasner (Ithaca: Cornell University, 1983), 175-76.
5. Jervis, "Cooperation," 186-214.
6. Tom Lansford, *Evolution and Devolution: The Dynamics of Sovereignty and Security in Post-Cold War Europe* (Aldershot: Ashgate, 2000), 48.
7. See Stephen R. Rock, *Why Peace Breaks Out: Great Power Rapprochement in Historical Perspective* (Chapel Hill: University of North Carolina, 1989).
8. Bandwagoning refers to the tendency for lesser states to ally themselves with a strong power in order to improve their capabilities while balancing refers to efforts by states to band together in opposition to great powers in order to prevent hegemony; Schweller, 72-73.

9.   Richard K. Betts, "Systems for Peace or Causes of War? Collective Security, Arms Control and the New Europe," *International Security* 17, no. 1 (Summer 1992): 12.
10. See Alexander George, *Forceful Persuasion: Coercive Diplomacy as an Alternative to War* (Washington, D.C.: United States Institute of Peace, 1991).
11. Jervis, "Security Regimes," 177-79.
12. Richard Rosecrance asserts that the ability of states to devote more resources to economics because of American security guarantees in the post-World War II era led to the rise of the "Trading State" which concentrated its resources on commerce and was able to gain far greater shares of the world economy than would otherwise have been possible. Examples of the trading state include Japan and Germany; Richard Rosecrance, *The Rise of the Trading State: Commerce and Conquest in the Modern World* (New York: Basic Books, 1986).
13. Weber, 322.
14. These costs may be overt or tacit. For instance, there may be concrete sanctions imposed upon a state that defects from a regime or that state may simply lose access to the benefits of membership.
15. Charles Lipson, "Is the Future of Collective Security Like the Past," in Downs, 105-31.
16. Weber, 322.
17. Ibid.
18. Walt, *The Origins of Alliances*, 12.
19. Glenn H. Snyder, "Alliance Theory: A Neorealist First Cut," *International Affairs* 44 (Spring 1990): 104.
20. Michael W. Doyle, "Balancing Power Classically: An Alternative to Collective Security?" in *Collective Security Beyond the Cold War*, ed. George W. Downs (Ann Arbor: University of Michigan, 1994), 158.
21. An example of this sort of shift occurred in the 1750s with shifts in alliances between London and Vienna to London and Paris, and between Paris and Berlin to Paris and Vienna; Doyle, 159.
22. Gulick, 61.
23. Jervis, "From Balance to Concert," 67.
24. Ibid.
25. Gilpin, *War and Change*, 27.
26. On the benefits of using coercion to exploit weaker states, see Thomas C. Schelling, *Arms and Influence* (New Haven: Yale University, 1966): 1-34.
27. Robert Axelrod and Robert O. Keohane use game theory to probe this issue. They conclude that if all states continue cooperation they would be better off, however, if defection occurs, the first state to defect gains the most. This creates incentives for individual states to be the first to defect if they perceive weaknesses in the structure of the alliance; Axelrod and Keohane, 229.
28. George W. Downs, "Beyond the Debate on Collective Security," in *Collective Security Beyond the Cold War*, ed. George W. Downs (Ann Arbor: University of Michigan, 1994), 2.
29. George W. Downs and Keisuke Iida, "Assessing the Theoretical Case Against Collective Security," in *Collective Security Beyond the Cold War*, ed. George W. Downs (Ann Arbor: University of Michigan, 1994), 18.
30. Kupchan, "Collective Security," 43.

31. Downs and Iida, 18.
32. See, for instance, Betts, 5-43.
33. George Downs and Keisuke Iida identify six theoretical arguments against collective security: "1) Collective security requires a substantial diffusion of power; 2) Variation in assessment of threats dramatically limits the range and efficacy of collective security; 3) The free-rider problem jeopardizes any collective security agreement; 4) Collective security cannot survive in the absence of an outside threat; 5) Collective security requires states to commit themselves to an inflexible course of action that is insensitive to context and self-interest; and 6) The logic of collective security is circular in the sense that its establishment requires that its consequence already exist;" Downs and Iida, 36.
34. Downs and Iida, 24.
35. Michael Hechter summarized the phenomenon of free-riders from a utilitarian perspective in the following manner: "Rational self-interest actors will not join large organizations to pursue collective goods when they can reap the benefit of other people's activity to pursue those ends. This means that the rational actor in the utilitarian model will always be a free rider whenever given the opportunity;" Michael Hechter, "Karl Polanyi's Social Theory: A Critique," *Politics and Society* 10, no. 4 (Fall 1981): 403.
36. Downs and Iida, 22-23.
37. Downs and Iida cite these factors as examples of how hegemonic powers can aid collective security systems; Ibid. Their arguments echo Robert O. Keohane's work on hegemonic cooperation and hegemonic stability theory; see Keohane, *After Hegemony*, especially Chapter 8, "Hegemonic Cooperation in the Postwar Era."
38. Kupchan, 49.
39. Robert Axelrod and Robert O. Keohane, "Achieving Cooperation Under Anarchy: Strategies and Institutions," *World Politics* 38 (1985): 234.
40. Under collective security systems, states have both rewards and potential punishments as incentives for cooperation. Punishments are implemented by the punishment regime, while rewards come in the form of payoffs from cooperation and the potential for future cooperation; Anatol Rappaport and Albert Chammah, *Prisoner's Dilemma: A Study in Conflict and Cooperation* (Ann Arbor: University of Michigan, 1965), 235.
41. Joseph S. Nye, Jr, "Nuclear Learning and U.S.–Soviet Security Regimes," *International Organization* 41 (1987): 385.
42. Note that in both cases the co-option of these states involved the "rehabilitation" of the states after their defeat in hegemonic bids. These efforts were undertaken in order to avert future conflict and maintain the relative stability of the contemporary system of states.
43. Bernard Law Montgomery, *The Memoirs of Field Marshall Montgomery* (New York: World Publishing, 1958), 447.
44. Ibid.
45. Under Article 5 of the Treaty, the memberstates agreed the ". . . an armed attack against one or more of them in Europe or North America shall be considered an attack against them all and consequently they agree that, if such an attack occurs, each of them, in exercise of the right of individual or collective self defense recognized by Article 51 of the Charter of the United Nations, will assist the Party or Parties so attacked by taking forthwith, individually and in concert with other Parties, such action as it deems necessary, including the use of armed force, to restore and maintain the security of the North Atlantic area;" NATO, "Article 5," *The North Atlantic Treaty*, Washington, D.C., 4 April 1949. Hence, while the

Treaty does pledge the United States to the defense of its NATO partners, it does not specify an American military presence in Europe.

46. Furdson, 187.

47. Adenauer described the EDC as both central to integration and an "indispensable prerequisite for peace in Europe;" Federal Republic of Germany, *Government Declaration by the German Federal Chancellor, Dr. Konrad Adenauer, Before the German Bundestag on 20 October 1953* (Bonn: Press and Information Office, 1953).

48. See Konrad Adenauer, *Memoirs, 1945-1966* (Chicago: Henry Regnery, 1966).

49. The year 1952 was initially set as the Joint Chiefs of Staff (JCOS) target date, while NSC 68 set the date as 1954, but for planning purposes, the JCOS continued to use 1952 as the date at which the Soviet threat would be the greatest, US, Senate Committee on Appropriations, *Hearings, Department of Defense Appropriations for 1953* (Washington, D.C.: GPO, 1953), 332-35, 385.

50. NATO, SACEUR, *First Annual Report* (Brussels: NATO, 1951), 2.

51. Lansford, *Evolution and Devolution*, 147.

52. On the negotiations surrounding the failed EDC and the ramifications of the proposals, see Edward Furdson, *The European Defense Community: A History* (London: MacMillan, 1980).

53. Arie Bloed, and Ramses A. Wessel, eds., *The Changing Functions of the Western European Union (WEU): Introduction and Basic Documents* (London: Martinus Nijhoff Publishers, 1994), xv-xviii.

54. U.S., Department of State, *Documents on Germany, 1944-1985*, no. 9446 (Washington, D.C.: Bureau of Public Affairs, 1986), 420-24.

55. The original members of NATO were Belgium, Canada, Denmark, France, Great Britain, Iceland, Italy, Luxembourg, the Netherlands, Norway, Portugal and the United States.

56. Denmark, Norway and the Netherlands opposed Greek and Turkish entry because the two nations were perceived to lack the democratic credentials of the other members and would "dilute" the cohesion of the alliance. Other members, namely France, were concerned over the potential for an intra-alliance conflict between the two states, especially in light of the Article 5 guarantee. Nonetheless, the United States was able to convince the other members to accept the necessity of membership for the two nations as a means of securing NATO's Mediterranean flank; Mark Smith, *NATO Enlargement During the Cold War: Strategy and System in the Western Alliance* (London: Palgrave, 2000), 79-82.

57. Ikenberry and Kupchan, 151.

58. On the tendency for states which carry a large per centage of the burdens of an international institution to press their strategic preferences and use the organizations to their advantage, see Snyder, 113.

59. For an overview of French strategic interests during the early and middle stages of the Cold War, see Simon Serfaty, *France, De Gaulle and Europe: The Policies of the Fourth and Fifth Republics Toward the Continent* (Baltimore: Johns Hopkins, 1968).

60. De Gaulle wanted complete shared command, even of the American nuclear forces deployed in Europe under the auspices of NATO – a situation that was completely unacceptable to the United States; Charles G. Cogan, *Oldest Allies, Guarded Friends: The United States and France Since 1940* (London: Praeger, 1994), 125.

61. Harrison and McDonough, 36.

62. Frank Costigliola, *France and the United States: The Cold War Alliance Since World War II* (New York: Twayne, 1992), 126.

63. Michael Harrison, *The Reluctant Ally: France and Atlantic Security* (Baltimore: Johns Hopkins, 1981), 115.

64. Ibid., 170; Ronald Tiersky, *The Mitterrand Legacy and the Future of French Security Policy*, McNair Papers, no. 43 (Washington, D.C.: INSS, 1995).

65. Axelrod and Keohane, "Achieving Cooperation," 102.

66. For Italy and Spain, support for the development of an autonomous European pillar was based on an attempt to gain recognition of their particular national concerns, mainly focused on North Africa. Meanwhile, Germany supported the WEU as a means to bring the French back into the fold of the Alliance by using the French participation in WEU discussions as a substitute for French involvement in NATO forums.

67. Robbin Laird, *The Europeanization of the Alliance* (Boulder: Westview 1991), 25-26.

68. Van Ham, 197.

69. Keohane and Nye, *Power and Interdependence*, 36.

70. Andrew Hurrell, "Explaining the Resurgence of Regionalism in World Politics," *Review of International Studies* 21, no. 4 (October 1995): 336-37. While states have engaged in multilateralism in order to reinforce state power, the "institutional enmeshment" may constrain some elements of state sovereignty as regionalism rises; see Mark W. Zacher, "The Decaying Pillars of the Westphalian Temple: Implications for Order and Governance," in *Governance Without Government: Order and Change in World Politics*, eds. James N. Rosenau and Ernst-Otto Czempiel (Cambridge: Cambridge University, 1992).

71. On the progress of cooperation and collaboration in Europe, see Simon Serfaty, *Memories of Europe's Future: Farewell to Yesteryear* (Washington, D.C.: CSIS, 1999).

72. Celeste A. Wallander, "Institutional Assets and Adaptability: NATO After the Cold War," *International Organization*, 54, no. 4 (Autumn 2000), 718.

73. See, for instance, Edward J. Marolda and Robert J. Schneller, jr., *Shield and Sword: The United States Navy and the Persian Gulf War* (Washington, D.C.: Naval Institute Press, 1998).

74. Institute for National Strategic Studies (INSS), "The Revolution in Military Affairs," *Strategic Forum*, no. 11 (November 1994), 3.

75. Stephan Iwan Griffiths, "Nationalism in Central and South-Eastern Europe," in *Security and Strategy in the New Europe*, ed. Colin McInnes (New York: Routledge, 1992), 64-65.

76. U.S. Committee for Refugees, *World Refugee Survey, 1997* (Washington, D.C.: Immigration and Refugees Services of America, 1997), 4-5.

77. While Germany is home to approximately 350,000 refugees from the former Yugoslavia, the fastest growing segment of the nation's foreign population come from states such as Afghanistan, Iran and Iraq; "Germany: Data, Ethnic Germans, Asylum," *Migration News* 5, no. 5 (February 1998).

78. Helmut Kohl, "Security in Tomorrow's World," speech at the 34th Munich Conference on Security Policy, 7 February 1998.

79. For an excellent overview of the potential for strife see Graham E. Fuller and Ian O. Lesser, *A Sense of Siege: The Geopolitics of Islam and the West* (Boulder: Westview, 1995).

80. In France, immigrants make up some 6.3 percent of the total population, and of these, some 40 percent are from North Africa. Of this number, some 600,000 are Algerians who have migrated to France since 1990, bringing France's Algerian population to some 800,000;

William Drozdiak, "Fleeing Kurds Cause Alarm in Europe," *Washington Post* (7 January 1998). Of France's immigrant population, *The Economist* states, "A formidable number of black and brown people, mostly of North African origin, mostly without qualifications and many of them unemployed, are growing up not as Frenchmen but as a sullen, excluded minority;" *The Economist, France Survey* (25 November, 1995), 11.

81. "France, Belgium: Suburbs, Algeria," *Migration News* 5, no. 2 (February 1998).

82. Andrew Jack, "French Planning Tougher Curbs on Immigration," *The Financial Times* (21 April 1996), 2; "French Parliament Debates Immigration Laws," *BBC News* (5 December 1998).

83. Oleg Bukharin and William Potter, "Potatoes Were Guarded Better," *Bulletin of the Atomic Scientists* 51, no. 3 (May 1995): 46-50.

84. Peter Van Ham, *Managing Non-Proliferation Regimes in the 1990s: Power, Politics and Policies* (New York: Council on Foreign Relations, 1994), 24.

85. WEU operations were only undertaken after considerable and often rancorous debates because the WEU had no standing forces. Therefore it had to make military arrangements with NATO and national forces on an *ad hoc* basis; Diego A. Ruiz Palmer, *French Strategic Options in the 1990s, Adelphi Papers* 260 (Summer 1991), 47.

86. Charles Krupnick "Not What They Wanted: American Policy and the European Security and Defense Identity" in Alexander Moens and Christopher Anstis, eds., *Disconcerted Europe: The Search for a New Security Architecture* (Boulder: Westview 1994), 120.

87. Colin McInnes, "The Future of NATO," in Colin McInnes, ed., *Security and Strategy in the New Europe* (New York: Routledge 1992), 87.

88. Indeed since all NATO operations have to be unanimously approved, CJTF preserved a tacit American veto over operations. At the same time, it allowed the United States to avoid certain operations while granting approval for any combination of states that might wish to undertake the mission.

89. NATO, NAC, *Declaration of the Heads of State and Government Participating in the Meeting of the North Atlantic Council*, press release M-1(94)3 (11 January 1994), 1.

90. These groups were established at the NATO Ministerial in Istanbul in June of 1994.

91. The WMD Center had six specific tasks: "to ensure a more vigorous debate at NATO leading to strengthened common understanding among Allies on WMD issues and how to respond to them; to improve the quality and quantity of intelligence and information sharing among Allies on proliferation issues; to support the development of a public-information strategy by Allies to increase awareness of proliferation issues and Allies' efforts to support non-proliferation efforts; to enhance military readiness to operate in a WMD environments and to counter WMD threats; to exchange information concerning national programs for bilateral WMD destruction and assistance–specifically how to help Russia destroy its stockpiles of chemical weapons; and to enhance the possibilities for Allies to assist one another in the protection of their civil populations against WMD risks; "Interview: Ted Whiteside, Head of NATO's WMD Center," *NATO Review*, vol 49 (Winter 2001/2002), 22.

92. The accord declares that the "provisions of this Act do not provide Russia or NATO, in any way, with a right of veto over the actions of the other nor do they infringe upon or restrict the rights of Russia or NATO to independent decision-making and action;" *Founding Act on Mutual Relations, Cooperation and Security between the Russian Federation and the North Atlantic Treaty Organization* (1997), 3.

93. On the creation of the EAPC see, NATO, "The Transformation of NATO's Defence Posture," *NATO Fact Sheet*, no. 22 (July 1997).
94. See NATO, "The Euro-Atlantic Partnership Council," *NATO Fact Sheet*, no. 19 (July 1997).
95. Robert Joseph, "Proliferation, Counter-Proliferation and NATO," *Survival*, 38, no. 1 (Spring 1996), 120.
96. Javier Solana, "On Course for a NATO of 19 Nations in 1999," *NATO Review*, 1 (Spring 1998), pp. 3-5; NATO, *NATO Basic Document: The Study on Enlargement* (Brussels: NATO, 1995).
97. Under the Membership Action Plan (MAP), approved at the 1999 Washington Summit, potential candidates are judged on a variety of criteria, including political and economic, military, resources, security issues and legal issues. For instance, under political criteria, aspirants must have resolved any outstanding border or minority disputes with neighboring states. Under military criteria, future memberstates have to have the ability to integrate their weapons and communications systems with NATO standards; NATO, *Membership Action Plan*, NAC-S(99)66 (24 April 1999).
98. The document also stated that one fundamental goal of NATO was to "develop effective cooperation with other European and Euro-Atlantic organizations as well as the United Nations. Our collective aim is to build a European security architecture in which the Alliance's contribution to the security of and stability of theses and other international organizations are complementary and mutually reinforcing, both in deepening relations among Euro-Atlantic countries and in managing crises;" NATO, *The Alliance's Strategic Concept*, NAC-S(99)65 (24 April 1999).
99. US, Department of Defense, "Background Briefing," *DefenseLink* (11 December 1998).
100. NAC, *Statement on the Defence Capabilities Initiative*, N-NAC-D-1(2000)64 (8 June 2000).
101. Lawrence Freedman, "Why the West Failed," *Foreign Policy* 97 (Winter 1994): 53-69.
102. Andrei Georgiev and Emil Tzenkov, "The Troubled Balkans," in Hugo Miall, ed., *Redefining Europe: New Patterns of Conflict and Cooperation* (London: Pinter, 1994), 54.
103. Besides NATO forces, IFOR included troops from European states such as Russia, Ukraine, Poland, Romania, Sweden, the Czech Republic, Lithuania, Latvia, Estonia, Austria, Finland and Hungary.
104. For an overview of NATO's role in the former Yugoslavia, see NATO, *NATO's Role in Bringing Peace to the Former Yugoslavia*, NATO Basic Fact Sheet, no. 4 (March 1997).
105. Leontiy P. Shevtsov, "Russian-NATO Military Cooperation in Bosnia: A Basis for the Future?" *NATO Review* 45, no. 2 (March 1997): 18.
106. Serbian atrocities in Kosovo escalated as the fighting increased in the region. See for instance, Amnesty International, *Crisis Report: Kosovo*, EUR70/48/98 (21 July 98).
107. Fred Abrahams, "The West Winks at Serbia Atrocities in Kosovo," *International Herald Tribune* (5 August 1998).
108. Mary Robinson, *Statement by the United Nations High Commissioner for Human Rights On the Situation in Kosovo* HR/98/14 (9 June 1998).
109. This includes investigations which have documented 526 mass graves and exhumed more than 5,000 bodies; NATO, *Kosovo: Facts and Figures* (5 December 2000).

110. On January 28, 1999, the British and French governments announced that they were willing to commit ground troops, but they were undercut by the Clinton Administration's public refusal to commit ground forces.

111. Daniel Plesch, "Kosovo: A Symptom of NATO's Strategic Failure," *Basic* (7 April 1999), 2.

112. On the European efforts at conflict prevention, see European Action Council for Peace in the Balkans and the Public International Law & Policy Group, "Kosovo: From Crisis to a Permanent Solution" (1 November 1997); and Stefan Troebst, "Conflict in the Kosovo: Failure of Prevention?" *European Centre for Minority Issues Working Paper, Number 1* (May 1998).

113. "The Ageing Alliance," *The Economist* (10/23/99), 6.

114. Alice Ackerman and Antonio Pala, "From Peacekeeping to Preventative Deployment: A Study of the United Nations in the Former Yugoslav Republic of Macedonia," *European Security* 5, no. 1 (Spring 1996): 84.

115. The Albanian population initially comprise 23 percent of Macedonians, however, the conflict in Kosovo caused this percentage to swell with in the influx of refugees; see for instance, Gazmend Pula, "Self-Determination: A Non-Confrontational Option for the Kosova Crisis" *Balkan Forum* 4, no. 3 (September 1996): 202.

116. UN, *Report of the Secretary-General of the United Nations*, S/1995/222/Corr. 1 (29 March 1995).

117. Lord Robertson, "Press Statement," PR/CP(2001) 168 (7 December 2001).

Chapter 3

Building a Consensus

Introduction

The terrorist attacks on 11 September 2001, represented a direct challenge both to the existing security paradigms of the major powers and the transatlantic security regime. In the aftermath of the Cold War, NATO evolved and reformed its mission capabilities to address changing threats. Instead of a strategic doctrine geared toward defending against a massive conventional attack, the Alliance developed forces which could be rapidly deployed to engage in a variety of operations such as those undertaken in the former Yugoslavia. Concurrently, NATO also endeavored to address broad security threats such as the proliferation of WMDs and terrorism. Nonetheless, few officials within the Alliance or its memberstates envisioned the potential devastation or loss of life that occurred on 11 September.

In the wake of the terrorist attacks, NATO's leadership had to formulate and implement an immediate response and devise long-term strategies to counter future terrorist activities. The immediate question facing the Alliance was whether or not to invoke Article 5 which would mandate a collective reaction to the attacks. Within the political bodies of NATO there was considerable debate over the optimum strategy and it fell to the leadership of the Alliance to coordinate the organization's reaction in such a way as maintain the centrality of NATO to European security.

NATO's Structure and Organization

NATO's decision-making structures are designed to ensure a variety of goals. First, political officials who represent each of the memberstates are responsible for all of the major decisions. The political bodies of the Alliance dominate those of the military and ensure civilian control of the military. Second, major decisions are made on the basis of consensus, not majority rule. Often the decision-making process is accomplished in relative secrecy in order to prevent the appearance of winners or losers through the machinations. Ideally the interests and opinions of each of the memberstates count equally. In practical terms, however, more powerful states such as the United States, Great Britain and France, tend to have greater influence. Third, and finally, the structures are designed to allow great flexibility and quick responses. The 1949 founding charter of NATO was written in such a fashion as to allow reform and restructuring in order to adapt to changed global circumstances.

Alliance leaders must always take into account the domestic impact of their decisions in both their own and their partners' countries. In addition, NATO has developed bilateral relationships with individual states, principally Russia, Ukraine, the states of Central and Eastern Europe and states in the Mediterranean region. The Alliance also has formal relations with regional organizations, mainly the European Union (EU). As such decision-making is further constrained and the ramifications of any NATO actions must be weighed against the "shadow of the future" in terms of relations with these states and entities. For instance, NATO expansion must be evaluated in the context of NATO-Russian relations. The following sections examine the formal structure of the Alliance and the major external agreements and actors which influence NATO in the context of building a consensus.

The Washington Treaty

The simplicity of the Washington Treaty has allowed the organization to evolve over time in order to adapt to new missions and new threats. The Treaty itself is a rather simple and straightforward document. The Treaty has a short preamble which lists the underlying principles of the Alliance as the determination to:

> safeguard the freedom, common heritage and civilization of their peoples, founded on the principles of democracy, individual liberty and the rule of law.
> They [the memberstates] seek to promote stability and well-being in the North Atlantic area.
> They are resolved to unite their efforts for collective defense and for the preservation of peace and security.[1]

The text of the Washington Treaty contains fourteen articles which define the rights and obligations of each of the memberstates. The articles also lay out the framework of the organization. The first article asserts the legitimacy of the organization under the UN Charter.[2] The second pledges support for institutional development in both the security and economic spheres. Article 3 calls upon the memberstates to maintain both collective and individual defense capabilities and provides the basis for joint defense planning. Article 4 establishes the framework for consultations between memberstates and the Alliance in times of threat. The fifth Article is the most significant as it contains the principle of collective defense, that an attack on one memberstate is an attack on all. The article requires all Alliance partners to come to the aid of a memberstate that is under attack.

The sixth article defines NATO's geographic boundaries and until the Cold War ended, the organization did undertake operations outside of these territorial limits.[3] Article 9 of the Treaty establishes the North Atlantic Council (NAC) as the political authority which controls the Alliance. The chairman of NAC is NATO's Secretary General.

Article 10 allows for the incorporation of new members with "unanimous" approval of the existing members. In addition, Article 13 allows any memberstate to withdraw from the Alliance with a minimum of one year's notice to the other parties, once the Treaty has been in place for 20 years.

Major Organs

The membership of NAC includes permanent representatives from each of the memberstates. Occasionally, during extremely important sessions, foreign ministers or even national leaders sit in place of the regular permanent representatives during NAC meetings. The result of these more senior meetings is usually a major reform or change within the Alliance. For instance, such senior meetings have taken place to approve the expansion of NATO or the adoption of new strategic plans.

NAC is the only body specifically authorized by the North Atlantic Treaty. However, it has the statutory authority to create agencies and bodies so that the Alliance can carry out its strategies and promote its interests. Since 1949, NAC has created a number of structures and committees to oversee the operations and strategic planning of NATO. All committees and military commands are under the authority of NAC. The Military Committee supervises the Alliance's military structures. It is comprised of the chiefs-of-staff of the member nations and their representatives. The Military Committee provides planning and guidance to the two main NATO commanders.[4]

The first of these commanders is the Supreme Allied Commander Europe (SACEUR). SACEUR is headquartered at Mons, Belgium and controls Alliance forces in Europe. The headquarters supervises the Alliance's nuclear deterrent forces in Europe, and controls the main land and air forces of the organization stationed in Europe. SACEUR is also responsible for training operations and exercises as well as maintaining the integrity of NATO's territorial boundaries.[5] The European command has been reorganized into three main sub-commands: Southern, Central and Northwest. The second major NATO command is the Supreme Allied Commander Atlantic (SACLANT). SACLANT is headquartered in Norfolk, Virginia, and has authority over NATO forces in the Atlantic. SACLANT is responsible for safeguarding the Alliance's sea lines of communication and supply and conducting amphibious operations and landing. SACLANT also oversees the deployment of NATO's seaborne nuclear deterrence.[6] Both commanders have considerable authority and can set standards for training and equipment and for the organization of forces. SACEUR and SACLANT also have direct command of the

NATO forces during operations. These positions have always been senior U.S. officers which has added to the aforementioned calls for greater European influence within the Alliance.[7] Since the end of the Cold War, the number of subordinate commands within NATO has been reduced from 65 to 20 to reflect decreases in manpower and assets and to give the Alliance a more streamlined command system.[8]

The senior political body under NAC is the Political Committee. The Political Committee meets regularly with different levels of seniority and advises NAC on political issues. In addition to the Political Committee, NATO's International Staff has both a Political Directorate and an Economics Directorate which also serve as consultative bodies for NAC and the Secretary General. The Economics Committee concentrates on issues which relate to defense spending and the economic consequences of defense policy. The Committee also reviews the budgets and budget proposals for the various agencies of the Alliance. This board has the added responsibility of developing the Alliance's overall budget and configuring the amounts that each memberstate contributes to the organization. NATO's overall budget and each agency's spending are reviewed by an international independent board of auditors which is selected by the Alliance partners.

Military planning and policy is overseen by the Division of Defense Planning and Policy, while procurement and equipment issues are overseen by the Conference of National Armaments Directors which reports to the Directorate of Armaments Planning, Programs and Research. The Alliance has endeavored to incorporate the impact of defense planning and operations on both the environment and civil societies through its Division of Scientific and Environmental Affairs.

The headquarters of NATO is located in Brussels, Belgium and serves as the permanent home for NAC. The complex also houses the delegations from each of the memberstates. Each delegation is comprised of a permanent political envoy and a national military representative. Both figures are supported by staffs of military and civilian advisers. The headquarters also contains the offices of the Secretary General and the International Military Staff, as well as a number of Alliance agencies which oversee communications and command functions. Some 3,150 are employed at NATO headquarters. Some 1,400 of these are members of national delegations and their staffs. Approximately 1,300 are civilian employees of various agencies and 450 are members of the International Military Staff.[9]

NACC/EAPC

In order to facilitate cooperation with the nations of Central and Eastern Europe in the wake of the Cold War, in 1991, at the Rome Summit, NATO created the North Atlantic Cooperation Council or NACC. This organization was designed as a forum to encourage and coordinate cooperation and collaboration between the Alliance and the states of the former Soviet bloc. Specifically, NACC was tasked with providing information on civil-military relations and civilian control of the military. NACC was the first tangible step by NATO in addressing the security concerns of the Central and Eastern European states. It also marked an expansion of the Alliance's role as a "loosely-constructed collective security organization."[10] NACC laid the foundation for the PfP program and other cooperative projects with non-NATO states.

By 1997, however, there was widespread dissatisfaction with NACC. The non-NATO members of the organization wanted more influence and more tangible results from their association with the Alliance. In response to criticisms of NACC, NATO inaugurated the Euro-Atlantic Partnership Council or EAPC in 1997. The EAPC includes the memberstates of NATO and the members of PfP.[11] Like the NACC, the EAPC provides a forum for discussions and exchanges on security and political matters. It played an important role in coordinating the Alliance's response to the crisis in Kosovo and unlike its predecessor, the EAPC develops concrete two-year action plans to organize collaboration between the Alliance and its PfP partners. The EAPC also oversees the operations of NATO's Euro-Atlantic Disaster Response Coordination Center (EADRCC) which is designed to assist in humanitarian operations in which the Alliance or its partners participate. Examples of operations of the EADRCC include flood relief efforts in the western regions of Ukraine and programs and measures to aid the refugees that resulted from the Kosovo Crisis.[12]

Permanent Joint Councils

In 1991, Russia joined the NACC, PfP and later joined the EAPC as a founding member. Russia contributed troops to the IFOR/SFOR operations in Bosnia and to the KFOR mission in Kosovo. Relations between NATO and Russia were formalized in 1997 with the signing of an accord which, among other things, established the NATO-Russia Permanent Joint Council (PJC) as a body to promote cooperation and collaboration between the former Cold War nemeses. The PJC meets monthly and coordinates activities between the Alliance and Russia. The Council also meets at the ministerial level on issues of significant importance to both parties. The PJC has initiated talks between Russian and Alliance officials on a host of issues, including humanitarian operations, nonproliferation concerns, disarmament and civil-military relations. There is now a permanent Russian mission at NATO headquarters in Brussels and a NATO office in Moscow.[13]

Concurrent with the development of relations between NATO and Russia was the opening of the relationship between NATO and Ukraine. At the Madrid Summit in 1997, NATO officials signed the Charter on a Distinctive Partnership with Ukraine. The Charter led to the establishment of a NATO liaison office in Ukraine's capital, Kiev, and a Memorandum of Understanding between Ukraine and NATO on civil emergency preparedness. NATO has also conducted seminars on civil-military relations and resource planning for the Ukrainian military. Ukraine is also a member of PfP and under that context, has contributed forces to NATO operations and participated in NATO training exercises.[14]

Mediterranean Cooperation Group

One of the "new" areas of concern for NATO in the wake of the Cold War was the Mediterranean region. There were three specific concerns to the Alliance: 1) the proliferation of WMDs in the region; 2) the ability of NATO to deploy or project power either in the area or through the region in areas such as the Middle East and Persian Gulf in light of conflicts in Kuwait and Iraq; and 3), the spread or potential spread of ethnic and substate conflict throughout the region, as exemplified by the ongoing violence in Algeria, and its potential to create refugees and conflict spillover.[15] In an effort to deal with security issues emanating from that region and to foster cooperation between the Alliance and states in the region, NATO initiated the Mediterranean Dialogue under the auspices of committee, the Mediterranean Cooperation Group (MCG).

NATO's Mediterranean Dialogue was based on a similar initiative undertaken by the WEU in 1992. The Alliance launched its project in 1994. Six Mediterranean nations, Egypt, Israel, Jordan, Morocco, Mauritania and Tunisia, joined the forum along with representatives from the NATO states.[16] The main goal of the MCG is to foster cooperation between partner states and NATO on security and economic issues.[17] Under existing arrangements, officers from the partner nations may take courses at both the NATO School and the NATO Defense College. In addition, there is an Annual Work Program which coordinates planning programs and exercises in civil-military relations, humanitarian operations and various aspects of defense cooperation.

WMD Groups

In response to the growing security threat posed by the proliferation of WMDs, at the 1994 Brussels Summit, Alliance leaders called for the creation of new bodies within NATO to study and recommend policies on WMD proliferation. As a result, NAC authorized the establishment of two new groups to analyze the ramifications of proliferation concerns.[18] The first of these bodies was the Senior Politico-Military Group on Proliferation (SGP). The SGP was tasked to study the political intricacies of proliferation and nonproliferation efforts. It has worked with Russia and other nuclear powers to develop common approaches to nonproliferation. The second body was the Senior Defense Group on Proliferation (DGP). This group was tasked to analyze the military issues surrounding proliferation and the efforts to counter the spread of WMDs. The DGP is also the work group that has developed the Alliance's main response strategies to the use of WMDs. Both groups meet en masse as the Joint Committee on Proliferation which is chaired by NATO Deputy Secretary General and which reports directly to NAC.[19] The work of the groups is enhanced through the capabilities and assets of the newly created NATO WMD Center.

NATO and the European Union

The drive for the Europeanization of the Alliance in the 1980s reinforced the initiative to create an ESDI. In 1999, the European Council summarized the political goals of ESDI as such:

> We are convinced that the Council should have the ability to take decisions on the full range of conflict prevention and crisis management tasks defined in the Treaty on European Union, the "Petersburg tasks". To this end, the Union must have the capability for autonomous action, backed up by credible military forces, the means to decide to use them, and a readiness to do so, in order to respond to international crises without prejudice to actions by NATO.[20]

These goals built upon existent trends within the EU. In the fall of 1998, British Prime Minister Tony Blair proposed a Common European Defense Initiative (CEDI). Germany and the other EU states endorsed CEDI in February of 1999. CEDI became the security component of the Common Foreign and Security Policy (CFSP) called for by the 1997 Maastricht Treaty.[21] At the Cologne Summit in June of 1999, the proposal received formal approval from the EU.

However, the new drive for ESDI did not come with the exclusionary traits of the past in regard to NATO. This new spirit of cooperation between the EU and NATO was represented in the comments of a German official: "It is obvious that we cannot build up a European Security and Defence Identity without a more institutional arrangement between the [EU] and NATO. The EU arms-length approach to NATO is a thing of the past."[22] The Chief of Political and Academic Affairs of the European Commission's Washington Delegation, Cameron Fraser described American support for ESDI in the following manner: "Our [the EU] efforts now are supported by the United States administration because they see the value of the Europeans taking on a greater share of the burden in dealing with European security issues . . . . It's a better rebalancing of the transatlantic relationship that we should see, not any threat to it."[23]

The embodiment of the drive for autonomous capabilities within the EU is the proposal for a European rapid reaction capability which give the Europeans the means to deploy their own military or non-military peacekeeping assets without American support or approval.   The Rapid Reaction Facility (RRF) called for by European Council at the Helsinki Summit in 1999, is designed to expedite the deployment of civilian assets to "deal with natural disasters, conflict prevention, and crisis management."[24] The RRF is conceived as a method to incorporate both governmental resources and those of NGOs, and to work with the military units of EU memberstates.[25] The ultimate goal of the RRF initiative would be to create a permanent standby force that could deploy up to 15,000 personnel trained in "human rights monitoring, civil administration, policing, conflict resolution, election supervision, media monitoring and local languages."[26] Many of the components of such a force would be available through existing civilian police forces.

The RRF would exist in tandem with a regular rapid reaction force known as the European Rapid Reaction Force (ERRF). At the Helsinki Conference, the EU agreed to develop a 50,000-60,000 member reaction force that could be deployed within 60 days and be maintained for a period of at least one year.[27] The French have called for an even larger multilateral force.[28] The purpose of the reaction force would be to take action in situations where NATO was not involved and the forces would be outside of the Alliance's military and political command structure. In this way, there would be no shared assets, as in the case of the WEU, and the U.S. would not be involved in the actual decision-making chain.

A variety of problems exist that must be overcome if ESDI is to be implemented through the establishment of the RRF and the ERRF. Lord Robertson summarized these impediments in the following manner:

This is not purely an issue of finding new money for defense. It is about getting a good return on investment - literally 'getting more bang for your buck.' Today, the European Allies spend about 60% of what the United States spends on defense, but nobody would suggest that the European Allies have 60% of the capability. We need to improve that return on investment, through innovative management, defense industrial consolidation, setting of priorities, and courageous decisions.

We must spend more wisely and if that doesn't free up enough resources, there is nothing for it but to call for more resources. But let me be clear - I am committed to ensuring that DCI delivers - that the capability shortfalls will be addressed.

To the extent that European Allies are prepared to support DCI, and make faster progress in improving their capabilities, they will also fare better in fulfilling the EU's Headline Goal. Even at the relatively modest level of 60,000 rapid reaction troops set at Helsinki, it is clear that European nations have some serious gaps in capabilities, such as strategic lift, air-to-air refueling and strategic intelligence. Hence, if Europe is not delivering as promised, we will have two gaps: a transatlantic capability gap, and a European credibility gap. This is hardly a recipe for a healthy 21st century Alliance. We must avoid such an outcome, and we must act now to avoid it.[29]

The ERRF has emerged as the cause of one of the most significant policy rows between Europe and the U.S. in recent history. The administration of George W.

Bush has signaled that it sees ERRF as potentially competing with NATO for resources. In addition, U.S. Secretary of Defense Donald Rumsfield has expressed concerns about the fact that the ERRF would have a separate planning organization for operations.[30] This could cause conflict with NATO operations, especially since many of the forces pledged to the ERRF are "double-hatted" or committed to both NATO and the European force.[31] British opponents of the ERRF contend that "the creation of the ERRF will undermine NATO, discourage American involvement in European peacekeeping operations."[32] While Washington has long supported the Europeans assuming a greater share of their defense burden, many in Congress and the Bush Administration assert that the ERRF would become a rival to NATO with overlapping functions and redundant capabilities. Nonetheless, the United States continues to officially endorse the creation of autonomous European security capabilities under the auspices of NATO.

In the wake of 11 September, one of the central questions facing the Alliance concerned the ability of the European states to contribute to any American-led attack and still continue plans to develop their autonomous capabilities. At the center of this question, as well as broader concerns over the relevancy of the Alliance to any military or political response to the 11 September attacks, was Lord Robertson, the Alliance's Secretary General. To the Scotsman fell the multifaceted task of leading NATO during one of its most significant tests. Lord Robertson would have to maintain a delicate balance which incorporated the interests of the Alliance members and partners on both sides of the Atlantic and which preserved the long term viability of NATO's role in transatlantic security.

The Secretary General

The Secretary General is the chief executive of NATO. In addition to serving as the chairman of NAC, the EAPC and the MCG, the Secretary General also chairs several other senior committees within the Alliance and is responsible for directing the day-to-day operations of NATO. He is also titular chair of a variety of major committees. The Secretary General must be a consensus maker who is able to broker compromises since NAC operates on the principle of unanimity. The power of the Secretary General is derived from his ability to propose initiatives and to direct discussions over subjects in various committees. The Secretary General also serves as the main spokesman for the Alliance and is its most visible representative. Throughout the history of the Alliance, the Secretary General has also been the focal point for resolving disputes between NATO members, including the ongoing series of disputes between Greece and Turkey and past rifts such as the French withdrawal from the Alliance's integrated military structure in 1966.

The Secretary General is chosen by NAC. The position is usually held by a senior political or diplomatic figure. As with other decisions of NAC, the choice of

Secretary General is usually the result of compromise and consensus-building. Since American officers dominate the military structures of the Alliance, by tradition, the post of Secretary General is always held by a European. However, Atlanticist nations have dominated the position and officials from the United Kingdom been the Alliance's chief executive on three out of ten occasions.[33]

Lord Robertson

Lord Robertson, George Islay MacNeill Robertson, became NATO's tenth Secretary General in 1999. His immediate predecessor, Javier Solana, a staunch Europeanist, resigned as Secretary General of the Alliance in order to take control of the fledgling efforts to develop a CFSP within the EU. Robertson's tenure has been marked by a consistent effort to maintain the centrality of NATO in European security and to develop new capabilities and functions for the Alliance. For Lord Robertson, the attacks on 11 September 2001 reinforced the importance of collective security and he was determined to ensure that NATO played a significant role in the fight against global terrorism.

Lord Robertson was born in 1946 in Port Ellen, Isle of Islay, Scotland. After he graduated from the University of Dundee with a degree in Economics, he went to work for a labor union and became responsible for the union operations in the Scottish whiskey industry. In 1978, he was elected to the House of Commons as a member of the Labour Party. He served in a variety of functions for the Party, including Opposition Spokesman for Scotland (1979-1980), defense (1980-1981) and Foreign and Commonwealth affairs (1981-1993). From 1993 to 1997, he was the Spokesman for Scotland in the Labour Party shadow cabinet. Following the election of Blair as Prime Minister in 1997, Lord Robertson was appointed Minister of Defense. In this position, Lord Robertson oversaw dramatic cuts in defense expenditures and the formulation and implementation of a new strategic vision for the armed forces of the United Kingdom. Lord Robertson also worked to improve cooperation between the U.K. and its European allies, especially in the realm of defense-industrial collaboration.[34]

During the Kosovo Crisis, Lord Robertson was the one of the most vocal European critics of the Serbian actions and called for a swift and overwhelming military response by the West. During the NATO air campaign, he worked closely with his American counterpart, Secretary of Defense William Cohen. As it turned out, the United Kingdom was the only ally to provide significant numbers of sophisticated precision-guided munitions during the campaign.

Lord Robertson's vocal support for NATO's operations in Kosovo made him the leading choice to succeed Solana when he resigned. Following custom, Lord Robertson was granted a life peerage by Queen Elizabeth II and made Lord Robertson of Port Ellen on 24 August 1999.[35] Initially, Lord Robertson's priorities centered around efforts to improve cooperation between NATO and Russia and to oversee the ongoing operations of NATO forces in the three Balkan operations. It was also expected that the new Secretary General would supervise the second round of NATO expansion in the post-Cold War era. However, the events of 11 September led to a dramatic recalculation of NATO's chief executive's priorities.

First Reactions

On one level, NATO's response to the attacks of 11 September 2001 was immediate and sure. On the afternoon of the attacks, Lord Robertson denounced the actions:

> I condemn in the strongest possible terms the senseless attacks which have just been perpetrated against the United States of America. My sympathies go to the American people, the victims and their families. These barbaric acts constitute intolerable aggression against democracy and underlie the need for the international community and the members of the Alliance to unite their forces in fighting the scourge of terrorism.[36]

Lord Robertson's condemnation was followed by similar statements from the major bodies and structures within the Alliance.[37] NAC's communique stressed the solidarity of the Alliance:

> The North Atlantic Council met tonight to express its solidarity with the United States of America at this moment of great tragedy and mourning. Our deepest sympathy lies with the victims, their families and all Americans. The NATO nations unanimously condemn these barbaric acts committed against a NATO member state. The mindless slaughter of so many innocent civilians is an unacceptable act of violence without precedent in the modern era. It underscores the urgency of intensifying the battle against terrorism, a battle that the NATO countries indeed all civilized nations must win. All Allies stand united in their determination to combat this scourge.
>
> At this critical moment, the United States can rely on its 18 Allies in North America and Europe for assistance and support. NATO solidarity remains the essence of our Alliance. Our message to the people of the United States is that we are with you. Our message to those who perpetrated these unspeakable crimes is equally clear: you will not get away with it.[38]

Individual Alliance partners also expressed solidarity with the United States. On 11 September, in the wake of the attacks, British Prime Minister Blair declared that the United Kingdom would stand "shoulder to shoulder" with the United States in punishing the perpetrators while German Chancellor Gerhard Schröder condemned the attacks as a "declaration of war on the free world."[39] In France, the often un-transatlantic *Le Monde* declared "we are all Americans!"[40] Official support for the

United States from the NATO allies was mirrored by support among the European public. Polls in the week after the attacks found that 80 percent of the Danes, 79 percent of the British, 73 percent of the French, 70 percent of the Portuguese, 66 percent of the Italians and Dutch, 58 percent of the Spanish and 53 percent of the Germans, felt that their countries should take part in any military attack undertaken by the United States.[41]

The central question for the Alliance was how to respond in practical terms that would enhance or compliment American efforts? Lord Robertson had to develop a meaningful approach which would demonstrate not only the solidarity of the Alliance, but also the relevance of NATO to both the immediate crisis and toward future terrorist threats. Just as the end of the Cold War had led to a broad and significant recalculation of the intricacies of national security, the attacks on 11 September also promised to change the security norms within the transatlantic region in just as dramatic a fashion.

The Article 5 Debate

Lord Robertson and most senior NATO officials perceived that the Alliance had four main tasks following the attacks. First, the Alliance had to provide demonstrable support for the United States. This would need to include both moral and material support in whatever manner necessary. In order to accomplish this, Robertson would have to develop and maintain a consensus among the Allies, many of whom had divergent interests. Second, with the emergence of terrorism as more than a marginal security threat, NATO had to proceed with policies that upheld the importance of the Alliance and showed that the organization was not irrelevant in the face of the emerging "new" threat of international terrorism. Throughout the Cold War and beyond, the United States had underwritten European security and now an opportunity had arisen whereby Western Europe could "repay" its transatlantic partner. Third, whatever policies and actions were undertaken, the relationship between NATO and Russia had to be sustained. This was especially important in light of the plans by the Alliance for future expansion into Central and Eastern Europe and the existing tensions which resulted from American plans for a missile defense system. Fourth, and finally, NATO had to continue to carry - out its existing missions. Principal among these missions were the ongoing operations in the Balkans, including the sensitive mission in Macedonia where the Alliance was endeavoring to forestall the outbreak of ethnic conflict. NATO also needed to proceed with the preparations necessary for the next round of expansion.

The first real test of Alliance solidarity arose quickly in the aftermath of the attacks. On Wednesday, the day after the attacks, NAC met to begin devising its reaction. The main issue before NAC was whether or not to invoke the Alliance's Article 5 provision which would require all NATO memberstates to come to the aid of the United States if requested. The irony was of course that Article 5 had been put in place originally at the insistence of the European states as a means to ensure that the United States would actually come to the defense of its European allies during the Cold War, even it if might the risk of nuclear war. As Robert Osgood wrote about the Washington Treaty:

> The founders of the Treaty, wary of America's history of isolation and conscious of Europe's dependence upon American intervention in two world wars, believed that a truly entangling alliance, formally binding the United States within the mutual obligations of several states, was essential to make America's commitment to come to the defense of Europe convincing to the potential aggressor and to the potential victims of aggression as well.[42]

Few expected that the first request for Article 5 cooperation would be to assist the United States in the aftermath of an attack on its soil.

To further complicate matters, there was uncertainty as to what the invocation of Article 5 might actually mean for the allies. On the one hand, if the attack could be proven to be the work of a national government, this would have simplified matters for the Alliance could have easily supported conventional military action against that government. On the other hand, if, as most believed, the attacks were the work of a substate or terrorist group, then a number of potential problems could arise. For instance, there were trepidations about invoking Article 5 in response to terrorist attacks since it might set a precedent whereby NATO partners called for Article 5 protection in the event of lesser terrorist activities.

At the 1999 Washington Summit, the United States had endeavored unsuccessfully to have NAC approve a counter terrorism role for NATO. However, opposition from the French and German delegations had prevented approval of this expanded role. One official noted that "We [the Germans and French] believed then, as now, that NATO's role was not about combating terrorism. This should be left up to democratic and civil institutions, involving the police, the judicial authorities and all diplomatic and political instruments."[43] Instead, NAC approved a compromise measure, Article 24, in its new Strategic Concept which broadened the scope of Article 5, but with qualifications. Article 24 of the Alliance's New Strategic Concept states:

> Any armed attack on the territory of the Allies, from whatever direction, would be covered by Article 5 and 6 of the Washington Treaty. However, Alliance security must also take account of the global context. Alliance security interests can be affected by other risks of a wider nature, including acts of terrorism, sabotage and organized crime, and by the disruption of the flow of vital resources. The uncontrolled movement of large numbers of people particularly as a consequence of armed conflicts, can also pose problems for security and stability affecting the Alliance. Arrangements exist within the Alliance for

consultation among the Allies under Article 4 of the Washington Treaty and, where appropriate, coordination of their efforts including their responses to risks of this kind.[44]

What was particularly troubling about an expanded NATO role in fighting terrorism, as part of an expanded vision of Article 5, was the potential for the Allies to be called upon to combat internal terrorism in states with ongoing conflicts such as Spain or Turkey. Turkey in particular was keen to use Article 5 to force the Allies to aid its struggle against the Kurdish separatist movement, the PKK while Spain wants to explore the possibility of using the Alliance against the Basque separatist movement, the ETA.[45]

The automatic nature of Article 5 could prove also troublesome or potentially embarrassing, especially if it became evident that the planning or conduct of the attacks originated within one of the NATO member- or partner-states. Issues of national sovereignty and the cohesion of the Alliance could be tested under such circumstances. In addition, several states, including France and Germany were concerned that Article 5 might force them to engage in military actions beyond the scope of an appropriate response. In other words, Article 5 might give the United States carte blanche to conduct military operations against a variety of groups who were not directly involved in the 11 September attacks and the NATO states would have to approve the military action.

In an era of constrained military outlays, there were concerns over the ability of the Alliance to provide any significant assistance to the United States and still maintain their other commitments, including plans for the creation of 60,000-member rapid reaction force, the ERRF, to be placed at the disposal of the European Union as called for by the Union's 1999 Helsinki Conference.[46] In fact, in June of 2001, just months prior to the attacks, Lord Robertson told *The New York Times* in an interview that "for the Europeans there is a clear message . . . if a crisis comes along, the capability will not be there."[47] NATO's Deputy Secretary General Sergio Balanzino chaired a committee charged with overseeing NATO's progress toward the Defense Capability Initiative (DCI) which found that in the Summer of 2001, Alliance members were only spending half what was needed to meet five main force goals which NAC had established at the Washington Summit.[48] The concern over capabilities extended to NATO's ability to oversee its existing operations in the Balkans and potentially develop and implement the strategy necessary to conduct a major campaign against international terrorism.

The Article 5 Decision

On the day after the attacks, NAC gathered to debate and formulate a response. The American delegation made it clear that it would seek the invocation of Article 5 if it could be proven that the attacks originated outside of the United States.

France, Italy, Spain and the United Kingdom strongly supported the American position. Germany, the Netherlands, Belgium and Norway initially opposed the invocation. German officials were concerned about an American "overreaction" while officials from the Benelux states and Norway were afraid of the long-term consequences of NATO assuming a counter-terrorism function.[49] However, Lord Robertson argued that one of the overriding concerns for the Alliance was to maintain its unity. Dissension in NATO could lead the United States to bypass the Alliance completely and permanently marginalizing NATO. One NATO official asserted:

> that would be the worst possible scenario, NATO would be accused of being divided over combating terrorism. What we realized this week was how the world has fundamentally changed. The attacks on the U.S. are the tip of the iceberg. All of us are vulnerable. We must close ranks. There is no other option.[50]

These sentiments were echoed in an essay written by two former members of the Clinton Administration's National Security Council, Antony J. Blinken and Philip H. Gordon, in the *International Herald Tribune*: "While the form of possible retaliation can and should be debated, neutrality is not an option."[51]

With strong support from the Secretary General and two of the three major Western European powers, the American bloc carried the day. Within just six hours of meeting on 12 September and 36 hours after the attack, NAC agreed to invoke Article 5 for the first time in the history of the Alliance, if and when it could be proven that the attacks originated with a group or government outside of the United States.[52] The more reluctant Allies were further persuaded by assurances from the United States that military action would be only one component of the campaign against terrorism and that armed attacks would be supplemented with diplomatic efforts and a broad-based campaign against the financial assets of terrorists through nation and international banks and other financial institutions. American officials also stressed the importance of cooperation with Russia and the possibilities for a closer relationship between the Cold War nemeses as a result of a broad-based campaign against international terrorism.[53] Finally, the Benelux states, France, Germany and Portugal received assurances that NAC would be able to further refine the threshold levels for Article 5 action and decide cases on an individual basis.[54]

Still, even the more vocal supporters of the United States went to lengths to ensure that NATO support for any American-led military response would be qualified and conditional. After championing NAC approval of Article 5, French Foreign Minister, Hubert Vedrine, asserted that the invocation of the all-for-one clause did not automatically force French military participation in American-led operations. Vedrine proclaimed that "Article 5 does not abolish the freedom of action of each ally."[55] Vedrine's stance was echoed by German Foreign Minister Joschka Fischer who also implied that Article 5 did not mean automatic military participation by German forces. Fischer also publically warned the United States against a "hasty reaction" to the attacks.[56]

Both Germany and France also indicated that they preferred any campaign to be coordinated through the auspices of the United Nations. In this, way, an armed response would gain greater credibility in the eyes of the Islamic world and could be counted on to have at least the tacit support of Russia and China as permanent members of the UN Security Council. The involvement of the UN might also expand diplomatic options and increase burdensharing. Clearly many of the NAC representatives wanted to demonstrate their support for the United States, and even contribute troops to any military actions, but they also wanted to ensure that any campaign undertaken was multifaceted and perceived as legally and morally justified in light of the attacks.

Furthermore, while NAC agreed to the invocation of Article 5, dissension arose over the level of proof necessary for the action. The United States quickly asserted that the genesis of the attacks lay with Osama Bin Laden and the Al Qaeda network of international terrorism. Two days after the attacks, President Bush publically declared war on Al Qaeda and international terrorism. The Bush Administration subsequently declared in a variety of venues and public statements that the world would be given clear and irrefutable proof that Bin Laden and Al Qaeda were responsible for the attacks.

A public display of such proof was very important to a number of the NATO allies who were wary of presenting the impression that the Alliance was going to war against Islam. There were sizable populations of Muslims in a variety of West European nations, including France, Belgium and Germany. Many of the allies had already experienced outbreaks of Islamic-based terrorism and did not wish to provoke new campaigns of terror.[57] French Prime Minister Lionel Jospin publically noted that there was no "war against Islam or the Arab-Muslim world."[58] All of the NATO partners, including the United States, were also sensitive to the need not to alienate Turkey, the only predominately Muslim nation within the Alliance.[59] NATO also wanted to maintain the progress gained in its initiatives such as the Mediterranean Dialogue. Furthermore, Alliance officials wanted to maintain friendly relations with Muslim nations such as Pakistan which would likely play important roles in any military action against the Al Qaeda network. Finally, the Alliance found it necessary to minimize damage already done by Italian Prime Minister Silvio Berlusconi's remarks on 26 September 2001 in which he characterized Western civilization as "superior" to the Islamic world.[60]

The United States and "Proof"

Even though a range of high ranking American officials, including President Bush and Secretary of State Colin Powell, had promised clear proof of the guilt of Bin

Laden and Al Qaeda, the Bush Administration became reluctant to make its information public. For instance, in a televised interview, Secretary of State Powell remarked:

> I am absolutely convinced that the al-Qaida network, which he heads [Bin Laden], was responsible for this attack. You know, it's sort of al-Qaida - the Arab name for it is 'the base' - its something like a holding company of terrorist organizations that are located in dozens of countries around the world, sometimes tightly controlled, sometimes loosely controlled. And at the head of that organization is Usama bin Laden. So what we have to do in the first phase of this campaign is to go after al-Qaida and go after Usama bin Laden. But it is not just a problem in Afghanistan; its a problem throughout the world. That's why we are attacking it with a worldwide coalition . . . . We are hard at work bringing all the information together, intelligence information, law enforcement information. And I think, in the near future, we will be able to put out a paper, a document, that will describe quite clearly the evidence that we have linking him to this attack. And also, remember, he has been linked to earlier attacks against US interests and he was already indicated for earlier attacks against the United States.[61]

Nonetheless, no white paper or other major document was made available to the public before the military strikes against Afghanistan commenced. After its initial pledge to make public information linking Bin Laden and Al Qaeda with the terrorist attacks, the Bush Administration changed its strategy at the beginning of October. It began to assert national security concerns as a motive for not releasing the information to the public. Specifically, the Administration claimed the need to maintain existing and gain new sources of intelligence as motivation to keep information secret. In response to a question on the previous promises of concrete proof, U.S. State Department Spokesman Richard Boucher proclaimed:

> Once again the American public has heard from its own government that we have amassed a considerable body of information, that we have reached a firm conclusion that Al Qaeda was responsible for this [the 11 September attacks], as the president said a week ago, and that we are being careful about the sources and methods of acquisition of information because we're in this fight for the long haul, we're going to need to continue to get information, and we're not going to do anything that would jeopardize our ability to find out about these networks so that they can't harm the American people.[62]

After the initial commitment to invoke Article 5, the Allies made clear that the action and future support was constrained by two points. First, clear proof needed to be presented to the Alliance before action was taken to formally invoke the collective security clause of the Washington Treaty. Such evidence was necessary to avoid the aforementioned perception that any military campaign that involved NATO was not taken to be a war against Islam. Second, the allies asked for continued consultations and involvement in the planning and conduct of operations.

Even British Prime Minister Blair, who was perceived as the closest ally of the United States in any potential military campaign, maintained that any military campaign "must and will be based on hard evidence" and his office assured his country's public that British and NATO support did not translate into a "blank check" for the United States to undertake any operations it saw fit.[63]

In spite of assurances of specific proof, what the allies received was initially fairly general. At a meeting of NATO's defense ministers in Brussels on 26 September, the allies received their first briefing from American officials on the attacks. American Deputy Secretary of State Paul Wolfowitz met with the NATO representatives. While the meeting was informal, in that there were no plans for major decisions to be made, many of the NATO ministers were disappointed with the materials presented by the United States. For instance, German Deputy Defense Minister Rudolf Scharping reported that he had expected Wolfowitz to present the ministers with a formal white paper outlining the evidence that the United States had linking Al Qaeda to the attacks.[64] British Defense Secretary Geoff Hoon reported that Wolfowitz "did not develop it [the evidence] further than the president [Bush]has done so far."[65]

While the lack of evidence was troubling for some of the Alliance partners, Lord Robertson tried to put the best face on the American showing, even remarking that he questioned the necessity for "an ally to produce evidence."[66] Nonetheless, a variety of Allies, led by Germany, requested that more legalistic proof be presented in the future. NAC representatives informed the Americans that such proof would be necessary to satisfy their domestic audiences. In fact, on the day following the meeting, the Belgian Defense Minister, Andre Flahaut predicted that it would take some time to develop the evidence necessary for an Article 5 decision and that the Alliance would spend considerable period formulating a response: "The U.S. has insisted on a certain autonomy and flexibility. We shall not expect a quick request of NATO's Article 5. There is a long time for preparation."[67]

On 2 October, NAC met with other American representatives. At a morning meeting, more formal evidence was presented by Frank X. Taylor, the United States Department of State Coordinator for Counter-Terrorism, who gave a classified briefing to the NATO ministers. The briefing lasted 40 minutes and included slides, but many NAC officials came away with the impression that the evidence presented did not rise to the level of legal proof necessary to hold-up in a courtroom.[68] Later that day NAC was again briefed by Wolfowitz who was joined by Deputy Secretary of State Richard Armitage. The NATO briefings occurred simultaneously with bilateral meetings between American and individual national officials in a variety of Western European states. The information included outlines of the terrorist network and a variety of circumstantial evidence which linked Al Qaeda and the terrorists on board the doomed airliners through money trails and bank transactions.[69] The British government summarized the four broad conclusions of the evidence as London saw it:

> 1) Usama bin Laden and Al Qa'ida, the terrorist network which he heads, planned and carried out the atrocities on 11 September 2001;
> 2) Usama bin Laden and Al Qa'ida retain the will and resources to carry out further atrocities;
> 3) The United Kingdom, and United Kingdom nationals are potential targets;
> 4) Usama bin Laden and Al Qa'ida were able to commit these atrocities because of their close alliance with the Taliban regime, which allowed them to operate with impunity in pursuing their terrorist activity.[70]

While several of the NAC representatives wanted more concrete evidence, they realized that it would have been politically damaging to NATO and to relations with the United States to reject the Article 5 request. NAC formally invoked Article 5 in response to the 11 September terrorist attacks at the 2 October meeting. Lord Robertson declared to the public and press that:

> The facts are clear and compelling. The information presented points conclusively to an Al Qaeda role in the 11 September attacks.
> We know that the individuals who carried out these attacks were part of the world-wide terrorist network of Al Qaeda, headed by Osama bin Laden and his key Lieutenants and protected by the Taleban.
> On the basis of this briefing, it has now been determined that the attack against the United States on 11 September was directed from abroad and shall therefore be regarded as an action covered by Article 5 of the Washington Treaty, which states that an armed attack on one or more of the Allies in Europe or North America shall be considered an attack against them all.[71]

Crossing the Rubicon

With the decision in place to invoke Article 5, NAC committed the Alliance to participate in any American-led campaign against the Taleban and Al Qaeda. However, the size and scope of involvement was not initially clear. While the United States asked for the Article 5 declaration, it did not immediately request substantial military or logistical support from the Allies. Instead the Bush Administration moved ahead fashioning a series of coalitions to support its efforts both diplomatically and militarily. Russian President Vladimir Putin signaled his belief that Bin Laden was behind the attacks and his country's willingness to support military action by the United States. On the day after NATO invoked Article 5, Putin stated that he was prepared to "profoundly change" Moscow's relationship with NATO in order to counter rising threats such as terrorism.[72] Even China indicated its support for the United States.

With Article 5 in place, NATO officials awaited requests from the United States for specific assets. Individually, various nations offered a variety of assistance, ranging from troops to the use of air bases or air space to intelligence sharing. To the NATO Allies, however, it quickly became evident that the United States would only use selective resources from its allies as the Bush Administration embarked upon a policy designed to ensure American control of the military operations in Afghanistan.

Notes

1. *North Atlantic Treaty*, Washington, D.C., 4 April 1949.
2. Under the UN Charter, regional collective security organizations were encouraged. The founding nations of the Alliance asserted that NATO's formation fulfilled this component of the UN Charter in regard to Western Europe.
3. *North Atlantic Treaty*.
4. Throughout the Cold War, NATO had three major military commands, but in 1994, NAC ordered the Allied Command Channel to be incorporated into the Allied Command Europe (ACE).
5. NATO, *NATO Handbook: Partnership and Cooperation* (Brussels: NATO, 1995), 169.
6. Ibid., 177.
7. Furthermore, by tradition, the second-in-command for SACLANT is a British officer.
8. NATO, *NATO Handbook Fiftieth Anniversary Edition* (Brussels: NATO, 1998).
9. Ibid.
10. Michael J. Brenner, "A United States Perspective," in Brenner, Michael, ed. *Multilateralism and Western Security* (New York: St. Martin's, 1995), 155.
11. The members of the EAPC are Albania, Armenia, Austria, Azerbaijan, Belarus, Belgium, Bulgaria, Canada, Croatia, the Czech Republic, Denmark, Estonia, Finland, France, Georgia, Germany, Greece, Hungary, Iceland, Ireland, Italy, Kazakhstan, the Kyrgyz Republic, Latvia, Lithuania, Luxembourg, Moldova, the Netherlands, Norway, Poland, Portugal, Romania, Russia, Slovakia, Slovenia, Spain, Sweden, Switzerland, Tajikistan, the former Yugoslav Republic of Macedonia, Turkey, Turkmenistan, Ukraine, the United Kingdom, the United States, Uzbekistan.
12. *NATO Handbook: Fiftieth Anniversary Edition*, Chapter 2.
13. NATO, "Russia-NATO Relations: NATO Fact Sheet" (9 February 2001), available online at www.nato.int/docu/facts/2000/nato-rus.htm.
14. NATO, "NATO-Ukraine: NATO Fact Sheet" (22 August 2001), available online at www.nato.int/docu/facts/2000/nato-ukr.htm.
15. Ian O. Lesser, *NATO Looks South: New Challenges and New Strategies in the Mediterranean* (Santa Monica: RAND, 2000), 2-3.
16. Algeria joined the Dialogue in February of 2000.

17. For an overview, see Ian O. Lesser, Jerrold D. Green, F. Stephen Larrabee and Michele Zanini, *The Future of NATO's Mediterranean Initiative: Evolution and Next Steps* (Santa Monica: RAND, 2000).

18. These groups were established at the NATO Ministerial in Istanbul in June of 1994.

19. Gregory L. Schulte, "Responding to Proliferation: NATO's Role," *NATO Review*, 43, no. 4 (July 1995), 15.

20. European Council, *Declaration of the European Council on Strengthening the Common European Policy on Security and Defence*, NR 122/99 (6 March 1999).

21. CFSP formally entered into force on 1 May 1999.

22. Brooks Tigner, "Solana Diplomacy Holds Key to Enhanced Security Role," *Defense News* (19 July 1999), 19.

23. Cameron Fraser, "What They Said: Cameron Fraser on CFSP, ESDP & the Balkans," *Europe*, 397 (June 2000), 2.

24. BASIC, "EU Plan for Rapid Reaction Facility: A Small But Important First Step" (December 1999).

25. European Council, *Proposal for a Council Regulation Creating Rapid Reaction Facility* (11 December 1999).

26. BASIC, *ESDI: Right Debate, Wrong Conclusions* (2000).

27. EU Presidency, *Presidency Conclusions Helsinki European Council*, DN: Pres/99/3000 (20 December 1999).

28. "Meet Your New European Army," *The Economist* (25 November 2000), 55-58.

29. Robertson, Barcelona Speech.

30. Richard Norton-Taylor, "Plans for EU Force are Confused, MPs Warn," *The Guardian* (11 April 2001).

31. The double-hatting arrangement was originally developed in order to give the WEU operational capabilities. Under this type of arrangement, units are pledged to more than one command or hat. For instance, NATO's Allied Rapid Reaction Corps (ARRC) which is made-up of British and Dutch amphibious units is double-hatted as Forces Available WEU (FAWEU) which means that the troops could be used in WEU operations.

32. Derek Brown, "The European Rapid Reaction Force," *The Guardian* (20 November 2000).

33. These include Lord Ismay, Lord Carrington and Lord Robertson. In addition, there have been two Dutch Secretaries General, Dirk U. Stikker and Joseph M.A.H. Luns (at 13 years, the longest serving Secretary General), two Belgians, Paul-Henri Spaak and Willie Claes, one Italian, Manilo Brosio, one German, Manfred Warner and one Spaniard, Javier Solana.

34. See Douglas Barrie and Theresa Hitchens, "Mergers Across Europe's Borders Spell Job Losses," *Defense News* (14 June 1999); U.K., Ministry of Defense, *Defense Diversification: Getting the Most Out of Defense Technology* CM3861 (London: HMSO, 1998).

35. The peerage is granted to enhance the prestige of the person entering office.

36. NATO, "Statement by the Secretary General of NATO, Lord Robertson," PR/CP(2001) 121 (11 September 2001).

37. For instance, on the day following the attacks, the EAPC issued the following statement:"We, the member nations of the Euro-Atlantic Partnership Council, gathered today to express our solidarity with the people of the United States of America following yesterday's tragic events. These brutal and senseless atrocities have caused suffering on a massive scale. Our deepest sympathies go to the victims and their families. We are appalled

by these barbaric acts and condemn them unconditionally. These acts were an attack on our common values. We will not allow these values to be compromised by those who follow the path of violence. We pledge to undertake all efforts to combat the scourge of terrorism. We stand united in our belief that the ideals of partnership and co-operation will prevail;" NATO, "Statement by the EAPC," PR/CP(2001) 123 (12 September 2001).

38. NATO, "Statement by NAC," PR/CP(2001) 122 (11 September 2001).
39. "Old Friends, Best Friends," *The Economist* (15 September 2001), 20.
40. Jean-Marie Colombani, "Nous sommes touts amèricains," *Le Monde* (12 September 2001).
41. "Gallup Poll on International Terrorism in the US" (17 September 2001), online http://www.gallup-international.com/terrorismpoll_figures.htm.
42. Robert Osgood, *NATO: The Entangling Alliance* (Chicago: University of Chicago, 1962), 25.
43. Judy Dempsey, "EU Doubts Grow Over 'Switch' in NATO Role," *Financial Times* (19 September 2001).
44. NATO, *The Alliance's Strategic Concept* NAC-S(99) 65 (24 April 1999).
45. Judy Dempsey, "NATO Help Likely To Go Beyond Bin Laden Attack," *Financial Times* (5 October 2001).
46. EU Presidency, *Presidency Conclusions Helsinki European Council*, DN: Pres/99/3000 (20 December 1999).
47. Michael R. Gordon, "Armies of Europe Failing to Meet Goals, Sapping NATO," *The New York Times* (7 June 2001).
48. The force goals included five broad areas: 1) logistics, 2) command and control, 3) mobility, 4) force and infrastructure survivability, and 5) "effective engagement" or the capability to deploy precision guided munitions; ibid.
49. Joseph Fitchett, "NATO Unity, But What Next," *International Herald Tribune* (14 September 2001).
50. Judy Dempsey, "NATO Quick to Set Historic Precedent," *Financial Times* (14 September 2001).
51. Antony J. Blinken and Philip H. Gordon, "NATO Is Ready to Play a Central Role," *International Herald Tribune* (18 September 2001).
52. Lord Robertson, Speech at the "Welt am Sontag Forum," Berlin (1 October 2001).
53. This was especially true in light of perceived links between the Al Qaeda network, the ruling Taliban in Afghanistan, and Chechyan separatists conducting their own terrorist campaign against Moscow.
54. Dempsey, "EU Doubts."
55. Judy Dempsey, "Use of Article 5 Marks Policy Shift for Europe," *Financial Times* (16 September 2001).
56. Ibid.
57. See Fuller and Lesser for an overview of the impact of Islamic fundamentalism on Western Europe.
58. Quoted in Suzanne Daley, "After the Attacks: In Europe; A Pause to Ponder Washington's Tough Talk," *The New York Times* (16 September 2001).

59. Turkey's relationship with the rest of Western Europe was troubled already as a result of the European Union's reluctance to allow Turkish membership in the organization and because of concerns over Turkey's human rights record and democratic credentials; see Zalmay Khalilzad, Ian O. Lesser and F. Stephen Larrabee, *The Future of Turkish-Western Relations: Toward a Strategic Plan* (Santa Monica: RAND, 2000).

60. Berlusconi would later claim that his remarks were taken out of context, Marina Harss, "Italy: Repairing the Damage," *The New York Times* (3 October 2001), A6.

61. Colin Powell Interview "Meet the Press" (23 September 2001) online http://www.state.gov/secretary/rm/2001/index.

62. Richard Boucher, "State Department Briefing," Washington, D.C. (4 October 2001).

63. Daley, "Tough Talk."

64. James Dao and Patrick E. Tyler," A Nation Challenged: The Alliance; Military Called Just One Element in War on Terror," *The New York Times* (27 September 2001).

65. Judy Dempsey and Alexander Nicoll, "NATO Leaders Warm to U.S. Flexibility," *Financial Times* (27 September 2001).

66. Dao and Tyler.

67. Dempsey and Nicoll.

68. The evidence was based on mainly circumstantial data that drew links between where the hijackers had studied and links in their backgrounds with Bin Laden and the Al Qaeda network; Judy Dempsey, "Evidence From U.S. 'Points' To Bin Laden," *Financial Times* (4 October 2001).

69. London prepared a summary of the evidence for the British public. The summary contained evidence which linked Bin Laden and Al Qaeda to the 1998 attacks on the American embassies in Africa and the 2000 attack on the USS *Cole*. The summary also outlined the support given Al Qaeda by the Taliban and overviews of videos and statements made by Bin Laden about the potential for attacks and "self-incriminating" statements made afterwards. Intelligence was also cited that Al Qaeda was planning a major attack on 11 September and that a number of the hijackers had ties to Al Qaeda and that a number were trained in Afghanistan; U.K., "Responsibility for the Terrorist Atrocities in the United States, 11 September 2001 (London: HMSO, November 2001).

70. Ibid.

71. NATO, "Statement by Lord Robertson" (2 October 2001).

72. Suzanne Daley, "NATO Says U.S. Has Proof Against Bin Laden Group," *The New York Times* (3 October 2001).

Chapter 4

The Call to Arms

A Broad Strategy

In the aftermath of the 11 September attacks, the Bush Administration signaled its intention to develop the kind of broad-based coalition of nations that the United States had arrayed against Iraq during the Persian Gulf War of 1991. At the core of this coalition of states was the NATO Alliance. For officials on both sides of the Atlantic, the centrality of NATO to any military operation against the Taliban and Al Qaeda was the key to preserving the Alliance as the cornerstone of the transatlantic security regime. For the Europeans, the attacks of 11 September provided an opportunity for NATO to demonstrate its utility to the United States and the organization's ability to counter new security threats. For the Americans, NATO participation provided any military operations with an enhanced degree of legitimacy and reaffirmed the transatlantic link in the face of new competition from emerging security structures in Europe such as the ERRF.

Euro-American relations have traditionally been complicated by the multi-layered manner in which they exist. For instance, at a broad level, there exist hemispheric relations between the United States and the European states en masse. This relationship has been characterized by U.S. support for European integration on political, economic and security issues and is usually expressed through interaction between the United States and the European Union, although it can also be perceived in trends such as the drive for the Europeanization of the Alliance or the establishment of an ESDI.[1] Yet, bilateral relations such as those between the United States and the United Kingdom or the United States and France often overshadow transatlantic relations, as was the case in the French withdrawal from NATO and as is the case in the continuing "special relationship" between the United States and the United Kingdom.[2] Concurrently, bilateral relations between individual European states can also impact the security and foreign policies of those nations.[3]

Coalition Lessons

In their security interactions with the Allies, successive administrations in the United States have been able to take advantage of the intricacies of European multi- and bilateral relations. In the post-Cold War era, the United States increasingly found it necessary to develop coalitions of the willing by relying on specific states that were willing to contribute forces or assets to operations. For instance, during the Gulf War, the United States did not seek troops or other military resources from each of its NATO partners, but instead relied upon those states, both within the Alliance and outside of it, that had capabilities which Washington found useful. The result was still the "largest and most capable international military coalition in a generation."[4] For example, the naval blockade of Iraq consisted of 60 ships from a diverse collection of states ranging from NATO partners to Argentina and Australia. During the Gulf War, problems arose when Washington sought to establish a unified command and control structure to coordinate the forces. The French and the Italians sought a separate role for the European naval units deployed under the auspices of the WEU. This independent role was opposed by the U.S. and the Atlanticist states in NATO (including the U.K., Canada, the Netherlands and Denmark). For the British, "political games were going on which had less to do with efficient execution of the blockade and rather more to do with eroding American domination of NATO and the newly formed Coalition."[5] Ultimately, the solution that the Americans employed was simply to deploy the WEU forces in a separate area.

Subsequent American-led military operations in Bosnia and Kosovo reinforced the problems inherent in multilateral coalitions without a unified command system. In both operations there were problems reaching a consensus on targets and the execution of missions.[6] There was an inordinate amount of political interference from NATO memberstates in the day-to-day operations of the air campaign in Kosovo.[7] The missions in Kosovo also demonstrated the uneven quality of European military capabilities, as there were only a handful of nations that had the precision-guided munitions and deployment capabilities that made them useful in air operations.[8] During the Kosovo campaign, the United States provided 70 percent of the aircraft and 80 percent of the total munitions expended during the conflict.[9] Testifying before the U.S. House of Representatives, British member of parliament, Iain Duncan Smith, the Shadow Secretary of State for Defence, stated that the "Kosovo conflict underlined the considerable gap in capability between the European and United States' forces."[10] A Defense Science Board report pointed out, "US and allied military commanders and other officials have expressed concern that with the USA's unmatched ability to invest in next-generation military technologies, it runs the risk of outpacing NATO and other allies to the point where they are incapable of operating effectively with US forces on future battlefields."[11] As *The Economist* reported:

> For the European governments, the spectacle of American power unleashed in their corner of the map was frightening and chastening. They found most of their weaponry humiliatingly obsolete when set against the American arsenal of stealth bombers and

precision-guided missiles. Once begun, this became an American war run from the White House and Pentagon over which the Europeans had little political influence.[12]

Consequently, the lessons of the Gulf War and the Balkan missions in regard to the hazards of coalition warfare were twofold: 1) it is difficult to establish a clear command and control structure with unified decision-making procedures; and 2) the majority of the Alliance partners lacked the military capabilities to allow them to be truly interoperable with sophisticated American military resources. In addition, the ability to gain consensus for action among the Allies presents an ever-present potential stumbling block for NATO action. Any effort to conduct a NATO-led military operation:

> would notably have to involve Euro-American agreement to mobilize Alliance assets and procedures. The great diversification of challenges to stability and security furthermore entails the likelihood that any specific problem would tend to be perceived as more or less salient by different members of the Western Alliance. Perceptions of the urgency of any given challenge will not converge, either within Europe or across the Atlantic. In fact, in a post-bipolar world, there are many reasons to suppose that they might differ.[13]

Such considerations reinforced the American preference to develop a unilateral command system for any operations.

Bandwagoning

According to the tenets of international relations theory, states tend to either bandwagon with or balance against hegemonic powers. During the Cold War, the states of Europe chose to bandwagon with the United States in order to balance against the Soviet Union. With the demise of the Soviet Union, many expected the states of Europe to chafe under American domination and initiate efforts to begin balancing against American security or economic primacy.[14] Indeed, many scholars and policymakers asserted that the drive for ESDI was a manifestation of renewed balancing pressures.[15] NATO, as a manifestation of American security primacy, should be one of the first casualties. John M. Goldgeier comments:

> Both the theory and history of international politics strongly suggests that NATO should have dissolved, not expanded. No alliance has ever survived victory; and the possession of overwhelming power in the hands of one state typically induces balancing, not bandwagoning, behavior among contenders. Thus, in the wake of the Soviet Union's self dismemberment, it was entirely reasonable to expect that the United States would either disengage militarily from Europe or be forced out by the Europeans, who should have

been eagerly defecting from the victorious American alliance to form a counter-hegemonic coalition.[16]

The balancing tendency should be especially evident in nations such as the United Kingdom which for centuries based its foreign policy on the principle of developing alliances or shifting coalitions to forestall hegemony. Throughout European history, Great Britain endeavored to balance in order to prevent hegemony on the European continent. Owen Harries points out that:

> bandwagoning with one superpower to thwart another and much less attractive superpower was one thing; bandwagoning with the sole superpower, the undisputed hegemon, is quite another. It goes against the long-established British tradition of attempting to balance – either alone or by the creation of a coalition – any power that is, or threatens to be, dominant. This, the classic principle of balance of power, has been the central tent of British policy for the last four centuries. Its logic has been summed up succinctly by the Israeli statesman, Abba Eban: 'The alternative to a balance of power is an imbalance of power, which has usually provoked wars and has never consolidated peace.'[17]

Nonetheless bandwagoning has continued even in the wake of the end of the Cold War. There are a number of reasons for this. First, as aforementioned, the end of the Cold War did not mean an end to all security threats faced by Western Europe and NATO continues to be the optimum means to counter these risks. Second, and related to the above point, is the absolute "fact" of American military superiority and advanced capability, and the necessity of NATO as a means for the Europeans to access that power. Third, the history of failure among the European states in their quest to develop CFSP, especially in light of the experiences of the EU in the former Yugoslavia. The potential for a meaningful autonomous European security identity is now, and will for the near-term future, be constrained by a lack of resources and defense spending. Fourth, the linkages existent in non-security areas, especially in the economic realm. Both Europe and the United States are joined in a variety of institutions which work to promote international economic stability. This commonality of interests will continue to spill over into the security sphere.[18] Fifth, and finally, states that are satisfied with the contemporary status quo tend to band together and work to maintain the stability of the international system. The transatlantic security regime has provided a number of benefits to its memberstates who have, in turn, indicated at a variety of junctures, their support for the continued existence of NATO. Even the drive for greater autonomy by the Europeans is designed to maintain the centrality of NATO. The German Minister of Defense, Rudolf Scharping commented that the drive for ESDI should be:

guided by two principles. Firstly, strengthening the transatlantic link will remain the central part of a policy aimed at achieving peace, security and democracy throughout the Euro-Atlantic area. No-one should believe that the importance of the new NATO and our American allies for European security would be reduced if Europe had a greater capacity for action. Secondly, generating a European Security and Defense Identity by strengthening the European pillar of the Alliance and creating the political and structural prerequisites for a European Security and Defense Policy of the European Union are two sides of the same coin.[19]

Bandwagoning with NATO also continues for structural reasons. While the primary mission of any alliance is to protect its members against external threats and the primary mission of a collective security system is to protect against internal threats, the secondary mission of both types of international arrangements is alliance or system management.[20] The United States continues to manage intra-alliance security relations through agenda setting and by building internal coalitions within NATO. In its management efforts, the United States is aided by the highly developed bureaucracy of the Alliance. NATO is staffed by a large number of bureaucrats who, in their own self-interest, have endeavored to promote the Alliance and insure its continued existence.[21]

As a result, a number of processes have developed which both benefit the memberstates and reinforce the importance of the Alliance. These tacit and overt procedures also tend to work toward the continuation of NATO. Ronald Krebs identifies four such processes:

1) States use the issue-linkage opportunities provided by the alliance to offer side payments, eventually reaching a mutually satisfactory compromise.

2) Participation in alliance functions generates increasing knowledge of and trust in others' benign motives, decreasing concerns of relative gains and perceptions of intra-alliance threat. Further, if more powerful states provide military assistance, the state's absolute level of security rises.

3) Joint force structures and planning reshape each member's military posture to reflect alliance interests, reducing the fear of attack and obviating security dilemma dynamics. Force specialization constrains members' abilities to use their forces for exclusively national objectives.

4) Military officers that interact regularly with their allied colleagues are socialized into a shared culture, transcending their national interest. These officers endeavor to shape their states' preferences accordingly.[22]

Hence, in the aftermath of the 11 September attacks, NATO as an institution generated its own pressure to approve the Article 5 declaration (as represented by the actions of Lord Robertson, the head of the Alliance bureaucracy) and to take concrete steps to assist the United States.

Concurrently, the United States actively sought the invocation of Article 5 and aid from the Alliance. However, the United States did not seek substantial military forces or assets from each of the Allies. Instead, the Bush Administration embarked upon a policy designed to maximize the political support from all Allied states and to utilize selected military assets from a limited number of NATO's memberstates. The nature of the foe engaged by the United States did not necessitate the deployment of massive numbers of conventional forces. Once the campaign in Afghanistan was initiated, the United States employed a strategy that emphasized air strikes and the use of highly trained special forces. Because of the ongoing specialization of forces within NATO (see point three above) only a limited number of NATO states had resources that the United States needed in the campaign.[23] Dutch military analyst Rob de Wijk observed that "NATO forces are not training for this kind of work [the Afghan campaign]" and that only France and the United Kingdom had significant numbers of the kind of special forces troops that the United States needed for the mission in Afghanistan.[24] Neither do the European states have the abundance of precision-guided munitions that the United States planned to utilize (again, with the limited exception of France and the United Kingdom). As in previous military campaigns in the Balkans, the United States worked to develop intra-Alliance bandwagoning[25] by developing an internal coalition to participate in the operations.

While the United States wanted the political endorsement that the Article 5 declaration entailed, it did not want to alienate members of the Alliance that may have found it politically difficult to deploy troops because of domestic considerations.[26] The United States clearly signaled that "the international coalition assembled to fight terrorism would assign different tasks to different countries, with many of the players involved in intelligence-gathering, police work, and bushwacking on money trails – but perhaps few actually joining in the military phase."[27] In this manner, the United States worked to manage the Alliance in such a fashion as to maximize its utility in the campaign against international terrorism, but maintain cohesion by continuing the utility of the Alliance for each of the memberstates. For the memberstates of NATO, the American-led campaign in Afghanistan provided concrete security benefits by limiting the ability of terrorist groups such as Al Qaeda from undertaking future operations against European targets.

Once NAC invoked Article 5, it was incumbent upon the Bush Administration to "pick and choose" the assets and forces that it would use in the military campaign in Afghanistan. American military planners faced an enviable dilemma as an increasing number of nations began to pledge troops and assets for a highly specialized campaign which would likely not need the wealth of resources that NATO could provide. Hence, the Pentagon began to fashion a coalition of willing forces from nations within NATO that were engaged in intra-Alliance bandwagoning.

The Combined and Joint Task Force System

With the end of the Cold War, NAC recognized that the removal of the Alliance's central external threat elevated not one, but a number of new threats to the forefront of security planning. However, these threats were not universally appreciated or accepted throughout the Alliance. For instance, regional instability in the Maghreb ranked much higher as a security concern for the southern NATO states, Spain, France, Italy and Greece, than it did for Canada or the United States. In response, NAC endeavored to develop a system to allow states to engage in selective operations without engaging the full capabilities of the Alliance. In effect, NAC sought to initiate procedures whereby states could bandwagon together to deal with specific threats or incidents while disinterested states could pass the buck and avoid participation. The operations of these internal coalitions would have access to the full institutional resources of NATO and the benefits of the missions, whether in terms of reduced threats or enhanced stability, would accrue to the entire Alliance.

In addition to developing an institutional capability to organize threat-specific or crisis specific coalitions, NAC also sought to mollify the potential problems of coalition operations. Specifically, NAC developed a system to allow for coalitions of the willing which would permit operations to be carried out with forces or assets from only those states wishing to participate. It was envisioned that this initiative would simplify the approval process for operations and streamline the decision-making procedures and the command and control structure.

This initiative was the Combined and Joint Task Force (CJTF) system. The "combined" refers to an operation involving the forces from two or more nations, while "joint" refers to a mission which includes two or more branches of the military (the navy and army or the air force and marines, so any combination of the four). The CJTF "is a multinational (combined) and multi-service (joint) task force, task-organized and formed for the full range of the Alliance's military missions requiring multinational and multi-service command and control by a CJTF Headquarters. It may include elements from non-NATO Troop Contributing Nations."[28]

CJTF would allow the use of NATO assets in out-of-area operations without changing the Washington Treaty.[29] For example, CJTF would allow NATO resources to be utilized in an operation led by the WEU or missions which involved PfP states. CJTF established the relationship of NATO and WEU assets as "separable but not separate."[30] This was accomplished through the "dual-hatting" system whereby selected personnel from one military unit could be assigned to another multinational unit.[31] For instance, national forces assigned to NATO could also be "dual hatted" with the WEU so that on paper one unit could be assigned to both structures.[32]

NATO formulated the CJTF as a:

> multinational, multi-service deployable task force generated and tailored primarily, but not exclusively, for military operations not involving the defense of Alliance territory, such as humanitarian relief and peacekeeping. It provides a flexible and efficient means where-by the Alliance can generate rapidly deployable forces with appropriate command and control arrangements.[33]

The CJTF initiative was designed to accomplish a variety of tasks. First, CJTF allows the development of flexible command and decision-making structures which can be adapted for specific missions. Second, the initiative allows NATO assets to be shared with other European security organizations. Third, CJTF allows non-NATO nations to contribute forces to operations in which NATO is involved. Fourth, and finally, CJTF avoids "duplication" and therefore increases the efficient use of resources.[34] While not formal CJTF operations, the military actions in Bosnia and Kosovo exemplify many of the characteristics of CJTFs.

CJTF missions could be undertaken in one of three broad patterns. A "NATO-only CJTF" would involve some coalition of the NATO memberstates. This type of operation allows NATO to undertake a military campaign, but gives individual memberstates an opt-out option so that they may avoid participation for political or other reasons. A "NATO-plus CJTF" would involve some or all of the NATO Allies and partners from the PfP or EAPC. This type of mission would allow NATO greater access to resources and provide a means to promote closer cooperation and collaboration between NATO and its partners. Finally, there could be a "WEU-led CJTF." Such a CJTF operation would allow the WEU access to NATO resources and assets, but give the Europeans formal control or authority over the operation. It would also allow the operation access to WEU resources including military forces such as the Eurocrops.[35]

In many ways, the CJTF concept is an effort by NATO to formalize a system that has traditionally been ad hoc in nature. History abounds with examples of temporary coalitions, but the CJTF system would institutionalize the manner in which NATO would arrange such future combinations of states.[36] CJTF would also formalize ESDI within the Alliance by allowing the European states access to NATO assets and resources without necessitating participation by American or other forces (hence, coalitions of the willing). European states would be able to engage in operations with American support, but without American troops. Still, the staunch Europeanist states, led by France, voiced concerns over the ability of the United States to "veto" CJTF operations, since any mission would still have to be approved by NAC. In order to mollify such concerns, at the 1996 Berlin Summit, the United States agreed to give the European memberstates of NATO "political control and strategic direction" of CJTF missions that the European states initiate.[37]

NAC determined that in order to formally implement the CJTF initiative, the Alliance had to develop ready-made headquarters units to serve as the nuclei for these operations. Consequently, the Alliance would have prepackaged command and control structures in place to operate a CJTF. In order to facilitate the development of these structures:

> headquarters 'nuclei' or core staffs are being established on a permanent basis within selected 'parent' headquarters of the NATO military command structure. The headquarters 'nuclei' join with 'augmentation' modules and 'support' modules appropriate to a particular operation to form a CJTF headquarters specifically structured to meet the requirements of the operation in question.[38]

The CJTF system developed from a 1993 American proposal at an informal meeting of the defense ministers in Travemünde, Germany. The concept was formally approved by NAC at the Brussels Summit the following year.

NAC established a "Policy Coordination Group" to study the politico-military issues raised by CJTF and to ensure that the initiative is developed in such a fashion as to ensure political control of the operations.[39] NAC also ordered the Alliance military staff to undertake a variety of trials of the concepts. This led to a number of CJTF training exercises, including Exercise Allied Effort in November 1997 and Exercise Strong Resolve in March 1998. In light of the success of these and other operations, NAC ordered the implementation of the CJTF system in 1999. In response, the Alliance began developing headquarters structures and command and control communications equipment so that NATO can began CJTF operations in 2004.[40]

In response to the 11 September attacks, many suggested that NATO form a counter-terrorist CJTF. This would allow those European states that wanted to participate in any American response to do so and permit other Allies to opt out of the operations, all-the-while preserving the unity of the Alliance. In calling for a NATO counter-terrorism CJTF, Stanley R. Sloan writes that:

> One advantage of the CJTF structure is that non-NATO allies can be invited to participate. All the countries that want to become NATO members as well as other European democracies would likely join in. And such a task force would provide a framework for enhanced NATO-Russia cooperation . . . . NATO could, in effect serve as a clearing house for existing and future allied contributions to the war on terrorism.[41]

In theory, such a CJTF would satisfy the interests of all nations involved. It would allow for intra-Alliance bandwagoning while the United States could maintain control and leadership of the campaign.

Such a CJTF would also allow the Bush Administration to undertake operations not only with those states that wanted to participate, but those who had useful capabilities outside of the Alliance. This would include states outside of NATO, mainly Russia. Concurrently, states that wished to avoid direct participation could do so, but still engage in support activities such as intelligence sharing or engage in non-military efforts to counter global terrorism. Concurrently, the Europeans would retain some degree of influence over operations through the participation of NAC in the CJTF process.

However, in an apparent effort to maximize U.S. control and influence in operations against international terrorism, the Bush Administration engaged in a strategy designed to avoid entanglement and keep its options relatively open. Even as officials of the Administration endeavored to gain pledges of both overt and tacit support from individual states and from international organizations, the Americans also signaled their intention to conduct the war on their own terms by limiting the influence of these same allies.

The Bush Administration faced a multifaceted challenge of its own making: to gain as wide a degree of support as possible all-the-while maintaining American control of the strategy and implementation of the anti-terrorism campaign and ensuring the centrality of NATO to European security. For the European Allies, the challenges centered around the need to demonstrate their relevance and utility to transatlantic security and bolster the existing security regime, while they concurrently maximize benefits in regards to both national interests and domestic audiences.

A Coalition of the Willing

The United States went to great lengths to gain the declaration of Article 5 from its NATO Allies. It also sought and received institutional support from other international organizations such as the European Union. Yet, when presented with the opportunity to formalize NATO support and involvement through a mechanism such as the CJTF system, the Bush Administration deliberately chose not to use the Alliance's integrated command structure to oversee any military action against the Taliban or the Al Qaeda network. Instead, it bypassed NAC and developed an ad hoc version of the CJTF that was both a coalition of the willing and yet an exclusionary coalition.

Like most decisions reached by NAC, the Article 5 declaration represented consensus and compromise. While the Allies supported military action and the majority were willing to commit troops, a number of states were hesitant to endorse a declaration that would bind them to undertake future military action. In order to mollify these concerns, Wolfowitz assured NAC that the United States would not ask for collective military action by all of the Allies. Wolfowitz instead informed NAC that the United States would only ask for military collaboration from those states willing to engage in combat operations.[42] In his briefing of the Allies, Richard Armitage reported:

> I didn't, as I said, come here to ask for anything. I came here to share with good Allies the information we have. I did point out that in this coalition building there is a continuum from, on the one hand, rhetorical or political support for activities on this global attack on terrorism. It runs the gamut to sharing of intelligence, sharing of financial information, perhaps overflight rights, etc. And at the far end of the continuum is the possibility of some military activity either together or unilaterally.[43]

By implementing such an informal CJTF, the United States could gain the proverbial best of both worlds: the U.S. could "pick and choose among its allies, fashioning the moral authority of an international coalition without having to deal with the problems of the whole alliance."[44] Concurrently, the Allies were also satisfied since the American operation seemed designed to allow those states willing to participate the ability to do so and those unwilling to commit troops or specific assets the option to remain outside of the military campaign while the cohesion and solidarity of the Alliance remained intact.

Nevertheless, those Allies who were part of the coalition of the willing did seek to maximize their influence and gain concrete measures to institutionalize NATO's response. The President of the NATO Assembly, Rafael Estrella summarized the declaration of Article 5 in the following manner:

> By invoking Article 5 we have signaled that the attacks of September 11 were attacks against all of us. We, the Alliance, were expressing the greatest possible solidarity with the U.S. in its hour of need. Important as it may be as symbolism, we have also assumed the responsibility to deliver concrete assistance. National as well as NATO resources and facilities are being made available to help the U.S. prepare the appropriate response to the cancer of terrorism, of which Bin Laden is the most terrible and visible symptom.
>
> We also need, not now, but in the fairly near future, to discuss the assumed, as well as the established terms of reference in Article 5, define exactly what we mean from now on by Article 5. That discussion is also a symptom of the profound change in the character of the Alliance which is now upon us.[45]

Estrella succinctly expressed the desire of certain Allies to contribute both national and institutional assets to the campaign, but also to more thoroughly define the Article 5 commitment.

A Coalition of Coalitions

In the aftermath of the 11 September attacks, states from around the world chose to bandwagon with the United States as a means to both maximize their relative security gains, by combating international terrorism, and to enhance their status, especially within international organizations such as the European Union. By the time the military strikes on Afghanistan began on 7 October 2001, all of the major global powers had indicated their support for the United States, including nations such as Russia and China with which the United States had security tensions prior to 11 September.

While the United States worked closely with NAC and NATO to formulate a coordinated response and to maximize the utility of the Alliance, the Bush Administration also made it clear that NATO and the internal coalition within the Alliance was but one of a number of coalitions that the Americans were developing. In remarks with Lord Robertson, President Bush outlined the global level of support given to the United States in the wake of the attacks:

> I want to remind my fellow citizens, the coalition goes way beyond NATO. Russia is sharing intelligence and offering strong diplomatic support. The organization of American States invoked the Collective Defense Clause of the Rio Treaty. Japan and Korea are offering logistical and other support.
>
> I had a great conversation with Jiang Zemin of China about his desire to join us in fighting terrorist activities. Military forces from Australia and New Zealand are standing by to assist in combat roles if needed.
>
> In Africa, the Organization of African Unity has moved quickly and strongly to condemn the attacks, and many are offering basic services, such as overflight and the sharing of intelligence.
>
> In the Middle East many nations, including Jordan, Egypt and Saudi Arabia are offering law enforcement, intelligence and other cooperation.
>
> In short, many nations understand what NATO expressed, that an attack on us is really an attack on legitimate governments and on freedom.[46]

One reason that NATO formed just one component of the American response to 11 September was that many aspects of the Bush Administration's campaign were non-military. This included efforts to freeze assets of known terrorist groups with links to Al Qaeda, intelligence sharing and broad law enforcement related activities, including border surveillance and a renewed emphasis on detaining illegal immigrants. U.S. National Security Advisor, Dr. Condoleezza Rice described this aspect of the American-led campaign:

> But this is a broad coalition in which people are contributing on very different and very many fronts. The key to the broad coalition is to remember that, while everybody understandably wants to focus on military contributions, this is not the Gulf War. An equally important part of this war on terrorism is the disruption of these terrorist cells abroad.
>
> If you imagine that there are cells out there in 60-plus countries that could be continuing to plot, continuing to look for ways to wreak havoc, the intelligence and law enforcement efforts that have resulted in over 300 arrests of known and suspected Al Qaeda operatives is as important to this war on terrorism and to trying to avoid another attack, either on ourselves or on others, as is the war in Afghanistan.
>
> And so I think that's what the president will say to this coalition. It's financial assets; it's intelligence and information sharing. That's the important point he will make.[47]

Rice's comments were echoed in a variety of forums as the Bush Administration sought to ensure awareness of the multi-faceted nature of the American campaign. Deputy Secretary of State Wolfowitz described the campaign as a series on ongoing and interrelated actions, including economic, diplomatic and military:

> First of all, we're going into a campaign, a sustained campaign which means it's going to be a long series of actions before we achieve success. And I think it's a mistake to isolate one form of action like law enforcement, from another like military, and another like diplomatic. In fact the record demonstrates over and over again that you're more successful when you combine your resources; that diplomacy backed up by meaningful threats of force is much more effective than diplomacy without it; that a political strategy that brings in those hundreds of millions of moderate Muslims who have to be shocked by this barbaric act that claims to be done somehow in the name of their religion.[48]

Over time, officials in the Administration ceased to refer to a single specific coalition against the Taliban and Al Qaeda and instead spoke of a coalition of coalitions. Many nations identified the campaign against international terrorism as proceeding along two fronts with multiple coalitions involved on each front. For instance, Jospin stated that:

> the fight against terrorism since the attacks of 11 September is being waged on two fronts: a comprehensive strategy, conducted on a world scale at the judicial, police, intelligence, economic and financial levels . . . . the second front is of course the armed riposte against bin Laden and his al-Qaida network, an operation of legitimate defense

recognized by the United Nations, planned and conducted essentially at [a] national level
by the United States, with the international community's approval and participation of a
number of countries.[49]

On one level the United States has worked to develop specific coalitions or bilateral
agreements on issues such as intelligence, law enforcement, financial oversight and
aid to both Pakistan and a post-Taliban Afghanistan, while on another level the
Americans sought a series of military coalitions for specific activities ranging from
the operations in Afghanistan to the anti-terrorist campaign in the Philippines.

The results of the Bush Administration's multi-phased strategy were compelling
and dramatic. By 30 September, a week before the military strikes commenced, the
United States had 46 multilateral declarations of support. This included the
conditional Article 5 declaration by NATO, the invocation of the collective defense
clause (Article IV) of the ANZUS Treaty between the United States, Australia and
New Zealand, and the passage of Security Council Resolution 1373 which required
all states to take action against terrorists and their financial networks.

More than 100 nations had offered intelligence cooperation with the U.S. and
the Administration had increased counterterrorism operations with 200 different
intelligence or security services around the world. This was in addition to the 30
nations that offered the United States cooperation and support in criminal
investigations. Furthermore, 27 countries, including the NATO Allies, granted the
U.S. overflight or landing rights for aircraft involved in military action against
terrorism. Most significantly, the Administration had obtained the close
cooperation of Pakistan and many of the major moderate Arab states, including
Egypt.[50]

The tangible benefits of the American diplomatic successes were wide and
varied. The U.S. Treasury Department was able to freeze 20 Al Qaeda accounts in
overseas banks. The few nations that had diplomatic relations with the Taliban,
Pakistan, Saudi Arabia and the United Arab Emirates, cut ties with the Afghani
regime. The United States was also able to secure economic support for Pakistan
from a variety of nations, such as Japan, as a reward for Islamabad's cooperation.
Worldwide there were approximately 200 arrests of persons suspected to have ties
to Al Qaeda. The United States also gained permission to utilize air bases in Saudi
Arabia, Kuwait, Oman and the island of Diego Garcia. American forces would
ultimately be granted base rights in the former Soviet Republics of Tajikistan and
Uzbekistan.

As the United States prepared to initiate military operations against the Taliban,
it continued to utilize this broad-based strategy. Efforts to secure the support and
backing of individual NATO Allies were undertaken concurrently with attempts to
build or maintain other coalitions. NATO would not be the only major source of
support for the American-led campaign in Afghanistan, but in the words of Bush,

"we're building a very strong coalition against terror. And NATO is the cornerstone of that coalition."[51]

Bandwagoning Against International Terrorism

The most vocal and visible signals of support for the U.S.-led campaign against international terrorism came from America's closest security ally, the United Kingdom. British Prime Minister Blair was present at President George Bush's address to a joint session of Congress and received a standing ovation and in the aftermath of Bush's comment "thanks, friend." Blair has also delivered some of the most harsh rhetoric witnessed outside of the United States. For example, in a speech to his Labour Party, Blair asserted that "we will put a trap around the regime. . . . And I say to the Taliban, surrender the terrorists or surrender power – that is your choice."[52]

Of all of the European allies, Blair has had the most significant influence in the formulation and implementation of the American response to 11 September. The British were among the earliest supporters of the invocation of Article 5 and were the first nation to pledge troops to any subsequent military action. Indeed, Blair emerged as an unofficial emissary of the United States to both the EU and to individual European states. Concurrently, Blair influenced American policy and was responsible, for instance, for Bush's decision to "defer" an expansion of the anti-terrorist campaign to include action against Iraq.[53]

Furthermore, Blair made a leadership bid among the European Allies and has generally used the period in the aftermath of 11 September to expand British security influence on both sides of the Atlantic. In one telling example of both Blair's efforts and the intricacies of European Union politics, the Prime Minister invited President Jacques Chirac and Chancellor Schröder to discuss the American-led campaign on 4 November, 2001. However, when news of the meeting emerged, the leaders of Italy, the Netherlands, Spain and Belgium, as well as the EU High Representative for foreign policy, Solana, also demanded to be invited. Following the meetings, those Union memberstates that were not invited complained publically at their exclusion. French Foreign Minister Vedrine tried to explain that four nations, France, Britain, Germany and Italy, had a "special role" to play in regards to Afghanistan and that "other European countries are ok with this."[54] The journal *The Economist* summarized the incident in the following manner:

> Behind the immediate fuss lies a serious structural issue. The EU's small countries have always seen the Union as their protection against a return to the politics of the inter-war years, when their fates were often decided – behind their back – in smoke-filled conference rooms in London, Paris and Munich. They are alarmed at the prospect of a big

countries' "directorate" that might stitch up EU decisions ahead of meetings of the whole club. Some, particularly the British, might respond that as a matter of fact France and Germany have long staged pre-summit meetings that have often decisively influenced later EU deliberations. But bilateral meetings are apparently one thing, gatherings of the larger countries another.[55]

One on level, the potential for domination by a bloc of states, especially because of the historical precedents in Western Europe, was one of the reasons that the smaller Atlanticist states such as Denmark and the Netherlands were staunch supporters of the American security presence in Europe. The United States represented a benign hegemon or balancing power to counter any internal coalition of the major three powers.

On an institutional level, support for the United States by NATO translated into substantial support by the European Union (since membership overlaps and many nations are members of both NATO and the EU).[56] However, in light of close collaboration between France, Germany and the United Kingdom, the Union's High Representative for Foreign Policy, Solana, worked diligently through the autumn to counteract the perception that power and decisionmaking remained concentrated at the various national capitals, and not with the EU in Brussels.[57]

France and Germany, the other two members of the dominant security triumvirate in Western Europe, also expressed staunch support for the United States and pledged military forces for any anti-terrorist operations. In both cases, domestic politics have significantly influenced the foreign policy decisions in regard to the 11 September attacks. In France, divided government has constrained policy formulation and created a dynamic whereby "alone among its neighbors, France is having great difficulty in defining its self-interest in the current conflict."[58] President Chirac is a member of the conservative Gaullist Party, while Prime Minister Jospin is a member of the Socialist Party.[59] The two figures have faithfully personified their party positions, as Chirac called for greater French activism in the war on terror, while Jospin urged caution about being drawn into an American "adventure."[60] Nonetheless, both supported French involvement in order to maintain the *grandeur* of the nation's foreign policy.[61]

For Germany, participation in military action in Afghanistan raised historical issues about the nation's constrained foreign policy in the wake of the world wars. Schröder pledged German troops would be available for any military action in a move which "represented a gesture of emancipation from the limited international role the country has played since the defeat of Hitler."[62] Schröder received the backing of the Bundestag which in a 565 to 40 vote approved German support for the war on terror. However the selective use of Allied forces by the United States meant that German forces were not used in the campaign in Afghanistan (although German troops were deployed to the NATO mission in Macedonia).[63] In this manner, Germany was able to contribute to the campaign in Afghanistan by providing forces to the Macedonia mission and thereby relieving NATO from having to divert assets away from the anti-terrorist campaign while it still maintained its commitments in other areas of the world.

A number of other NATO memberstates also pledged military forces. Italy, Norway and Spain pledged forces, as did NATO's only predominately Muslim state, Turkey. Canada also pledged troops, aircraft and naval units.[64] Constraints prevented the deployment of some nations forces. For instance, by national law, Belgium is only allowed to deploy 1,000 troops outside of its borders, a limit already met through its participation in NATO operations in the Balkans.[65]

Other NATO states offered a variety of assistance ranging from permission to use air space to monetary support. Hungary granted landing and overflight rights to U.S. military aircraft.[66] Meanwhile Poland organized a conference of Central and Eastern European states in Warsaw in an effort to gain the cooperation of these 17 states with the United States on issues such as money laundering, intelligence sharing and efforts to "control the movement of persons and goods."[67] A number of nations outside of NATO, including Australia and Japan also offered to contribute assets to the campaign in Afghanistan.

System-Wide Interests and the War on Terror

Far more so than was the case with the United States, European governments recognized the security importance of combating international terrorism. A variety of West European states including, France, Germany, Italy, Spain and the United Kingdom, have been forced to undertake long-running campaigns against both indigenous and foreign terrorist organizations. Indeed, in the wake of the end of the Cold War, terrorism emerged as one of the few visible and direct threats to peace and stability in the transatlantic region. The March 1995 nerve gas attack on a Tokyo subway by the Japanese religious sect Aum Shinri Kyo demonstrated the potential for the use of WMDs by terrorist or substate groups. Furthermore, the attacks on 11 September demonstrated the capability for terrorist organizations to inflict massive casualties.

This trend toward ever more damaging and costly terrorist incidents will only continue. As Stuart J. Kaufman points out, writing four years before the 11 September attacks, "as the average state decreases in size [and power], while sophisticated weaponry becomes less and less expensive, the relative influence of nonstate actors is likely to rise. Thus technology may increasingly favor terrorists over states."[68] The attacks of 11 September demonstrated that terrorist groups do not even need access to highly sophisticated military technology to do great damage, but may be increasingly able to use non-military technology to conduct attacks. Indeed, the attacks on the World Trade Center and the Pentagon are in some respects a reflection of the rise of "superterrorism." Superterrorism can be defined as:

> Committing violent acts using advanced technological tools to cause massive damage to populations and/or to public and private support networks. It includes all forms of nuclear, chemical, and biological attacks except small chemical poisonings. It encompasses the use of plastic explosives (although fertilizer bombs are still considered a conventional terrorist tactic). It also includes cyber-crime designed to knock out security, economic, and emergency systems.[69]

One of the main differences between superterrorism and more traditional forms is that "the 'new' terrorism is characterized – among other things – by its unprecedented potential for violence, which is aimed at making many victims, by martyrdom and by the use of modern technology. The known networks are international and they exhibit a large degree of ethnic diversity."[70] Hence, contemporary terrorism may increasingly be marked by efforts to produce a greater number of civilian casualties and an almost total abandonment of attacks on military targets.

The proliferation of superterrorism has been facilitated by the increasingly transnational nature of the threat. Al Qaeda is a prime example of the global and crossborder nature of superterrorism. Headquartered in Afghanistan, Al Qaeda developed a network that included operatives in some 60 nations, substantial training facilities in Afghanistan, millions of dollars in assets and the capability of carrying out operations such as the attacks on the American embassies in Tanzania and Kenya and the attack on the U.S.S. *Cole* in Yemen.

The nature of Al Qaeda makes it extremely difficult to counter the group: "In effect, Bin Laden is the chief executive and chief financial officer of a loosely affiliated group of radical terrorists, who share resources, assets and expertise, and who can come together for an operation and then disperse. *Al-Qaida* [italics in original] is simply the most visible head of a hydra." [71]

The global nature of superterrorism has necessitated a transformation in the way nations deal with the threat. Traditionally in the United States, although less so in Europe, terrorism was seen as primarily a law enforcement issue. However, this changed in the wake of 11 September. The Bush Administration took dramatic steps to better coordinate domestic anti-terrorism efforts, including the establishment of a new Cabinet level post, that of Homeland Security. Domestic American initiatives occurred simultaneously with multinational efforts to facilitate intelligence sharing. Such measures are critically important in light of the importance of intelligence to counterterrorism efforts. Frank J. Cilluffo and Daniel Rankin point out that:

> Perhaps the most important tool in counter-terrorism is intelligence. Accurate and timely information, coupled with proper analysis is the lifeblood of the campaign against terrorism. Every aspect of the campaign from diplomatic, military, financial and political operations to the provision of warnings about future attacks relies largely on our intelligence. More specifically, the breadth, depth and uncertainty of the terrorist threat demands significant investment, coordination and re-tooling of the intelligence process across the board for the pre-attack (warning), trans-attack (pre-emption) and post-attack ("whodunit") phases.[72]

The transnational threat of superterrorism in many ways is analogous to the Cold War threat faced by Western Europe. The security threat requires a transnational and transatlantic response since the ability to counter superterrorism is beyond that of any one state, even the United States. However, a major difference between the Cold War and the war on terrorism is that the Europeans are demanding greater influence in the development of any broad strategy devised to combat the new threat. Hence the drive for the development of autonomous capabilities for the European Union and the drive for participation in the American-led campaign in Afghanistan by the major Western European powers.

Since there was no direct large scale conventional military threat against Europe, with the demise of the Soviet Union, the Alliance should have been able to recalculate and refocus its energies toward other threats, including terrorism. To a certain extent, the Alliance has recast itself and taken on new missions (see Chapter 2). However, the unwillingness of the United States to take a significant leadership role in fashioning new strategies to counter international terrorism before 11 September prevented the meaningful development of a counterterrorism role for NATO.

Nevertheless, in the aftermath of the 11 September attacks, new impetus was added to efforts to recalculate a counterterrorist role for the Alliance. The threat of superterrorism has increased pressure to develop more holistic approaches to security that would begin "with ever-closer cooperation between law-enforcement and national-security agencies . . . . The attacks on the United States reinforce the call for an integrated approach involving diplomatic, military and economic elements."[73] NATO is one of the few security organizations that has the capability to coordinate these varied approaches. The dramatic increase in intelligence sharing that occurred in the aftermath of the 11 September attacks is but one example of the potential for new roles or missions for the Alliance.

The Convergence of Transatlantic Interests

Although the major European states endorsed the invocation of Article 5 and offered various forms of assistance to the United States, as previously mentioned, this support did not come in the form of a "blank check."[74] Instead the Europeans sought substantial input in the formulation and implementation of the military strategy against the Taliban in Afghanistan. By the time the military campaign commenced, consensus had developed among the European states and the United States on a variety of issues.

First, all of the European states, including even the most pliable of America's allies, have insisted that the anti-terrorism campaign encompass a variety of approaches. The necessity to incorporate other international organizations into the campaign against terrorism was noted by NATO itself at a December 2001 Ministerial: "The struggle against terrorism will involve a wide range of international organizations," and "we support the efforts of the United Nations with its central role in this field, and those of the European Union, the Organization for Security and Cooperation in Europe, the G-8, and other financial institutions."[75]

In this regard, the actions undertaken by the Bush Administration in its initiatives to include nonmilitary measures, including financial, diplomatic and law enforcement, have won the praise of the Europeans and ensured continued support. French Defense Minister Richard summarized the European approval of the American strategy:

> Our American friends have thoughtfully emphasized that defeating terrorism can only proceed from a large array of means – financial, political, diplomatic, judicial, police and intelligence-related . . . – of which military force is only one among others. All the indications we have had in the last weeks emphasize particularly the requirement of higher efficiency and more intense co-operation in police tasks, investigation and judicial procedures. This will imply a solid political energy in all our European democracies.[76]

Second, European states, particularly France and Germany, stressed the importance of ensuring that any NATO action against the Taliban and Al Qaeda was not perceived as a "war against Islam." In their condemnations of the attacks and pledges of support for the United States, many NATO Allies even explicitly commented on this fact. For example, in Hungary's official note of support for the initiation of the attacks on Afghanistan, it is noted that "the Government considers it important to recall that [the] fight is not pursued against Islam, but terrorism."[77] NATO issued the following statement on the issue:

> Our fight is not against Islam or the innocent people of Afghanistan. Our countries are helping to provide humanitarian assistance to the Afghan people, who have suffered under

the cruelty of the Taliban regime. Our fight, the fight of the international community, is against the terrorists, their networks and those who harbor them, as stated in Resolution 1368 of the UN Security Council.[78]

This concern was shared by Washington for obvious reasons and the Bush Administration early on embarked upon a diplomatic offensive designed to woo moderate Arab states and maintain the support of Muslims both within the transatlantic region and in the broader global context. Concurrently, both the United States and its European partners engaged in efforts to reassure Muslims within their territory that the campaign was not directed against Islam. For instance, Blair penned an open letter to the Islamic Society of Britain in which he stated that "the horrific attack in America was not the work of Islamic terrorists," but "the work of terrorists pure and simple," and Britons "must not honor them with a religious justification, or a badge of faith."[79] Meanwhile, the French government initiated a series of regular meetings between French Islamic groups and the interior and foreign affairs ministers.[80]

Third, the Europeans accepted that NAC invocation of Article 5 would not translate into a broad call to arms for all of the states within the Alliance. Instead, NATO military action would involve a coalition of the willing along the lines of an informal CJTF. This relieved the few NATO partners that did want to commit troops to American-led campaign of any pressure to do so while it also simplified the command and control structures and streamlined the decision-making procedures of the operation. It also allowed the NATO partners to contribute to the operation against the Taliban and Al Qaeda in indirect ways which best reflected their particular assets and capabilities. Once the military campaign began on 7 October 2001, the United States provided the overwhelming majority of the forces and assets, but the NATO Allies did provide a substantial amount of assistance, some overt and some tacit, which facilitated the operation and reinforced the utility of the Alliance.

Notes

1. See Jeffrey Gedmin, ed., *European Integration and American Interests: What the New Europe Really Means for the United States* (Washington, D.C.: American Enterprise Institute, 1997).
2. For a post-World War II overview of the Anglo-American special relationship, see John Drumbell, *A Special Relationship: Anglo-American Relations in the Cold War and After* (London: Palgrave, 2000).

3.   See, for instance, Douglas T. Stuart and Stephen F. Szabo, eds., *Discord and Collaboration in a New Europe: Essays in Honor of Arnold Wolfers* (Washington, D.C.: Johns Hopkins, 1994).

4.   Gary G. Sick and Lawrence G. Potter, "Introduction," in Gary G. Sick and Lawrence G. Potter, eds., *The Persian Gulf at the Millennium: Essays in Politics, Economy, Security, and Religion* (New York: St. Martin's, 1997) 1.

5.   Theodore Craig, *Call for Fire: Sea Combat in the Falklands and the Gulf War* (London: John Murray, 1995), 168.

6.   Suzanne Daley, "NATO Quickly Gives the U.S. All the Help That It Asked," *The New York Times* (5 October 2001).

7.   Wesley Clark, *Waging Modern War: Bosnia, Kosovo, and the Future of Combat* (Washington, D.C.: PublicAffairs, 2001).

8.   During the Kosovo operation, such capabilities were almost entirely limited to the United Kingdom and France.

9.   The Europeans have less than 10 percent of the mobile defense assets that the U.S. possesses; Jonathan M. White, "European Defense: Not more Tanks, More Cops," *BASIC* (23 November 1999).

10. Iain Duncan Smith, "European Common Foreign, Security and Defense Policies – Implications for the United States and the Atlantic Alliance," *Congressional Testimony Before the House Committee on International Relations, 105th Congress* (10 November 1999).

11. As reported by Bryan Bender, "US Worried by Coalition 'Technology-Gap'," *Jane's Defence Weekly* (29 July 1998): 8.

12. "The Ageing Alliance," *The Economist* (10/23/99), 6.

13. Jérôme Paolini, "A French Perspective," in Michael Brenner, ed., *Multilateralism and Western Strategy* (New York: St. Martin's, 1995) 105-106.

14. On the potential for balancing against the United States, see John Mearsheimer, "Back to the Future: Instability in Europe After the Cold War," *International Security* 19, no. 3 (Summer 1990): 5-56; or Christopher Layne, "The Unipolar Illusion: Why New Great Powers will Arise," *International Security* 17, no. 4 (Spring 1993): 5-51.

15. For instance, Kenneth Waltz contends that one of the rising great powers that will challenge the United States is the "European Union or Germany leading a coalition." For Waltz, however, the key is German leadership since the divergent interests of the EU are likely to preclude the development of coherent foreign and security policies; see Kenneth N. Waltz, "Structural Realism After the Cold War," *International Security* 25, no. 1 (Summer 2000): 5-42.

16. John M. Goldgeier, "Not Whether But When: Book Review," *Political Science Quarterly* 115, no. 2 (Summer 2000), 315.

17. Owen Harries, "The Anglosphere Illusion," *National Interest* 63 (Spring 2001), 135.

18. For an expansion of these four points, see Robert J. Lieber, "No Transatlantic Divorce in the Offing," *Orbis* 44, no. 4 (Fall 2000): 571-85.

19. Rudolf Scharping, "NATO and Perspectives of European Security," Speech at Columbia University, New York (3 November 2000).

20. Waltz, "Structural Realism," 22.

21. Gunther Hellmann and Reinhard Wolf, "Neorealism, Neoliberal Institutionalism, and the Future of NATO," *Security Studies* 3, no. 1 (Autumn 1993), 20.

22. Ronald R. Krebs, "Perverse Institutionalism: NATO and the Greco-Turkish Conflict," *International Organization* 53, no. 2 (Spring 1999), 351.
23. For a more thorough discussion of the trends toward military specialization within the Alliance, see Lansford, especially pages 167-172.
24. Suzanne Daley, "NATO, Though Supportive, Has Little to Offer Militarily," *The New York Times* (20 September 2001).
25. Here I define intra-Alliance bandwagoning as coalescing or joining with the dominant power within an alliance or coalition to support its policies rather than balancing against the hegemonic power in an effort to expand or maintain the influence of the lesser actors.
26. Included among these states was Germany, because of its historical and legal constraints on deploying troops overseas.
27. Howard LaFranchi, "Despite Talk of Coalition, US Mostly Goes it Alone, *The Christian Science Monitor* (29 October 2001).
28. *NATO Handbook: 50th Anniversary Edition*, Chapter 12.
29. NATO, "NATO's New Force Structures," *NATO Basic Fact Sheet*, no. 5 (Brussels: NATO, 1996).
30. NATO, NAC, *Declaration of the Heads of State and Government Participating in the Meeting of the North Atlantic Council*, M-1(94)3 (11 January 1994), 1.
31. Charles Barry, "NATO's Combined and Joint Task Forces in Theory and Practice," *Survival* 38, no. 1 (Spring 1996), 81.
32. WEU, International Secretariat, *Structure and Functions: European Security and Defense Identity (ESDI) and Combined Joint Task Forces (CJTF)* (October 1995), 15.
33. NATO, "The Combined and Joint Task Force Concept: NATO Fact Sheet" (8 August 2000).
34. Anthony Cragg, "The Combined and Joint Task Force Concept" A Key Component of the Alliance's Adaptation," *NATO Review*, 44, no. 4 (July 1996), 8-9.
35. Barry, 92-3.
36. Ibid., 82.
37. Bruce Clark, "Europe Secures Greater Role in NATO Operations," *Financial Times* (4 June 1996), 1. In addition, at the Berlin Summit it was decided to reduce the number of standing elements at NATO headquarters and establish mobile headquarters that would form the nuclei of future CJTF missions; Bruce Clark, "NATO Seeks to Bridge Ambiguity Gap," *Financial Times* (6 June 1996), 2.
38. NATO, "The Combined and Joint Task Forces Concept."
39. Cragg, 8.
40. *NATO Handbook: 50th Anniversary*, Chapter 12.
41. Stanley R. Sloan, "Give NATO a Combined Task Force Against Terrorism," *International Herald Tribune* (13 November 2001).
42. Suzanne Daley, "NATO Says U.S. Has Proof Against Bin Laden Group."
43. NATO, "Press Availability: U.S. Deputy Secretary of State Armitage and NATO Secretary General Lord Robertson," Brussels (20 September 2001).
44. Ibid.
45. NATO, "NATO Allies 'Must Face New World Order'," *NATO Press Release* (6 October 2001).

46. George W. Bush and Lord Robertson, Press Briefing, Washington, D.C. (10 October 2001).
47. Condoleezza Rice, Press Briefing, Washington, D.C. (8 November 2001).
48. Paul D. Wolfowitz and Joschka Fischer, Press Briefing, Pentagon (19 September 2001).
49. France, Ministry of Foreign Affairs, "Replies by M. Lionel Jospin, Prime Minister, to Questions in the National Assembly," Paris (6 November 2001).
50. U.S., White House, "Operation Enduring Freedom Overview: Campaign Against Terrorism Results, Period Covered 14-30 September 2001," Fact Sheet (1 October 2001).
51. Bush, Press Briefing.
52. Brian Knowlton, "Give Up Terrorists or Quit, Blair Warns Taliban," *International Herald Tribune* (3 October 2001).
53. Martin Walker, "The Blare of Blair," *Europe*, 411 (November 2001), 2.
54. France, Ministry of Foreign Affairs, "War on Terrorism/UK/Europe: Interview given by M. Hubert Vedrine, Minister of Foreign Affairs to 'France Inter–Questions Directes'," Paris (8 November 2001).
55. "Guess Who Wasn't Coming to Dinner," *The Economist*, 361 (10 November 2001), 48.
56. Eleven nations that are members of NATO also belong to the European Union include Belgium, Denmark, France, Germany, Greece, Italy, Luxembourg, the Netherlands, Portugal, Spain, and the United Kingdom.
57. "Javier Solana: The EU's Voice in Foreign Affairs Talks Loudly–But Lacks a Stick," *The Economist*, 361 (17 November 2001) 52.
58. John Vinocur, "Europe's Leading Nations Use Afghan Conflict to Enhance World Role," *International Herald Tribune* (12 October 2001).
59. The two will likely meet in the presidential election in May 2002.
60. Vinocur.
61. Historically, French foreign policy has been based on the idea of a "civilizing mission" whereby it was incumbent upon the nation to spread culture and economic benefits around the world. This rationale formed the basis for the empire and continues to impact the domestic consensus on foreign policy and engagement in the World; see, for instance, Philip Gordon, *A Certain Idea of France* (New York: St. Martin's, 1993).
62. Vinocur.
63. Some 600 German troops formed the core of the NATO mission, Operation Amber Fox, in Macedonia; Victor Homola, "Germany: Macedonia Mission is Approved," *The New York Times* (29 September 2001).
64. Canada also faced a domestic controversy over participation as the nation's Prime Minister, Jean Chrètien, faced criticism for what many in the public and press considered to be a "slow reaction" to the attacks; "Canada and the War on Terrorism: A New Face to the Fore," *The Economist*, 361 (13 October 2001), 39.
65. Suzanne Daley, "NATO, Though Supportive, Has Little to Offer Militarily," *The New York Times* (20 September 2001).
66. Hungary, Ministry of Foreign Affairs, "Statement by Minister of Foreign Affairs Mr. János Martonyi Concerning the Evidence presented by the USA On Those Who Carried Out the Terrorist Attacks on September 11, 2001," Budapest (2 October 2001).
67. Poland, Ministry of Foreign Affairs, "The World After September 11 and Polish Foreign Policy: Polish Foreign Minister Wlodzimierz Cimoszewicz's Remarks at CSIS," Washington, D.C. (14 December 2001).

68. Stuart J. Kaufman, "The Fragmentation and Consolidation of the International System," *International Organization* 51, no. 2 (Spring 1997), 200.
69. Glen E. Schweitzer and Carole C. Dorsch, "Superterrorism: Searching for Long-Term Solutions," *Futurist* 33, no. 6 (June/July 1999), 40.
70. The Netherlands, "Plan of Action for Combating Terrorism and Promoting Security," 5125137/501/RTT (5 October 2001).
71. Frank J. Cilluffo and Daniel Rankin, "Fighting Terrorism," *NATO Review* 49 (Winter 2001/2002), 13.
72. Ibid., 14.
73. Robert Hall and Carl Fox," Rethinking Security," *NATO Review* 49 (Winter 2001), 9.
74. Daley, "Tough Talk."
75. NATO, "Statement on Combating Terrorism: Adapting the Alliance's Defense Capabilities," Press Release (2001) 173 (18 December 2001).
76. Alain Richard, "The European Union: A Rising Feature on the International Stage," Speech at the Welt am Sonntag Forum, Berlin (2 October 2001).
77. Hungary, "Statement by the Government of the Republic of Hungary Concerning the American-British Operation Launched in the Framework of the International Fight Against Terrorism" (Budapest: 7 October 2001).
78. NATO, "NATO's Response to Terrorism: Statement Issued at the Ministerial Meeting of the North Atlantic Council Held at NATO Headquarters, Brussels," M-NAC-2 (2001) 159 (6 December 2001).
79. Tony Blair to the Islamic Society of Britain, London (5 November 2001).
80. France, Ministry of Foreign Affairs, "Statement by the Ministry of Foreign Affairs Deputy Spokesman: Foreign and Interior Ministers' Meeting With French Moslems," Paris (4 October 2001).

Chapter 5

The Military Response to
11 September

Operation Enduring Freedom

As they prepared for military strikes against Afghanistan, American military officials wanted to ensure that they had a clear chain of command and that the decision-making process would be in the hands of American military officers, namely, the commander of U.S. Central Command, Army General Tommy Franks. The actual attacks on the Taliban regime would follow the pattern of previous operations whereby military action began with concentrated airstrikes. Although the overwhelming majority of forces used in the attacks were American, NATO provided a variety of both direct and indirect military assistance to the United States. Actual combat operations began on 7 October 2001, with air and cruise missile attacks launched by both American and British forces.

The first strikes included 15 land-based bombers and 25 carrier-based U.S. aircraft. In addition, British and American naval units fired 50 cruise missiles.[1] These strikes were directed against a variety of targets, such as airfields, air defense systems, barracks and training facilities and were designed to give the coalition forces control of the Afghan skies and the ability to conduct operations at will.[2] As the campaign progressed, attacks began to be concentrated on major concentrations of Taliban troops and other military facilities. Even as Taliban and Al Qaeda targets were attacked, the United States also initiated airdrops of humanitarian rations in an effort to demonstrate that the Afghan people were not the targets of the attacks and that the operation was not "a war against Islam." Concurrently, negotiations were initiated with anti-Taliban factions in Afghanistan in order to foster popular revolt and begin the process of developing a moderate, post-Taliban government.

Within a month of the initiation of hostilities, coalition forces had conducted a variety of operations, including both military and humanitarian missions. By 1 November, coalition forces had carried out some 2,000 combat sorties and dropped more than one million humanitarian ration packets to the Afghan people.[3] American Secretary of Defense Rumsfield declared that the initial goals of the air campaign were:

1) To make clear to the Taliban that harboring terrorists carries a price;
2) To acquire intelligence to facilitate future operations against al-Qaeda and the Taliban;

3) To develop useful relationships with groups in Afghanistan that oppose the Taliban and al-Qaeda;

4) To make it increasingly difficult for the terrorists to use Afghanistan freely as a base of operation;

5) To alter the military balance over time by denying to the Taliban the offensive systems that hamper the progress of the various opposition forces; and

6) To provide humanitarian relief to Afghans suffering oppressive living conditions under the Taliban regime.[4]

For the campaign, eventually code-named "Operation Enduring Freedom," the United States faced an interesting dilemma: Alliance partners and other nations pledged far more troops and resources than the United States could utilize. There were only limited military targets in Afghanistan and the Pentagon did not plan to deploy large numbers of ground troops. Instead, the campaign would utilize highly trained special forces and special operations troops of which even the NATO Allies only had a limited number.

The United States also made extensive use of its highly sophisticated, precision-guided weapons. These weapons include various types of smart weapons that are guided by either satellites or by spotters on the ground, such as the JDAM (Joint Direct Attack Munitions--which are one ton bombs that are guided by satellites to targets that have been pre-spotted by ground forces). More than 70 percent of the ordnance used in the aerial campaign was precision-guided.[5] The campaign also showcased U.S. aerial power and such weapons as the B-1 and B-2 bombers, as well as the venerable B-52 bomber.

The majority of ground combat was by anti-Taliban forces, led by the main opposition group, the Northern Alliance. Coalition special forces provided both training for the anti-Taliban troops and served to coordinate the air campaign, often calling in close air support strikes on the behalf of their Afghan allies.[6] These strikes included the use of U.S. Air Force AC-130 gunships which were able to deploy an enormous amount of munitions against ground troops and proved to be highly effective during the campaign. Although the lengthy bombing campaign led to charges of inactivity and some second guessing among domestic audiences, on 9 November 2001, Northern Alliance forces were able to capture the strategic town of Mazar-e Sharif whose fall signaled the beginning of a rapid collapse of the Taliban and Al Qaeda forces.[7] Within four days, Northern Alliance forces were able to capture the Afghan capital of Kabul and advance into the South while anti-Taliban Pashtun forces rose up against the regime. Some 1,200 American Marines established a base of operations near Kandahar (at the same site of the early U.S. special operations raid) on 25 November. There were other limited deployments of troops, including forces from the American Tenth Mountain Division in Northern

Afghanistan. By early December, the Taliban regime had been essentially defeated with its leadership in hiding and anti-Taliban forces in effective control of most of the nation. Following meetings in Bonn, Germany, Hamid Karzai, an opposition leader from the Kandahar Province was chosen interim leader of broad, coalition government for Afghanistan. In addition, arrangements were put in place for the deployment of an international peacekeeping force, led by the United Kingdom. Nonetheless, while the regime was destroyed and the main infrastructure of the Al Qaeda more or less eradicated, the two leading figures of the regime, Mullah Omar and Bin Laden, remained at large.

A combination of factors ensured that the United States would be able to undertake Operation Enduring Freedom without asking for significant assistance from its NATO Allies. The campaign in Afghanistan utilized only a small number of ground troops and only a limited number of forces overall. For instance, including those troops mobilized for airport and other domestic security functions, the United States only had to mobilize 67,793 National Guard and Reserve forces for Operation Enduring Freedom.[8] This number was only a third of the forces mobilized for the Gulf War. Also, the highly technical nature of the war limited the capability of the Allies to contribute meaningful resources. The United States made extensive use of sophisticated weaponry, including precision-guided bombs, drones, and electronic warfare equipment. Indeed, perhaps "the main lesson of Afghanistan, according to American and European officials and experts, is that small U.S. combat teams on the ground and high-performance aircraft with precision-guided weapons can be coordinated under almost any conditions."[9]

Furthermore, the limited number of forces also allowed the United States to ensure a centralized command structure and avoid external influences in decision making. Philip Gordon succinctly summarized the broad U.S. policy which saw:

> European support as politically useful but not particularly significant militarily. In this case it was reinforced by what many Americans saw as a key 'lesson' of Kosovo. Whereas many in Europe saw the Kosovo air campaign as excessively dominated by the United States and American generals, most Americans – particularly within the military – saw just the opposite: excessive European meddling, with French politicians and European lawyers interfering with efficient targeting and bombing runs, and compromising operational security. This time, the Bush team determined, would be different.[10]

The outcome of the military campaign seemed to confirm the utility of the American approach. After the demise of the Taliban, one of the main lessons that emerged was that "a military hub-and-spoke command operation has worked far better for Washington than the consensus decision-making on which it had to rely during the NATO air campaign over Kosovo and Serbia in 1999, which left many in the U.S.

Defense Department deeply frustrated."[11] While NATO did not provide substantial direct military assistance to Operation Enduring Freedom, the invocation of Article 5 initiated a variety of Alliance assistance which facilitated the military success of the campaign in Afghanistan.

American Requests From NATO

Following the series of meetings in late September and early October in Brussels where the officials of the Bush Administration presented evidence against Bin Laden and the Al Qaeda network to NAC, the Administration also made eight specific requests of the Alliance. None of the requests required substantial deployments of national or NATO forces and most were in line with ongoing efforts by the Bush Administration to develop both military and non-military coalitions in the fight against international terrorism. Following the NAC invocation of Article 5, NAC approved the U.S. requests and agreed to undertake the measures both individually and collectively. As such NATO served a mechanism for the United States to coordinate both military and non-military measures among the Alliance and aid in efforts to secure cooperation with non-NATO states. In addition, the measures cleared the way for the redeployment of American forces that were involved in ongoing NATO operations.

First, the partners agreed to bolster intelligence cooperation and sharing on matters related to terrorism and counterterrorism. This cooperation was to be implemented on both a bilateral and multilateral level under the auspices of a variety of NATO agencies. It built upon existing patterns of intelligence sharing within the Alliance. This request was in line with broad efforts by the United States to promote such cooperation globally and to develop a variety of anti-terrorist coalitions on non-military matters, including law enforcement, financial transactions and border control (see Chapter 4). In order to carry out the pledge, NATO undertook a variety of steps which resulted in "increased exchanges of information and intelligence."[12] The Alliance also instituted a variety of measures to improve the ability of the Alliance to cooperate with other international bodies, including European Union. One result was the ability of the Union to draw up its own list of terrorist organizations.[13]

Second, the Allies agreed to "provide, individually or collectively, as appropriate and according to their capabilities, assistance to Allies and other states which are or may be subject to increased terrorist threats as a result of their support for the campaign against terrorism."[14] The Bush Administration pressed for such a broad declaration as a tangible signal of international support for the nations in Central Asia that had agreed to support the campaign and in the event that military operations spread beyond Afghanistan and the military coalition needed to secure facilities for operations. It also served as an enticement for cooperation from Alliance and partner states. As an embodiment of this pledge, NATO pledged to "deepen our relationships with our Central Asian and Caucasian Partners , as well as with our partners in the Mediterranean Dialogue."[15]

Third, the United States gained assurances from the Allies that they would increase security measures to protect American and other Allied "facilities" within their borders. This was a response to both real and future concerns. On one hand, American planners hoped the resolution would prompt partner states to increase security for its facilities in Europe. After military strikes commenced, the European states initiated a variety of measures to fulfill this pledge. Belgium implemented "extraordinary" security measures around NATO and American military facilities, as did other Allies such the United Kingdom, Germany, France, Italy and Turkey.[16] On the other hand, it also relieved the United States from assuming all of the relative costs of significantly increasing security at its bases, a policy which could limit, albeit on a minor level, the resources available for use in combat operations.

Fourth, NAC agreed to replace assets that were currently being used in Allied operations, but were needed to support Operation Enduring Freedom. This would allow the United States to shift assets from current missions in areas such as the Balkans or the Mediterranean and redeploy them in Operation Enduring Freedom. For instance, Greece offered to supply troops to offset planned withdrawals of American forces from NATO missions in the Balkans.[17] The reallocation of resources would also allow the United States to limit the number of reserve and National Guard troops called to active duty.

Fifth, the Alliance would "provide blanket overflight clearances for the United States and other Allies' aircraft, in accordance with the necessary air traffic arrangements and national procedures, for military flights related to operations against terrorism."[18] This measure would reduce uncertainty when planning operations by guaranteeing permission to use airspace. When the American-led attacks began, some 40 nations gave the coalition permission to use their airspace for operations.

Sixth, the Allies consented to open their ports and airfields to the United States and other NATO partners for operations related to the anti-terrorist campaign, including allowing these facilities to be used for refueling. Like the previous point, this agreement allowed for more streamlined planning and formulation of missions, especially the transfer of assets from one theater to another.

Seventh, in one of two decisions which involved the deployment of NATO assets, NAC approved the stationing of units from the Standing Naval Forces in the Eastern Mediterranean to establish a NATO presence. Eighth, and in the second measure related to a deployment of Alliance forces, the Allies agreed "to deploy elements of its NATO Airborne Early Warning force to support operations against terrorism."[19]

In response to NATO's actions, American Secretary of State Powell expressed the thanks of the United States:

> It's been my pleasure today to once again host my colleague and dear friend Lord Robertson, secretary general of NATO. On this occasion I was able to thank him, as the president did earlier, on behalf of the American people for the strong support that we received from NATO in this time of crisis, within 24 hours after the events of September the Eleventh, NATO had acted.
>
> And NATO has continued acting in the four weeks since, providing strong support not only in terms of statements coming out, but in terms of the invocation of Article 5 and providing us the kind of support that we will see manifested later this week when NATO AWACS aircraft will be coming to the United States to help us with surveillance, when NATO naval forces will be moving into the eastern Mediterranean to take up some of the slack; when individual countries in NATO work with us to assist us in dealing with the situation with respect to terrorism; but above all, with all of the NATO nations making commitments under the Article 5 invocation to give us overflight rights and other things that have proven so helpful to our efforts.[20]

Powell also expressed the belief that such actions demonstrated the continuing utility of the Alliance:

> I think these actions show the viability of the alliance, shows that the alliance is growing, the alliance has a role to play. More and more nations want to become a part of the great alliance which has done such a brilliant job of preserving the peace and which is finding new missions for the future that will make it as vital as it has been in the past.[21]

Although the measures that the Alliance agreed to take did not lead to the deployment of massive amounts of NATO troops or assets, they did provide substantial direct and indirect support for the American-led military campaign in Afghanistan.

AWACS Deployment

NAC approval of the American requests led to two major deployments by the Alliance. Although they did not involve the deployment of NATO resources in combat missions, these operations did demonstrate that the Article 5 invocation was more than a symbolic or purely political action. Indeed, the deployments had practical military applications. Lord Robertson described the deployments as a means to allow American forces to be redeployed in Operation Enduring Freedom:

> Following a specific request from the United States, the Allies today agreed that five AWACS aircraft, together with their crews, will deploy to the United States to assist counter-terrorism operations. This deployment, which was agreed to by acclamation this morning [8 October 2001], will allow U.S. aircraft currently engaged in these operations in the United States to be released for operations against terrorism elsewhere.[22]

In many ways the deployment of the AWACS aircraft was an expression of the progress and shared capabilities of the Alliance. The aircraft are part of the NATO Airborne Early Warning Force (NAEWF) which was created by the Alliance in 1980. NAEWF operates under the auspices of the Supreme Headquarters Allied Powers Europe (SHAPE), and is tasked to support the operations of both major Alliance commands, SHAPE and the Supreme Allied Command Atlantic (SACLANT). The early warning unit is composed of two main elements. The first unit is a multinational force based at Geilenkirchen, Germany, and consists of 17 Boeing E-3A aircraft. These aircraft are owned and operated by NATO. Their crews are completely integrated with personnel from 12 different Alliance nations forming 30 crews.[23] The E-3A component has 2,500 personnel and 450 support staff. The element alternates between German and American command.

The second component of the NAEWF is the Airborne Early Warning Squadron, Number 8 of the Royal Air Force (RAF). This unit is based at Waddington in the United Kingdom and consists of seven E-3D aircraft. Its crews are supplied entirely by the RAF. NAEWF's mission is to "provide aircraft and trained aircrews to deliver a surveillance and/or control platform wherever and whenever directed."[24]

The five NAEWF AWACS aircraft and one training cargo plane were placed under the command of the North American Aerospace Defense Command or NORAD and stationed at Tinker Air Force Base in the state of Oklahoma, U.S.A. The NATO AWACS begin operations on 12 October 2001. The deployed forces numbered 196, and 31 civilians who were part of the support staff (each aircraft normally has a crew of 17).[25] The AWACS planes were tasked to support air surveillance operations to protect the continental United States. Meanwhile, American AWACS craft were deployed in Operation Enduring Freedom. Since NAEWF aircraft were involved in support of the NATO missions in the Balkans, Paris agreed to "backfill" by providing French AWACS aircraft for the operation in Bosnia-Herzegovina under the fourth point of the eight-point support agreement issued by NAC.[26]

Naval Deployment

In addition to the AWACS deployment, NAC also ordered the deployment of a naval task force to the Eastern Mediterranean. On 10 October 2001, American Air Force General Joseph Ralston, SACEUR, issued a statement to the press:

> NATO assets presently on exercise off the coast of Spain were re-assigned today to a new mission. Effective immediately, the Standing Naval Force Mediterranean (STANAVFORMED), consisting of nine ships from eight NATO countries, will set sail to provide an allied military presence in the eastern Mediterranean and to demonstrate our resolve.
>
> These two actions [the deployment of the AWACS and STANAVFORMED] underline the unwavering commitment of the 19 NATO nations to fight terrorism. Of course, we stand ready to provide any additional support requested by the United States, on order of the North Atlantic Council.[27]

The naval force was engaged in a training exercise off the coast of Spain before it was deployed in the NATO-led support mission that was dubbed Operation Active Endeavor on 26 October 2001 (the actual naval force is known as Task Force Endeavor).

By stationing forces in the Eastern Mediterranean, NATO signaled its readiness to expand its role and deploy more assets if needed since STANAVFORMED's primary mission is to be able to deploy rapidly to an area of "tension or crisis" and it "forms the nucleus around which to build a more versatile and powerful naval force, whenever required."[28] One of the more significant aspects of the Mediterranean operation is the prepositioning of forces which will allow for quicker deployment. This is true of the NATO units in the Eastern Mediterranean and both NATO and American forces in Europe. In testimony before a joint congressional committee it was noted that:

> Rotational naval forces in the Mediterranean can reach the Red Sea to conduct strike operations in Southwest Asia nine days faster than forces deployed from the eastern United States. Air Force aircraft and personnel deployed in Europe allow forces to respond more quickly to address small-scale conflicts in the area and to reduce the burden on airlift and sealift, than if the units came from the United States.[29]

In this fashion, the IRFs serve as a tool for potential operations if there was an expansion of the campaign in Afghanistan or if there was the need for an immediate military escalation in response to further terrorist activities. In addition to "showing the flag" for NATO, the deployment would also free American assets for Operation Enduring Freedom.

STANAVFORMED was established in 1992 when eight members of the Alliance agreed to create a permanent naval reaction force in the Mediterranean.[30] The unit is part of the range of NATO's Immediate Reaction Forces (IRFs) which were developed in the aftermath of the Cold War in order to give the Alliance out-of-area capabilities. STANAVFORMED is commanded by British Commodore Angus Sommerville and consists of nine ships.[31] As stipulated in the sixth point of NATO's eight-point support plan, Alliance states have agreed to open their ports and air facilities to the NATO naval forces during their deployment. During the period of its deployment, STANAVFORMED was involved in monitoring 1,000 merchant ships and undertook a rescue mission to save 84 workers on an oil rig on 4 December 2001.

In order to ensure a constant NATO presence in the region, it was decided to rotate STANAVFORMED with NATO's other major naval IRF, the Standing Naval Force Atlantic (STANAVFORLANT). STANAVFORLANT consists of 11 ships from 10 Alliance partners.[32] The Atlantic flotilla is commanded by Portuguese Commodore Fernando Melo Gomes. On 6 December 2001, STANAVFORLANT replaced STANAVFORMED in the Eastern Mediterranean. Under current plans, the two task forces will rotate every three months in order to allow the ships to be refueled and refitted.[33]

By stationing naval units in the Mediterranean, NATO endeavored to demonstrate its military utility. Concurrently, its forces also continue to fulfill other missions. Christopher Bennett summarizes Operation Action Endeavor in the following manner:

> These forces . . . have not been involved in combat operations, but have demonstrated Alliance resolve and participation in the campaign against terrorism. Moreover, they are available for other missions, including participation in diplomatic initiatives, such as under the Alliance's Mediterranean Dialogue, NATO's forum for discussion and cooperation with countries in the wider Mediterranean region.[34]

Cooperation in the Balkans

Alliance cooperation and support for the American-led campaign was also highly evident in NATO actions in the Balkans. The Alliance undertook a number of specific efforts in this regard. To begin with, NATO-led operations in Macedonia and Kosovo forestalled two major crises and contributed to regional peace and security. Lord Robertson explained the Alliance's actions at a meeting of NATO's foreign ministers:

In Serbia, without fanfare, we oversaw the reopening of the Ground Safety Zone around Kosovo, heading off a predicted major conflict there. Our missions in the former Yugoslav Republic of Macedonia have demonstrated that a modest number of NATO troops can avert a bloody civil war. Today, we paid tribute to the men and women of Task Forces Harvest and Fox, whose work has been the model of crisis prevention.

In Kosovo, NATO forces have created a peaceful environment without which the recent successful elections, the first free and fair elections in Kosovo history, could simply not have been held. And NATO continues to support the stabilization process in Bosnia-Herzegovina, preparing the way for an increasing transfer of tasks to civilian authorities.[35]

NATO peacekeeping successes in the Balkans paved the way for other actions. For instance, NATO intelligence operations were able to detect and "smash" Al Qaeda cells operating in the Balkans, specifically in Kosovo and Bosnia.[36]

NATO also agreed to troop reductions in the Balkans in order to allow American forces to be shifted elsewhere. The ongoing SFOR Operation consisted of some 18,000 troops. At a meeting of NATO defense ministers in Brussel in December 2001, the American Secretary of Defense asked the Alliance to reduce the number of troops in SFOR by 6,000 troops or about one third. Rumsfield asked that the reductions be proportional. With approximately 3,100 American troops in SFOR (and about 8,100 in all of the Balkan operations), this would free up about 1,000 troops for service elsewhere and still maintain the core of the mission.[37] The United States was careful to note that it was not requesting a complete withdrawal of forces from Bosnia and that the withdrawal would be a gradual phased operation that could be part of a larger reorganization of the NATO missions in the region.[38] Greece has even requested that the NATO presence in the Balkans be reduced to a "token level."[39]

Bilateral Military Assistance

In addition to support on a multilateral level, NATO also served as a forum to facilitate bilateral assistance from its Alliance partners. The habits of collaboration that were internalized by the Alliance partners during the history of the organization created both the institutional framework and the general climate necessary for cooperation on broad issues and specific missions. As the forum which served as the coordinating mechanism for such cooperation, NATO's influence extends to even those missions of Alliance partners in which the organization itself is not involved. For instance, one of the keys to the ability to conduct combined operations is interoperability. This extends to both equipment and military procedures.

The Alliance defines interoperability as "the ability of systems, units and forces to provide services to and accept services from other systems, units or forces and to use the services so exchanged to enable when to operate effectively together."[40] In order to facilitate interoperability between Alliance members and potential new members, NATO developed the PfP Planning and Review Process (PARP). PARP developed 20 criteria for interoperability which include the "commonality of fuel requirements, replenishment in harbour, commonality of airfield procedures and something as basic, but so very important, as NATO land map symbology."[41]

Indeed, one of the cornerstones of the Alliance is interoperability. The Alliance's handbook describes the importance of interoperability in the following manner:

> Operational interoperability directly influences the combat effectiveness of NATO forces, particularly those involving multinational formations. Standardization of equipment, supplies and procedures is thus an overall force multiplier which has to be taken into account in the design and production of systems and equipment. The minimum objectives needed to obtain combat effectiveness are interoperability and commonality of procedures. These requirements have a direct bearing on logistic support for standardized equipment. Sufficient flexibility also has to be provided in order to facilitate the participation of non-NATO nations in NATO-led operations.[42]

In order to establish such high degrees of interoperability, NATO serves as a forum to negotiate bilateral and multilateral Standardization Agreements (STANAGs). Such agreements are usually the result of multilateral negotiations which take place over long periods of time and incorporate training and practical experiences, as well as Alliance and other military studies. These STANAGs cover a wide-range of areas, but are concentrated in three areas: 1) Operational standards; 2) Material standards; and 3) Administrative standards. NATO defines these standards in the following manner:

> A) **Operational standards** are those standards which affect future and/or current military practice, procedures or formats. They may apply among other things, to such matters as concepts, doctrine, tactics, techniques, logistics, training, organization, reports, forms, maps and charts.
>
> B) **Material standards** are those standards which affect the characteristics of future and/or current material to include telecommunications, data processing and distribution. They may cover production codes of practice as well as material specifications. Material includes complete systems, including command, control and communications systems, weapons systems, sub-systems, assemblies, components, spare parts and materials and consumables (including ammunition, fuel, supplies, stores and consumable spares).

C) **Administrative standards** primarily concern terminology – which apply to both the "operational" and the "material" fields – but this category also includes standards which facilitate Alliance administration in fields without direct military application (e.g., reporting of economic statistics).[43]

The degree of interoperability among the Allies is all the more notable for the size of the Alliance and the varying degree of capabilities which range from the high level of technological sophistication of the United States to the numerically limited capabilities of Luxembourg. Multilateral interoperability can be sub-divided into:

Allies who agree to accept certain standards and to work together towards standardization where formal standards do not exist;
Partners who may be presented with Allied standards to which to aspire;
Other allies/friends of NATO members who may be aware of NATO standards and make use of them when they are commonly available – other alliances may of course derive their own standards and *modus operandi* may be developed among friends;
ad hoc coalition partners for whom Allied standards may or may not be available or acceptable.[44]

In addition, within each category, there are further sub-categories which include military headquarters and units, supra and inter-governmental organizations and headquarters, non-governmental organizations, private volunteer organizations, private military and security companies, civil authorities and the leadership of the parties involved.[45]

The operations in Afghanistan brought together all of the above categories, and necessitated steps to ensure some degree of interoperability. While the short duration of the military campaign did not test the entire range of interoperability needs, the subsequent peacekeeping operations will in that they involve a greater number of actors and a greater level of categories of interaction.

During the Cold War, operational interoperability was "never tested in combat," but it was a central component of numerous Alliance exercises and was achieved in areas such as 'intelligence gathering" and "air operations."[46] In addition, the Alliance developed a high degree of "doctrinal and cultural interoperability" which may give multilateral coalitions in which it is involved a higher degree of "political strength." [47]

Interoperability has also been one of the important features in ensuring combat cohesion and in ensuring the capability of non-NATO partners, such as those in the PfP program, to participate in NATO-led operations. With the development of initiatives such as CJTF and the practical experiences of NATO-led operations in Yugoslavia, NATO's need for interoperability was heightened. Nonetheless, the practical exercises and the operations themselves demonstrated the relatively high degree of interoperability of NATO. This high degree of interoperability among Alliance forces, both in terms of equipment and operating standards, reinforces the capability of Allies to undertake missions even outside of the auspices of NATO.

Anglo-American Cooperation

The two nations within the Alliance with the highest degree of interoperability are the United States and the United Kingdom. The two states have cooperated closely on a number of military operations including the NATO-led missions in the Balkans, the administration of the No-Fly Zone over Iraq, and Operation Enduring Freedom. British submarines launched Tomahawk cruise missiles on the first day of combat operations during the campaign in Afghanistan. In NATO, only the United States, the United Kingdom and France have the full range of expeditionary capabilities (air, land, sea and special operations) that allow them to engage in significant overseas campaigns.

These capabilities are expressly detailed in the British Strategic Defense Review and the American military strategic concept JV 2010, initiated by the Joint Chiefs of Staff in 1998. These studies demonstrate the doctrinal similarities between the two nations and the conscious effort to ensure interoperability.[48] The result of cultural, doctrinal and military interoperability between the U.S. and the U.K. led to close cooperation in the Afghan military campaign as the British were prepared to operate within the American command structure.

The British military actions in Operation Enduring Freedom were designated "Operation Veritas." The British Secretary of State for Defense, Geoffrey Hoon, enunciated the goals of the coalition from the British perspective:

1) To bring Usama bin Laden and Al Qaeda to account
2) To prevent Usama bin Laden and Al Qaeda posing a continuing terrorist threat
3) To ensure that Afghanistan verifiably ceases to harbor and sustain international terrorism and the associated terrorist training camps
4) And, since Mullah Omar has not complied with the United States' ultimatum, we require sufficient change in the leadership there to ensure that Afghanistan's links to international terrorism are broken.[49]

Hoon also stated that "since 11 September, the United Kingdom has stood beside our closest ally, the United States" and that the United Kingdom would "conduct this campaign together for as long as it takes."[50] Such staunch support was very important to the United States. In response to a question about the impact of British participation, Wolfowitz commented that "having one country that is with us 100 percent the way the U.K. is is fantastic."[51] These sentiments were echoed by a number of other American officials. For instance, in a joint press address with his British counterpart, Rumsfield made the following comments:

> Well, there's no question but that it is an enormous advantage to have our friend and ally [the U.K.] aboard on this exercise and engaged both in the planning and the discussion about it, but also physically involved, as the minister [Hoon] said, in several different ways. They do have considerable expertise in a number of areas, as you know well, and they bring a great deal of experience and talent and skill and training to this effort. And we're delighted and grateful.[52]

During the build-up to the military campaign, the British dispatch a variety of assets to engage in military operations. This included three nuclear-powered submarines that were used to launch tomahawk cruise missiles on 7 October and then again on 13 October when coalition forces targeted 17 Taliban and Al Qaeda targets. In addition, the British deployed a naval task force to the region, led by the aircraft carrier, the HMS *Illustrious*.

Besides the carrier and submarines, the British naval force included an assault ship, a frigate and a destroyer, and seven support vessels. Also included with the task force was a Royal Marine commando unit. British special operations forces, including the elite units the Special Air Service (SAS) and Special Boat Service (SBS), operated throughout Afghanistan during the campaign, staging raids and engaging in intelligence gathering activities.[53] The elite teams also trained anti-Taliban forces. In addition, as anti-Taliban forces gained control of large areas of the nation, British forces were deployed to help maintain order and to protect humanitarian operations.

One of the most significant contributions of the British to the military operations involved participation in air missions. British aircraft, including the Tristar and the VC-10 tanker, are compatible with U.S. aircraft and provided refueling services during each of the air sorties. These operations extended the range of coalition aircraft and expanded the ability of the air units to respond to emerging targets. In addition, reconnaissance and surveillance aircraft, such as the E-3D Sentry AWACS, Nimrod MR2 maritime reconnaissance craft and the Canberra PR9, flew operational sorties throughout the campaign and helped identify concentrations of Taliban forces for attack. Finally, RAF C-130 Hercules aircraft were used for transport activities.

France

France also offered to participate in the military operations and offered air, naval and ground assets to the coalition. By November, France had 2,000 troops deployed in the region. The French military also established a liaison office with U.S. Central Command to coordinate operations and ensure smooth relations between the military commands.[54] This included naval assets (a frigate, supply ship and two minehunters and a mobile support vessel), reconnaissance and surveillance aircraft, special operations forces and a mine sweeping unit. French air assets, including Mirage aircraft, were stationed in Dushambe, Tajikistan.

Nonetheless, French participation was limited even when compared with that of the United Kingdom. French military forces were engaged in intelligence gathering operations. The limitations on participation were mainly as a result of French demands for a multilateral command structure. Prime Minister Jospin, summarized French demands in the following manner:

> Over and above the facilities provided, the cooperation on intelligence which is proving fruitful, and support already given to the U.S. forces, offers in three areas – air, naval and special forces – have been made. We are ready to bolster our support, particularly naval support, at short notice, if requested to do so. This being the case, France's participation in new operations necessitates our full involvement in the definition of the objectives and military planning and, with respect to our own forces, our approval of them.[55]

Jospin's comments were echoed by Chirac who stated on 6 November, "as I've said and I'll say again, we are absolutely ready to send special forces provided, of course, firstly that we know the nature of the mission and, secondly that we're involved in the planning of it."[56]

However, ultimately the French demands were rebuffed by the Bush Administration. The limited role of the French military during the campaign met with domestic anxiety about the nation's global role. An essay in the *International Herald Tribune* noted that "with its military contibution so far limited to reconnaissance, intelligence and refueling missions, France has been confounded by the dilemma of how to look politically useful, innovative and important on the scale of Germany and Britain."[57]

As the military campaign progressed and the anti-Taliban forces gained territory, French forces did take on a greater role. On 17 November, 58 French soldiers were deployed to Mazar-i Shariff as part of a larger force that number 300. These troops were engaged in humanitarian operations and were tasked to provide security for mine-clearing operations around the area's airfield and around the city itself.[58] France also offered to contribute up to 1,000 troops to the international peacekeeping mission to Afghanistan that was developed in the wake of the fall of the Taliban.

Nonetheless, the French government found itself essentially cast as an outsider and embarked upon a public campaign to act as the "balancer" in the coalition and ensure that the United States did not expand military operations unnecessarily. A spokesman for the Foreign Ministry declared "if the U.S. asks for a strike elsewhere, we will have to retain our authority to consider it."[59]

Canada

The Canadian government of Prime Minister Jean Chrétien initially faced domestic criticism for responding slowly. However, on 7 October, Chrétien announced the dispatch of a significant military force.[60] The Canadian military contributions were dubbed Operation Apollo. Canadian forces included approximately 2,000 service personnel, including members of the nation's elite anti-terrorist unit Joint Task Force 2 (JTF2) and an additional 1,000-member light infantry unit held in reserve. Specific military assets included a naval task force (two frigates, a destroyer and a supply ship), six aircraft for surveillance and transport, and a third Canadian frigate which was assigned to operate with one of the U.S. carrier battle groups operating in the region.[61]

Turkey

Turkish support of the coalition was extremely important to the Bush Administration in its efforts to ensure that the campaign in Afghanistan was not perceived as a war against Islam. Indeed, Turkey was an eager partner in the campaign against international terrorism, partially in reaction to the nation's own campaign against domestic terrorism. For example, Turkey supported expansion of NATO's counter-terrorism role and worked closely with the United States to identify people and groups with links to Al Qaeda within the country.[62] Turkey also supported the U.S. decision to not halt the bombing campaign during the Muslim holy month of Ramadan.[63]

As with a number of other Allies, Turkey opened its airspace to American aircraft and then issued a "blanket clearance for landing to and takeoff from a number of Turkish airfields."[64] This was especially significant since the air base at Incirlik, Turkey serves as one of the main American bases in the region. Turkey also agreed to send 90 special forces troops to participate in coalition military operations in Afghanistan. The Turkish forces were tasked to train Northern Alliance troops and to engage in intelligence and small-unit combat missions.

Other Bilateral Support

Other NATO nations provided a variety of forms of assistance. Norway offered to contribute troops and to "participate in NATO operations if the USA should ask for Allied support."[65] Meanwhile, Norway assumed Lead Nation status in the KFOR operation. Norway deployed an extra 200 troops, in addition to the 1,000 troops already serving as part of KFOR.[66]   Dutch naval units participated in the STANAVFORMED and the government offered to deploy aircraft in support of Operation Enduring Freedom.   The Dutch also dispatched the frigate HNLMS *Philips van Almonde* to Bahrain and placed the ship under the auspices of U.S. Central Command to support American missions in Afghanistan.   A variety of other Allies, including the Czech Republic, Italy, Poland and Spain, pledged troops and other military assets for use in the campaign in Afghanistan.[67]   In addition, Germany offered to provide 3,900 troops and other resources.[68]

In a demonstration of the U.S. strategy of building a coalition of coalitions, two non-NATO states, Australia and Japan also participated in the military operations in Afghanistan.   Australia provided a military contribution on the same level as several of the more substantial NATO partners.   The Australian contribution was made up of some 1,550 service personnel, naval frigates and support vessels and air assets, including reconnaissance and surveillance aircraft, tankers and F/A-18 fighters. Australia also deployed special operations forces.[69]   Australia's deployment was authorized following the 14 September 2001 invocation of Article IV of the Australia, New Zealand, United States (ANZUS) Treaty.[70]

Japan also made a military contribution to the coalition.   On 9 November 2001, Japan dispatched two destroyers and a supply ship to operate in tandem with American forces in the Arabian Sea.   These ships were later joined by another destroyer and supply ship, meanwhile, eight aircraft were also deployed to the region to operate with coalition forces.   The Japanese constitution states that the nation "renounces the use of force to settle international disputes" and special legislation had to be passed in order to allow the deployment.[71]   The Japanese government also had to take steps to mollify Chinese and South Korean concerns over the re-militarization of Japan.[72]   In a further effort in support of the United States, Japan, like the NATO Allies, agreed to increase security around American bases and facilities in the country.[73]

A number of states, including Italy, Spain and Portugal, deployed naval assets as part of NATO's Mediterranean naval operations in support of Enduring Freedom. This was in addition to a number of individual naval assets that were deployed with the American naval forces stationed in the Indian Ocean.   At the height of the campaign, there were more than 80 coalition naval vessels deployed in the Arabian Gulf.   The overwhelming majority of these ships were American, however, as aforementioned, there were British, Canadian and French flotillas, and vessels from Italy, the Netherlands, Australia and Japan.   The French, Italian and Dutch established liaison missions on board the American flagship, the USS *Theodore Roosevelt*.

The coalition was able to utilize the high level of interoperability, including communications capabilities, and the extensive experience of the forces working together. The coalition naval forces conducted operations and patrols to seal off escape routes of Taliban and Al Qaeda leaders.[74] In addition, several nations, including the United Kingdom, France, Italy and the Netherlands, allowed their air assets to be used in the air campaign where they carried out surveillance and reconnaissance and refueling missions, in addition to some ground support missions.[75]

During the ongoing operations, "every country maintains their national prerogative out here, they [the coalition partners] aren't told what to do," said American Admiral Mark Fitzgerald (the commander of the *Roosevelt* Battle Group), "we have to meld all these national concerns and use each nation's vessels and airplanes together."[76] The Americans had to take into account different national restrictions on the kind of mission that each country's forces could participate in. For instance, Japan's vessels were not allowed to undertake combat operations, but could only participate in supply and support missions. In this way, the coalition forces in the Arabian Gulf operated as an ad hoc CJTF.

The Endgame

Although the NATO Allies may not have provided significant military assets during the actual military campaign, they did provide the means to complete the operation by providing a peacekeeping force to bolster the interim Afghan government. On 20 December 2001, the UN Security Council authorized the deployment of a peacekeeping force and the United Kingdom volunteered to serve as the lead nation for the mission. The operation would involve as many as 5,000 to 6,000 troops and work in tandem with the American military, indeed the force would be technically under the operational command of the United States.[77]

However, this division of labor led to some tensions between the NATO Allies, particularly on the part of the Germans and the French. The Germans have objected to fact that the UN-sponsored mission would still be under the command of the United States.[78] The German government specifically requested that the American military operations be separated from any UN-sponsored peace mission.[79] The French were displeased with the overall division of labor as they had sought a greater role in the military operations. For French policymakers concerned with issues of rank and global status, the perception of being relegated to "clean-up" after American actions was unacceptable. To Paris, the word from Washington seemed to be: "We'll do the cooking and prepare what people are going to eat, then you will wash the dirty dishes."[80]

The UN-sponsored mission, which would be stationed in Kabul, was tasked to support the interim government of Hamid Karzai and maintain public order. The force would also train Afghan security forces and undertake joint patrols with government troops. In addition, almost half of the British-led force would consist of engineers and other specialists who would assist in the rebuilding and repair of the infrastructure of Kabul.[81]

The limited nature of the UN operation was the result of two main constraints. First, none of the nations involved wanted to have troops stationed in the country for a long period of time in light of the potential for casualties. Second, the interim government was opposed to the presence of the troops and only international pressure (mainly American pressure) led the Afghans to consent to allow the mission.

Ultimately, either 15 or 16 nations will contribute troops to the mission. The United Kingdom would supply the largest number of troops with some 1,800 soldiers. Other NATO Allies would provide the bulk of the remaining troops, including Germany with 800, followed by France with 550, Italy and Spain with 300 each, and Greece and the Netherlands with 100 each. Allies such as Belgium, Denmark, Norway, Portugal and Turkey also offered small contingents. A variety of non-NATO states will also participate in the operation, including Austria, Finland, New Zealand, Romania and Sweden. After a three-month deployment, the British plan to turn over the command of the mission to the Turks who will supply additional forces at that time.[82]

The Role of the Alliance

The United States could have undertaken the military operations in Afghanistan without the help or assistance of its NATO and coalition partners. It had the military assets and capabilities, and the strategy relied more on the anti-Taliban forces inside Afghanistan than on conventional NATO forces. Nonetheless, the Allies did provide a variety direct and indirect support in both the campaign in Afghanistan and in the larger counter-terrorism effort.

The deployment of Alliance resources, including AWACS aircraft in the United States, special forces units in Afghanistan and the naval deployments to the Mediterranean and Arabian Sea, did significantly bolster the ability of the Bush Administration to conduct Operation Enduring Freedom. NATO actions both increased the capability of the coalition and freed up American resources for use in Afghanistan. NATO's military support and combat actions were facilitated by the high degree of interoperability within the Alliance. This allowed for both close cooperation during the combat operations in Afghanistan and in the naval mission in the Arabian Sea.

In addition, the actions of key Allies such as the United Kingdom and Germany were important in the diplomatic efforts to provide a settlement in the aftermath of the fall of the Taliban. These efforts included Germany's hosting of the conference of anti-Taliban officials which developed a post-Taliban interim government. They also included the British willingness to lead the UN-sponsored peacekeeping mission. Meanwhile, Allied support extended to a variety of non-military operations, including diplomatic initiatives and efforts to develop institutional frameworks to counter international terrorism. One of the driving forces behind these efforts and the concrete support provided by the Alliance during the military phase of Operation Enduring Freedom was the need to demonstrate and maintain the relevance and centrality of NATO to the transatlantic security regime.

Notes

1. United States, Department of Defense, Central Command, "Operation Enduring Freedom Update" (8 October 2001), http://www.centcom.mil/operations/Enduring_Freedom.
2. Brian Knowlton, "Bush: 'Battle Joined'," *International Herald Tribune* (8 October 2001).
3. United States, Department of Defense, "Statement of the Secretary of Defense," No. 560-01 (1 November 2001).
4. Ibid.
5. In comparison, 30 percent of the munitions used in Kosovo were precision-guided while only 10 percent of the ordinance in the Gulf War was precision-guided; Joseph Fitchett, "High-Tech Weapons Change the Dynamics and the Scope of Battle," *International Herald Tribune* (28 December 2001).
6. Special operations forces from a variety of coalition states, including the United States and the United Kingdom, also undertook a variety of specific missions. The most noted of these operations was the 19 October 2001 deployment of approximately 300 U.S. Army Rangers and Special Forces (Green Berets) units which captured an airfield and raided Taliban Supreme Leader Mullah Omar's headquarters near Kandahar. The raid was mainly an intelligence operation, but it also demonstrated the capability of the coalition to insert and extract troops anywhere in Afghanistan. The Allied forces only suffered minor injuries.
7. The complaints about the pace of the war led Rumsfield to issue a press statement that "this is a task that will take time to accomplish . . . . Americans have seen tougher adversaries than this before – and they have had the staying power to defeat them." In the same release, Rumsfield stated "in the end, war is not about statistics, deadlines, short attention spans, or 24-hour news cycles" instead it is about "will – the projection of will, the clear, unambiguous determination of the President and the American people to see this through to certain victory;" U.S., Department of Defense, "Statement of the Secretary of Defense."
8. This included 32,214 for the Air National Guard and Air Force Reserve, 22,643 for Army National Guard and Army Reserve, 9,485 for the Navy Reserve, 1,557 for the Marine Corps Reserve, and 1,894 for the Coast Guard Reserve; United States, Department of Defense, "National Guard and Reserve Mobilized as of January 9," News Release No. 013-02 (9 January 2002).
9. Fitchett, "High-Tech Weapons."

10. Philip H. Gordon, "NATO After 11 September," *Survival* 43, no. 4 (Winter 2001-2002), 4.

11. David M. Malone, "When America Banged the Table and the Others Fell Silent," *International Herald Tribune* (11 December 2001).

12. NATO, "Statement on Combating Terrorism: Adapting the Alliance's Defense Capabilities, Issued at the Meeting of the North Atlantic Council in Defense Ministers Session Held in Brussels," Press Communique PR/CP(2001) 173 (18 December 2001).

13. The European Union list included the Basque separatist group the Eta and the radical Irish group, the Real IRA, as well as radical groups in the Middle East such as Hizbollah and Islamic Jihad; "Brussels Draws Up List of Terrorist Organizations," *Financial Times* (28 December 2001).

14. NATO, "Statement to the Press By NATO Secretary General Lord Robertson on the North Atlantic Council Decision on Implementation of Article 5 of the Washington Treaty Following the 11 September Attacks Against the United States," Brussels (4 October 2001).

15. NATO, "Statement on Combating Terrorism."

16. Barry James, "Allies Urge Their Citizens to Keep a Low Profile," *International Herald Tribune* (8 October 2001).

17. "Greek Troops to Serve in Afghanistan," *International Herald Tribune* (19 December 2001).

18. NATO, "Statement to the Press."

19. Ibid.

20. United States, Department of State, "Colin Powell Holds Media Availability With NATO Secretary General George Robertson" (10 October 2001).

21. Ibid.

22. NATO, "Statement by the Secretary General of NATO Lord Robertson," Press Release (2001) 138 (8 October 2001).

23. The twelve nations included Belgium, Canada, Denmark, Germany, Greece, Italy, the Netherlands, Norway, Portugal, Spain, Turkey and the United States.

24. NATO, NAEWF, "Our Mission and Base" (1 October 2001), available online http://www.e3a.nato.int/info/mbase.htm; Specifically, "when operating at an altitude of 30,000 feet, a single E-3 aircraft can continuously scan more than 312,000 square kilometers of earth's surface. Operating well within Western airspace, such aircraft can provide early warning about low-flying intruders into the NATO area as well as high altitude coverage extending deep into the territory of a potential aggressor. While the Force's principal role is air surveillance, it provides economical communications support for air operations including counter-air, close air support, rescue, reconnaissance and airlift as well as surveillance and control. Aircrews can exchange information with ground- and sea-based commanders, since E-3As and E-3Ds can use maritime mode radar to detect and monitor enemy shipping. The AEW radar is able to look down and separate moving targets from the stationary ground clutter that confuses other radars. It adds the ability to detect and track enemy aircraft operating at low altitudes over all terrain, and to identify and give directions to friendly aircraft operating in the same area. In addition, its mobility allows it to be deployed rapidly where it is most needed, and makes it far less vulnerable to attack than ground-based radar;" NATO, NAEWF, "The NATO Airborne Early Warning & Control Force" (25 March 1999).

25. Interestingly, the largest national contingent in the NAEWF forces were from the United States (74 troops), followed by Germany with 55, and 22 from Canada; NATO, NAEWF, Press Release 0110-01 (10 October 2001).
26. NATO, Press Release (2001) 138.
27. NATO, SACEUR, "SACEUR Statement to the Media" (9 October 2001).
28. NATO, AFSOUTH, "NATO Naval Force Deploys to Eastern Mediterranean," Press Release 22 (9 October 2001).
29. Joseph A Christoff, "Report to the Congressional Committee: European Security–U.S. and European Contributions to Foster Stability and Security in Europe on 28 November 2001," GAO -02-174 (Washington, D.C.: GAO, November 2001), 11.
30. The eight permanent nations include Germany, Greece, Italy, the Netherlands, Spain, Turkey, the United Kingdom and the United States. Other nations also contribute to STANAVFORMED on a temporary basis.
31. STANAVFORMED includes one frigate from each of the following states: the United Kingdom, the United States, Germany, Italy, the Netherlands, Spain and Turkey. The force also includes a Greek destroyer and a Turkish auxiliary oiler.
32. STANAVFORLANT consists of one frigate from each of the following states: Belgium, Denmark, the Netherlands, Norway, Portugal, Spain and the United States. Germany, Italy, and the United Kingdom each contribute one destroyer and the Netherlands also contributes an oiler.
33. NATO, AFSOUTH, "NATO Maritime Forces Exchange Duties," Press Release 32-2001 (6 December 2001).
34. Christopher Bennett, "Aiding America," *NATO Review* 49 (Winter 2001/2002), 6-7.
35. NATO, "Press Statement by NATO Secretary General, Lord Robertson, Foreign Ministers Meeting," Brussels (6 December 2001).
36. Ibid.
37. Vernon Loeb, "Rumsfield Asks NATO for Bosnia Troop Cuts," *International Herald Tribune* (19 December 2001).
38. U.S., Department of State, "Background Briefing at NATO Headquarters" (18 December 2001).
39. Barry Schweid, "Greece Urges Less Troops in Balkans," *Associated Press* (11 January 2002). Greece was the one NATO Ally that opposed the Alliance's bombing campaign in Kosovo because of its support for the Orthodox Serbs and opposition to the Muslim Albanian separatists.
40. Klaus Naumann, "From Cooperation to Interoperability," *NATO Review* 44, no. 4 (July 1996), 17.
41. Ibid, 18.
42. *NATO Handbook: 50th Anniversary Edition.*
43. NATO, *NATO Logistics Handbook* (Brussels: NATO, October 1997), chapter 17.
44. Michael Cadnor, "Hanging Together: Interoperability Within the Alliance and With Coalition Partners in an Era of Technological Innovation," *NATO Fellowship* (Brussels: NATO, June 1999), 21.
45. Ibid., 22.
46. Ibid., 8.

47. Ibid., 13.
48. Ibid., 25.
49. Geoffrey Hoon, "Operation Veritas," Speech to the House of Commons, London (1 November 2001).
50. Ibid.
51. U.S., Department of Defense, "News Transcript: Deputy Secretary Wolfowitz Interview With London Sunday Telegraph" (26 October 2001).
52. U.S., Department of Defense, "News Transcript: Secretary Rumsfield Media Availability With Secretary Hoon" (30 October 2001).
53. See, for instance, Richard Norton-Taylor, "Marines and SAS to Stage Raids Inside Afghanistan," *Guardian Unlimited* (27 October 2001).
54. France, Ministry of Defense, "Terror Attacks: A Permanent French Liaison Mission in the U.S.," Press Release (15 October 2001).
55. France, Ministry of Foreign Affairs, "Replies by M. Lionel Jospin, Prime Minister, to Questions in the National Assembly (Excerpts)," Paris (6 November 2001).
56. France, Ministry of Foreign Affairs, "Press Conference Given by M. Jacques Chirac, President of the Republic, at the United Nations Headquarters," New York (6 November 2001).
57. John Vinocur, :Voiceless in the War on Terror, France Faces Waning Global Influence," *International Herald Tribune* (6 November 2001).
58. Jon Henley, "French Troops Fly in to Help Aid Effort: Protection Party Heads for Mazar-i-Sharif," *The Guardian* (17 November 2001).
59. France, Ministry of Foreign Affairs, "Statement by the Ministry of Foreign Affairs" (9 October 2001).
60. "A New Face to the Fore," *The Economist* 361 (13 October 2001), 39.
61. Canada, Ministry of Foreign Affairs and International Trade, "Backgrounder: Canada's Action Against Terrorism Since September 11" (3 January 2002).
62. Turkey, Ministry of Foreign Affairs, "Measures Taken by the Republic of Turkey Against Terrorism: Report to the Security Council Established Pursuant to Resolution 1373 (2001)" (December 2001).
63. In explaining his decision, Turkish Prime Minister Bulent Ecevit stated that "terrorism has no Ramadan, no flags, no feasts;" Douglas Frantz, "Turkey Says Troops to Join U.S. Campaign and Train Anti-Taliban Forces," *The New York* (2 November 2001).
64. Ibid.
65. Norway, Office of the Prime Minister, Kjell Magne Bondevik, "Statement to the Storting on the Situation Since the Terrorist Attacks Against the USA" (8 November 2001).
66. Norway, Ministry of Defense, "KFOR 5–Norway's Role as Lead Nation" (8 January 2002).
67. U.S., Department of State, "The United States and the Global Coalition Against Terrorism, September-November 2001 – A Chronology," Fact Sheet (Washington, D.C.: U.S., Department of State, Office of the Historian, 2001); Elizabeth Williamson, "NATO's New Members Support U.S. Aims With Poland Likely to Send Military Units," *Wall Street Journal* (5 November 2001).
68. Deployment of troops in combat operations was delicate subject for the German government, both because of the nation's history legacy and domestic politics. Polls indicated that 60 percent of the public opposed the deployment of ground troops in

Afghanistan. In light of these constraints, the decision was instead made to deploy German troops in NATO's mission to Macedonia; Arie Farnam, "Bombings Hit Unintended Target: European Opinion," *Christian Science Monitor* (14 November 2001), 7.

69. Australia, Ministry of Defense, "Australia's Military Contribution to the International Coalition Against Terrorism," Fact Sheet (8 January 2002).

70. In announcing its decision, the Prime Minister's office stated "the Government has decided, in consultation with the United States, that Article IV of the ANZUS Treaty applies to the terrorist attacks on the United States. The decision is based on our belief that the attacks have been initiated and coordinated from outside the United States;" Australia, Office of the Prime Minister, "Application of ANZUS Treaty to Terrorist Attacks on the United States," Media Release (14 September 2001).

71. The special law, the Anti-Terrorism Special Measures Law, allowed the nation's Self-Defense Force to participate in missions in non-combat roles, such as refueling and transport; "Japan Rises to the Occasion," *Christian Science Monitor* (1 November 2001).

72. Nayan Chandra, "Japan's Navy is Back, and There's No Cause to be Alarmed," *International Herald Tribune* (22 November 2001).

73. U.S., Department of State, Richard Boucher, "Press Statement: Japan – New Counterterrorism Legislation," Washington, D.C. (29 October 2001).

74. Paul Garwood, "Allied Providing Protection in Gulf," *Associated Press* (6 January 2002).

75. Ibid.

76. Ibid.

77. In discussing the British-led mission, Ministry of Defense officials stated that whatever operations the peacekeeping force undertook "would be in cooperation with the Americans, they are the big brother;" James Meek, Richard Norton-Taylor and Michael White, "No. 10 Retreats on Plan to Send More Troops," *The Guardian* (20 November 2001).

78. Carola Hoyos and Gwen Robinson, "Multinational Peacekeeping Force Approved," *Financial Times* (21 December 2001).

79. Carola Hoyos, Andrew Parker and Hugh Williamson, "Anti-terrorist Coalition threatened With Split," *Financial Times* (20 December 2001).

80. Joseph Fitchett, "U.S. Allies Chafe at 'Cleanup' Role," *International Herald Tribune* (26 November 2001).

81. Alexander Nicoll, "Troops' Role is to Help Interim Rulers," *Financial Times* (11 January 2002).

82. Alexander Nicoll, "UK Outlines Plans for Afghan Troop Deployment," *Financial Times* (10 January 2002).

Chapter 6

Burdensharing

Introduction

As the military operations in Afghanistan progressed, questions arose over the military utility of the Alliance. The overwhelming majority of the military missions during the campaign were undertaken by the United States. While a number of the NATO Allies offered various types of security assistance, only a few states were actively engaged in the operations at a substantial level. There was close collaboration between the United States and the United Kingdom, but many policymakers on both sides of the Atlantic perceived that Operation Enduring Freedom reinforced the security primacy of the United States and demonstrated the limited capabilities of most of the Western European Allies. The Europeanist states within the Alliance saw the American domination of the Afghan campaign as further proof of the necessity to develop autonomous security capabilities for the European Union. On the other hand, the more ardent supporters of NATO, the Atlanticist states, stressed the direct and indirect contributions of the Alliance to the boarder framework of transatlantic security and the comprehensive effort to combat international terrorism.

While the NATO Allies did not contribute a substantial percentage of the troops involved in the military campaign in Afghanistan, they did provide substantial support, especially in the form of naval and air assets. Furthermore, the Allies were willing to provide higher numbers of personnel, if the United States had requested them. For the Bush Administration, however, the nature of the campaign in Afghanistan did not require large numbers of ground troops (including American forces). Instead, the Americans utilized a strategy that emphasized the use of sophisticated and high-technology weapons. The Bush Administration sought to maximize the political and diplomatic support provided by the Alliance. As such, in addition to its military role, the Administration endeavored to use NATO both directly and indirectly as a means to accomplish its non-military goals in the broad campaign against international terrorism. In this manner, the Administration restored one of the Cold War functions of the Alliance – that of a bridge between the United States and its West European Allies. However, in the ongoing campaign, Washington sought to expand the function of NATO to also serve as a bridge between the United States and a variety of other bodies, including the European Union, and other states, including Russia. In pursuing these objectives, the Administration reinforced the importance of the Alliance and further solidified its role as the cornerstone of transatlantic security.

In summarizing the impact of 11 September 2001, Lord Robertson rejected the suggestion that the attacks and the resultant American campaign marginalized the Alliance and instead suggested that:

> Some pundits made the mistake of thinking that the transatlantic relationship was coming to an end. In their view, the transatlantic link was simply a marriage of convenience – or more accurately, a shotgun wedding imposed by the Soviet Union. And that now, Europe and North America were ready to file for divorce. 11 September 2001 shattered that myth. Indeed, one of the clearest results of those tragic events has been a total affirmation that Europe and North America remain what they have been for over five decades: a rock-solid community of shared values.[1]

In other words, NATO remains the embodiment of the values, principles and norms of the transatlantic security regime. Furthermore, the events of 11 September 2001 and the subsequent campaign in Afghanistan reinforce the need for the Alliance to improve its capabilities in order to undertake new missions beyond its Cold War and immediate post-Cold War functions. Such improvements or reforms offer the optimum means to respond to the changing security challenges faced by the memberstates and their allies. They also offer the best method to ensure the future centrality of the Alliance.

Bridge Functions

Since the development of the transatlantic security regime, cooperation and interdependence have formed the core for interaction among memberstates in institutions such as NATO. Such cooperation and collaboration extended far beyond the military sphere and has been responsible for the broad stability in the region. Indeed, Robert O. Keohane contends that "European stability is closely linked to institutionalization."[2] Through linkage strategies such institutionalization extends to a variety of issue-areas beyond security, including trade, culture and politics, and it serves as a means to reconcile the former Cold War enemies.[3] Concurrently, bi- and multi-lateral cooperation also continues to serve as a means to harmonize security relations within the security regime as it did during the Cold War. For instance, even during the period of French estrangement from the Alliance, Franco-German military collaboration provided a forum for tacit French involvement in regional security and the dissemination of tactical and strategic doctrine as well as a forum for the discussion of security issues.[4]

Within NATO, the interplay between civil and military cooperation and collaboration has progressed significantly. During the 1960s, many, including even NATO Secretary General Dirk Stikker criticized the heavy influence of the military when compared with the significance of the Alliance's political organs.[5] However, the post-Cold War era witnessed the rise of the Alliance's political structures and functions as its military role declined in importance following the demise of the Soviet threat.

There was considerable debate over the ability of the Alliance to undertake new missions in the aftermath of the Cold War. However, NATO demonstrated that it could move beyond the defensive posture and doctrine that it developed during the Cold War. With the adoption of the Alliance's New Strategic Concept in 1991, NAC embraced a variety of new missions and functions for the Alliance.[6] By the mid-1990s, NATO reformed so that it could deploy forces out-of-area in new missions, including humanitarian operations, and develop increased ties and relations with the former states of the Warsaw Pact. The challenge for NATO in the new century is to continue to improve its political role by increasingly adopting non-military functions. Michael Brenner contends that:

> The imperative for the West today is to maintain that civic community (indeed, for the EU countries, to deepen it) while extending the range of its constructive influence – and, eventually, boundaries – eastward to embrace the liberalizing countries of the former communist world. That is an ambitious undertaking that exceeds even the postwar project of collective institution–building. Moreover, it calls for a political concert as much as for a continued military alliance. That is the magnitude of the task confronting the Western allies as they struggle to adjust the terms of their own relationship.[7]

In many ways, the post-attack actions and policies of the Alliance are demonstrative of its efforts to expand its security institution-building beyond the pure military realm. In fact, various officials from the Bush Administration asked NATO to undertake a variety of non-military actions which supported such short- and long-term goals. In an essay for *NATO Review*, the journal's editor, Christopher Bennett, suggested that the Alliance could contribute in five main areas which reinforce the ability of the United States to lead the anti-terrorist campaign and which elevate the future capabilities of NATO itself. These five areas include: 1) humanitarian and peace operations in the aftermath of the campaign; 2) non-proliferation efforts to counter the acquisition of WMDs by both states and substate actors; 3) improvements in civil emergency capabilities among the Alliance partners; 4) coordination efforts and activities with other regional and international organizations; and 5) improved relations with Russia.[8]

Humanitarian and Peace Operations

In addition to direct military Assistance from the Alliance, the United States requested that NAC develop contingency strategies for any potential humanitarian operations in Afghanistan. This task emerged as the principal Alliance support effort that did not involve direct deployment of forces for potential combat operations under Article 5. As discussed in Chapter 5, while the United States intentionally bore the brunt of the combat operations in Afghanistan, it fell to America's NATO Allies to develop and oversee the post-combat peace operations. This type of mission combines both military and humanitarian functions and it has grown increasingly common for the states of Western Europe and for NATO itself. Non-combat military operations of this type include a wide range of specific operations. For instance, peace operations may involve peacekeeping, peace-enforcement and conflict prevention missions. Peacekeeping missions involve the deployment of forces to resolve conflict through peaceful means, peace-enforcement operations involve the deployment of troops with the "option to use force," while conflict prevention missions involve the deployment of forces with the consent of at least one of the parties in order to forestall the outbreak of hostilities.[9] Humanitarian operations include disaster relief, refugee or displaced person assistance, and humanitarian aid.[10] These missions "are launched to save lives, assist and protect victims without distinction, in an independent, impartial, neutral and efficient way, according to needs and giving priority to the most vulnerable victims. Humanitarian operations are carried out with full transparency and consent of the authorities concerned."[11]

Increasingly, the difference between peace operations and humanitarian missions has been diminished, as have the distinctions between the organizations that conduct the operations:

> traditionally, humanitarian organizations have carried out humanitarian activity and military forces have conducted purely military activities. Recently though, functions have become blurred. The number of humanitarian actors has also increased. Coordination among actors has been rendered more difficult. The delivery of humanitarian assistance and protection has become more complex in nature and more dangerous to carry out with traditional means.[12]

The increased intricacy of such missions and the expanded number of actors has "required a complex interweaving of civil, humanitarian and military structures."[13] During a variety of missions in the Balkans in the 1990s, NATO served as coordinating body which brought together inter-governmental organizations (IGOs), military units and non-governmental organizations (NGOs), as well as private volunteer organizations (PVOs). NATO bought a number of capabilities to such missions, since: "military resources and expertise such as logistical support, specialized skills, manpower, provision of security and of access to victims are a useful means of supporting the emergency response capacity of humanitarian organizations, in accordance with the above-mentioned principles."[14]

The expansion of humanitarian and peace operations reflects the growing recognition on both sides of the Atlantic that substate conflict impacts the security and stability of regional and international systems. Speaking on the Bosnian conflict in 1999, former NATO Secretary General Solana stated that:

> The first lesson of Bosnia is perhaps the most difficult to learn–that, in today's Europe, even local conflicts can be an international problem. In fact, with the end of the Cold War, regional conflicts now pose the greatest challenge to peace and stability in the Euro-Atlantic area. They do not affect only the warring parties themselves. They also threaten stability far beyond their point of origin. They threaten to draw in other countries. They cause large, potentially destabilizing, floods of people. And they result in violations of human rights from which we cannot, nor should not, avert our eyes.[15]

As the perception that substate conflict posed a significant security threat to stability, there was a corresponding increase in the number of humanitarian operations designed to end or prevent such conflict. This increase was also facilitated by changing paradigms over national sovereignty.

Since the end of World War II, the importance of individual human rights has risen in stature through the adoption of international instruments such as the 1948 Universal Declaration of Human Rights. Governments that routinely or egregiously violate these rights, as in the case of genocide or ethnic cleansing, are increasingly seen to have lost their political legitimacy and become "an international outlaw."[16] Finally, in the contemporary era, states and international organizations are seen to have both a legal and moral duty to take action when such human rights violations occur. During the debate over what course of action to take in regard to Serb actions in Kosovo, the notion of a legal obligation served as the main justification for NATO intervention. Charles W. Kegley, Jr., and Gregory A. Raymond write that "according to NATO officials, the entitlement for protection against genocide gives rise to these legal obligations *erga omnes*" and every "member of the international community has legal standing to call for a state to observe these obligations and to impose sanctions if wrongful acts continue."[17]

Refocusing for New Missions

In the post-Cold War era, international bodies have sought to develop measures and capabilities to prevent or forestall substate conflict. In 1992, UN Secretary General

Boutros Boutros-Ghali ordered the international body to incorporate preventive diplomacy into UN peace operations.[18] One concrete manifestation of the increased emphasis on preventive diplomacy is the ongoing NATO mission in Macedonia. Concurrently, IFOR, KFOR and the various missions in Macedonia have demonstrated the capabilities of the Alliance and its willingness to engage in such operations.

Among the lessons learned from the Balkans were the need for military and command flexibility and the ability to develop broad coalitions which include NATO memberstates, partners, international bodies and civilian groups.[19] The operations also demonstrated the importance of military interoperability. Such interoperability makes NATO uniquely capable of undertaking multilateral missions. Furthermore, NATO operations mirrored smaller, but equally successful missions undertaken by other European institutions such as the OSCE.[20] NATO's brief history of success in peace operations set the stage for the British-led peacekeeping mission in the aftermath of the military campaign in Afghanistan.

The American preference for a British-led operation reflected the broad levels of dissatisfaction with traditional UN operations. This dissatisfaction is the result of a number of factors, including four broad factors: "1) infighting between UN departments; 2) lack of professionalism; 3) lack of UN resources and funding; and 4) lack of a shared understanding of the situation."[21] In addition, there were two major military concerns about UN-led operations, the lack of interoperability among the forces involved and a fragmented chain of command.[22] Daniel Byman suggests that "the United Nations, preferable as a vehicle for intervention given its legitimacy, is notoriously weak in using force rapidly and decisively," and that for any peacekeeping mission in Afghanistan "U.S. forces will be needed in the background to reassure the peacekeepers that they will not be abandoned and to assist in the most difficult operations."[23]

In response to perceived deficiencies, even the UN itself has called for reforms of its peace support operations. Specifically, the UN Department of Peacekeeping Operations has called for the adoption of five goals in order to improve operations, including: "1) enhancing the rapid deployment capability for peacekeeping operations . . . . 2) strengthening the relationship with Member States and legislative bodies . . . . 3) reforming the Department's management culture . . . . 4) reorienting the Department's relationship with field missions . . . . 5) strengthening relationships with other parts of the United Nations system."[24]

Peace Support Capabilities Within the Alliance

Unlike many UN operations, the NATO-led missions demonstrated the high degree of interoperability and cohesiveness of the Alliance. Missions in the Balkans also demonstrated the enormous military and non-military capabilities of NATO. For instance:

> the NATO force in Albania in 1999 was able to construct refugee camps for 5,000 people in 3 weeks. The airport at Tirana was improved by the installation of navigation aids, which increased capacity from 8 to 100 aircraft per day. At Durres port NATO troops increased the depth of the port and improved the handling capacity from 12 ships to 18 ships per day. Within Albania NATO built over 200 km of roads and, with 1,700 transport vehicles available, were capable of delivering 1,000 tons of supplies per day. Not least NATO were able to provide a command and control capability through the deployed Brigade Headquarters and extensive use of Liaison Officers that ensured that best use was made of available resources.[25]

Efforts to develop increased capabilities for humanitarian and peace operations were widely supported by the Europeanist states within the Alliance. For instance, Belgian defense officials have praised the "new balance" within NATO between the "traditional tasks and the new tasks of NATO."[26] Concurrently, Italian priorities for the Alliance include "making wider use of crisis management and peace-keeping missions, even outside the traditional geographical perimeter of the Alliance."[27] NAC officials recognized the unique qualities that the Alliance could deploy in peace support and humanitarian operations.

Bennett describes these qualities when he writes that "the unique cooperation among NATO's armed forces that underpinned the success of both the coalition campaign against Iraq a decade ago and the ongoing peace-support operations in the Balkans could prove extremely beneficial in difficult conditions"[28] (such as a peace support operation in Afghanistan). NATO success in the Balkans in peace operations has also reinforced the effort by the European Union to develop autonomous capabilities to undertake its own operations outside of the scope of the Alliance. Meanwhile, within the Alliance, the 11 September 2001 attacks refocused NAC efforts to develop the capabilities of NATO to undertake these types of operations.

On 13 November 2001, NAC issued orders to both the military and civilian organs of the Alliance begin developing contingency plans for a range of humanitarian missions in Afghanistan if the American military operations were able to dislodge the Taliban.[29] The significance of the request was that it underscored the capabilities of the Alliance. NATO was the only multilateral security organization with the capability to deploy forces quickly and the credibility to undertake the operation. The high degree of interoperability allows Alliance forces to deploy rapidly and to work together—a legacy of 50 years of joint and combined training exercises and the practical lessons learned from the missions in the Balkans. These factors also allowed the British-led peace operation to begin deployment in

Afghanistan while coalition forces continued to conduct military operations in the country.

NATO provided the forum to facilitate planning, the military experience and training and the operational interoperability necessary to undertake the post-combat mission in Afghanistan. NAC officials recognized this mission as essential to complement the combat operations. While the peace support mission is not a formal NATO operation, the majority of nations involved are NATO or partner states.[30] NAC planners recognize that, at present, only the Alliance can bring the resources and capabilities necessary to embark on these multilateral operations with a high degree of speed and credibility.

Significantly, the multi-national force negated the necessity for a similar wholly national force from the United States. While American troops continue to operate and conduct missions in Afghanistan, they are not committed to a long-term presence in the country which accomplishes two important considerations. First, the troops are able to be deployed elsewhere if there is an expansion of the military campaign. This is significant since the troops deployed in the country are highly-trained and specialized forces of which even the United States only has a limited number. Second, the temporary nature of the deployment also mutes domestic concerns in the United States over long-term involvement in Afghanistan.[31] Although there were minor tensions created by the impression of a division of labor within the Alliance because of the dominance of the United States in the combat operations (see Chapter 5), NATO's role in the formation of the Afghan peace operation demonstrates the continuing capability of the Alliance to evolve and embrace new functions.

NATO and WMDs

The second major area that NATO has been able to provide nonmilitary assistance to the United States in its campaign against international terrorism has been the formulation and implementation of broad strategies to counter the proliferation of WMDs. Because of the potential use of WMDs by terrorist groups or substate actors, the United States has been particularly interested in bolstering the non-proliferation efforts and capabilities of the Alliance. Although the events of 11 September 2001 reinforced American attempts to counter WMDs, successive administrations in Washington had endeavored to expand the role of NATO in this area since the end of the Cold War. This included support for a variety of new structures within the Alliance (see Chapter 3) such as the SGP and the DGP which operate as part of the JCP.

These efforts were in response to perceptions that WMDs may increasingly be the weapons of choice of terrorist groups and substate actors, in addition to lesser state actors.[32] The American Department of Defense describes these security threats as "asymmetrical warfare" and predicts that such strikes are likely to increase since:

> countering an adversary's strengths by focusing on its weaknesses – is not a new concept. Because of U.S. and allied conventional force superiority, some states may see asymmetric strategies, such as the employment of biological or chemical agents, as a means of avoiding direct engagements with dominant U.S. conventional forces and a way to "level the playing field." This strategy also applies to particular terrorist groups intent on inflicting a large number of casualties or causing panic, if such groups judge that conventional means are inadequate and they do not fear political or military retaliation.[33]

With the ever increasing gap between the United States and other international actors in the field of military technology, the Alliance will continue to face asymmetrical warfare attacks, such as those on 11 September 2001. This is especially true if groups develop new methods of converting non-military devices into alternative forms of WMDs.[34]

U.S. Non-Proliferation Efforts

In 1994, NAC acknowledged the seriousness of the potential threat posed by WMDs, including biological, chemical, nuclear weapons and the delivery systems for each weapon type. At the June NAC/NACC ministerials in Istanbul, Turkey, NAC issued the *Alliance Policy Framework on Proliferation of Weapons of Mass Destruction* which identified the proliferation of WMDs as a direct threat to international security and the spread of ballistic missile technology as a "problem requiring special consideration."[35] The *Policy Framework* also called for the Alliance to develop both political and military means to counter the threat.

On the political side, such measures included support for existing non-proliferation efforts and regular consultations and on the military side, the *Policy Framework* called for the Alliance to seek "to improve defense capabilities of NATO and its members to protect NATO territory, populations and forces against WMD use, based on assessments of threats (including non-state actors)."[36] The *Policy Framework* led to the establishment of the SGP and the DGP and elevated Alliance concern over WMDs.

At the 1999 Washington Summit, the United States proposed a new WMD initiative to improve coordination between agencies and memberstates of the Alliance. The Americans wished to elevate efforts to counter WMD proliferation within the Alliance. Speaking before NATO's defense ministers, U.S. Secretary of State, Madeleine Albright stated that:

> The Summit should address the threat posed to our populations, territory and to our military forces by weapons of mass, or WMD. We [the United States] have proposed a comprehensive WMD initiative that builds on the successful work we inaugurated at the 1994 summit. The initiative is designed to ensure that we can effectively address the threat posed by the proliferation of such weapons and their means of delivery. Our plan is to increase information and intelligence-sharing in the Alliance, accelerate the development of capabilities to deter and protect against potential WMD use, and underscore our shared commitment to prevent proliferation.[37]

The initiative had five main goals: 1) to facilitate the sharing and exchange of information on WMDs and proliferation issues; 2) to expedite defense planning for operations in WMD environments; 3) to broaden Alliance efforts at non-proliferation; 4) to increase the ability of memberstates and allies to protect civilian bodies form WMD attack and to coordinate responses to such attacks; and 5) to establish a WMD Center to coordinate strategies and non-proliferation efforts.[38]

At the heart of the American proposal was the suggestion to improve intelligence sharing. This initiative was opposed by France.[39] Several other members of the Alliance supported the French position which was based on the premise that existing multinational bodies, including the UN and the OSCE, should take leadership roles in the global counter-proliferation campaign and that the United States might be using the threat of WMDs to develop or justify renewed actions against the regime of Saddam Hussein in Iraq or against Iran.[40] Meanwhile, Germany and Canada initiated a proposal to reexamine NATO's nuclear policy and called for NAC to entertain a proposition to adopt a no-first-use policy of nuclear weapons (even to deter WMDs).[41]

In the end, NAC agreed to establish the WMD Center in an effort to implement the goal of intelligence sharing and to coordinate the "politico-military approach to the following tasks: encouraging debate and understanding of WMD issues in NATO; enhancing existing programs to increase military readiness to operate in a WMD environment; and increasing the exchange of information on WMD destruction assistance programs among allied countries."[42] The new strategic outlook marked the first time that the Alliance gave its military assets a "role" in forestalling the proliferation of WMDs.[43]

Once in office, the Bush Administration continued the broad campaign to enhance counter-WMD proliferation efforts through bilateral and multilateral means. For instance, the Administration worked with its closest ally, the United Kingdom, to develop both direct and indirect strategies to counter the threat of

WMDs. Speaking to Parliament, Baroness Ramsay of Cartvale broadly summarized the bilateral efforts:

> The Prime Minister and President Bush agreed that we should work to obstruct and deter new threats resulting form the proliferation of weapons of mass destruction and their means of delivery. A key element of this strategy would be to continue nuclear arms reductions where possible and strengthened WMD and missile proliferation controls and counter-proliferation measures. The Foreign Secretary and Secretary of State Colin Powell agreed last month [February 2001] to establish a counter-proliferation task force to take forward the proliferation aspects of this work.[44]

On a multilateral level, the United States initially faced resistence among several of its NATO Allies in expanding the Alliance's role in counter-proliferation efforts following two actions that seemed to run counter to non-proliferation initiatives which occurred in the aftermath of the 1999 Washington Summit. The first of these events was the 1999 U.S. Senate rejection of the Comprehensive Test Ban Treaty (CTBT). The second was the decision by the Bush Administration to unilaterally withdraw from the 1972 Anti-Ballistic Missile (ABM) Treaty in order to proceed with programs designed to establish a National Missile Defense (NMD) system. The NMD initiative has been particularly troubling to Europeanist states within NATO as they perceive that it might signal a return to American unilateralism, despite offers by the Bush Administration to include the Allies within any such system. The Allies were also concerned over the potential impact of NMD on relations between the United States, and the European Allies, and states such as Russia and China.[45] Improved relations between the United States and Russia in the aftermath of the 11 September 2001 attacks have quelled much of the disquiet over the potential impact of NMD (see below), nonetheless, many Allies continue to perceive NMD as a possible signal of American withdrawal from the transatlantic security regime.

Post 11 September 2001 WMD Strategy

Following the September attacks, the United States requested that NATO expand its anti-WMD efforts. In response, the Alliance agreed to increase cooperation and coordination to counter the potential use of WMDs by terrorist groups or substate actors among a wide range of fields, including collaboration on political and military issues and even in medical areas.[46] Specifically, the Alliance has developed procedures to expand the exchange of information between the Allies on WMD matters. The Alliance's WMD Center has been tasked with serving as the coordinating body for the enhanced efforts.

In order to assist the WMD Center, the United States Central Intelligence Agency (CIA) has increased it intelligence sharing with the Allies under the auspices of the Center and the Bush Administration has also expanded intelligence cooperation from the Departments of State and Defense. These American actions have been reciprocated by the Allies. In addition, the Center has conducted briefings with the EAPC and nations involved in the Mediterranean Dialogue, and it has engaged in bilateral discussions with both Russia and Ukraine.[47] However, the small size and resources of the Center may limit its effectiveness (the Center's staff consists of ten members, three from the international military staff and seven "national experts" from memberstates).[48] In addition, there remains opposition to a broad counter-proliferation role for the Alliance from nations led by France that support strengthening international non-proliferation efforts under the auspices of the United Nations or other bodies.

Civil-Emergency Planning and Response

The third major area of NATO support for the United States has been in the realm of civil-emergency planning and response strategies. The threat of the use of WMDs is but one of a myriad of emerging security threats that planners within the Alliance seek to address. With the end of the Cold War, there has been a marked increase in Alliance efforts to foster civil-emergency planning and to undertake exercises to prepare NATO military units to undertake a support role in response to non-military crises. In many ways, such planning also reflects the increasing number of peace support and humanitarian operations that the Alliance is involved in. It also is a reflection of the recognition that attacks directed against primarily civilian targets, such as the 11 September 2001attacks against the World Trade Center, are increasingly likely and that the military has a legitimate role to play in the emergency response and recovery efforts beyond its role in defending against such attacks.

Since the end of the Cold War, the Alliance has undertaken a variety of steps to improve its capabilities in regard to civil-emergency planning and operations. At the heart of the ability of NATO to undertake such missions lie broader questions of civil-military relations. Since its foundation, NATO was worked to ensure civilian control of the military. This tradition has coexisted with the even older custom whereby military assets have been used to assist civilian organs during times of national or regional emergencies. Neill Wright, the United Nations High Commissioner for Refugees, Deputy Coordinator for South-Eastern Europe summarized the intersection between the military and civilian agencies in the following manner:

There is a long-standing tradition of military forces assisting civilian actors. The military are after all recruited from civil society, and although additional laws may apply while they are serving, they remain members of civil society when not in uniform. During national emergencies, the military are called upon to assist in maintaining law and order if the situation exceeds the response capacity of the police. They are often used for natural, technological or environmental disaster response. Their standing response capacity and unique skills can also exceptionally be called upon when strikes disrupt public services or utility supplies. In these circumstances, as well as during their use in conflict, they remain responsible to their civilian masters–their government.[49]

With increased deployment of Alliance assets in peace support and humanitarian operations, civil-military relations have become increasingly institutionalized through the establishment of permanent structures and the development of doctrines and strategic planning for these missions. Such institutionalization has been designed to improve the capability of military units to operate within the parameters of civilian environments in order to conduct missions and achieve goals without creating friction with civilian agencies or populations. Hence, one specific goal of NATO exercises and doctrine in this field is to "create civil-military conditions that will offer the Commander the greatest possible moral, material and tactical advantages."[50]

These trends toward greater institutional capabilities reflect the growing acceptance that one of NATO's primary roles in regional security in Europe will be as an agency to deal with civil-emergencies ranging from natural disasters to relief efforts in the event of substantial WMD attacks. Multinational response, coordinated through institutions, provide capabilities and assets that are often beyond those of a single nation. They may also provide an enhanced degree of legitimacy to operations since such missions are usually undertaken under the auspices of the United Nations or the 1994 Oslo Guidelines and with the military participation of organizations including NATO or the OSCE.[51]

In order to facilitate the continuing process of developing an institutional role in civil-emergency operations, NATO has created a variety of agencies and undertaken both practical exercises and real missions.[52] The Alliance's Division of Security Investment, Logistics and Civil Emergency Planning is charged with coordinating NATO's programs in this field through its Civil Emergency Planning Directorate. The Directorate has a variety of main tasks:

1) Providing staff support to the Senior Civil Emergency Planning Committee and the nine civil emergency planning boards and committees responsible for developing crisis management arrangements in the areas of civil, sea land and air transport; energy; industry; food and agriculture; civil communications; medical care; and civil defense;

2) Developing arrangements for the effective use of civil resources in support of Alliance security objectives and for the protection of civil populations; and

3) Developing arrangements and encouraging active participation of Partner countries in CEP [civil-emergency planning] activities.

The Director of Civil Emergency Planning also oversees civil-emergency planning activities undertaken in the context of the EAPC, Partnership for Peace, the NATO-Russia Permanent Joint Council, the NATO-Ukraine Commission, the Mediterranean Cooperation Group and the Euro-Atlantic Disaster Response Coordination Center (EADRCC).[53]

To further enhance the ability of the Alliance to act as a coordinating body for civil emergencies, in 1994, the Committee of the Chiefs of Military Medical Services (COMEDS) was created. The chair and secretary of COMEDS is provided by Belgium and the committee is physically housed in the offices of that nation's Surgeon General.[54]

Following the attacks on the United States, the civil-emergency planning agencies and bodies of the Alliance met on 25 and 26 October 2001 in order to address the issues raised by the terrorist incidents and develop more thorough response strategies in the event of future attacks against Allied or Partner states. Among the initiatives approved was an agreement to develop a thorough "inventory" of the assets and competencies of each of the Allied and Partner states so that NATO would be better prepared to protect or assist civilian populations in the event of a nuclear, biological, chemical or other devastating attack. Specifically, the inventory would detail transportation, medical and appropriate scientific capabilities.[55] Finally, the meetings confirmed the EADRCC as the main coordinating body for civil-emergency response efforts by the Alliance.

Institutional Cooperation Beyond NATO

The fourth main area of nonmilitary support from the Alliance has been NATO's efforts to serve as a coordinating body between the United States and other international institutions. As aforementioned, the Bush Administration signaled soon after the 11 September 2001 attacks that it intended to develop a coalition of coalitions. In a report to Congress, the Congressional Research Service affirmed that the "use of diplomacy to help create a global anti-terror coalition is a central component of the Bush Administration response to September 11 events."[56] In this broad diplomatic campaign, the Administration asked NAC to improve relations and coordination with other European bodies such as the OSCE and the EU.

These organizations provide capabilities which could enhance, and in some cases, complement, the assets and abilities of the Alliance. For instance, the involvement of other international organizations increased the legitimacy of the broad goals of the American-led campaign while international instruments such as the 1999 United Nations Convention on the Suppression of Terrorist Bombings and the 2000 United Nations Anti-Terrorism Financing Convention provide international legal justification for American actions.[57] Concurrently, the Administration also sought to bolster its own series of campaigns by ensuring that other international and regional bodies adopted the policies and strategies advocated by the United States. Within the broad framework of transatlantic security, in many ways the OSCE and the EU exist as the main complementary institutions outside of the NATO/WEU tandem.

OSCE

The OSCE has been successful by employing five broad strategies. First, the organization empowers its negotiating teams with broad mandates to settle both political and military disputes. Second, OSCE missions bring enormous resources in the form of international aid and international legitimacy to crises. Third, the OSCE tends to use relatively small teams of diplomats who are familiar with the people and areas in conflict. Fourth, the organization dispatches its teams directly to the conflict area rather than holding international conferences at remote locations. Fifth, and finally, OSCE missions tend to focus on long term conflict resolution instead of quick or temporary settlements.[58]

As a result, the OSCE provides a unique, but limited, forum that can supplement and enhance the military abilities of the Alliance. Furthermore, the OSCE is more inclusive with a larger membership that includes Russia and the states of the former Soviet Union, and a broader geographic area.[59] The OSCE has undertaken a variety of successful missions in Central and Eastern Europe. For example, the OSCE dispatched an 18-member team to Georgia to mediate a dispute in Southern Ossetia and was later instrumental in drafting a new constitution for the newly-independent republic. In addition, an eight-member OSCE team negotiated an settlement of the crisis in the Transnistria and arranged a end to the dispute. The organization also negotiated the agreement that led to the withdrawal of Russian troops from Moldova.[60] Other examples of operations in which the OSCE was involved include the Chechyan crisis in Russia and the Albanian crisis where the organization worked with NATO to resolve the nation's internal turmoil.[61]

The OSCE has also worked closely with the Alliance in the NATO-led operations in the Balkans. Such cooperation remains vitally important for the Alliance, especially as the Alliance considers proposals to draw down the NATO military presence in Bosnia Herzegovina and Kosovo. One manifestation of the importance of the OSCE is that increased cooperation between the two organizations is one of the main long-term goals of the EAPC.[62] As the Alliance presence decreases, the OSCE and the EU will remain in the areas and continue to oversee reconstruction aid and peace support missions.[63]

The EU

While the OSCE provides a useful, though limited, mechanism to enhance regional security in Europe, the EU stands at the opposite extreme with an enormous degree of potential resources. While in many ways NATO and the EU have experienced a degree of rivalry within the institutional framework of the transatlantic region, the United States is increasingly in favor of a greater role for the Union in international security. This trend has been accelerated by the 11 September 2001 attacks. The Bush Administration has sought to promote an increased security role on the part of the EU in order to ameliorate the unequal burdensharing presently existent in European security. Concurrently, the Administration also seeks to have the EU assume a more robust role in the ongoing counter-terrorism campaign.

On one level, deep cooperation already exists between NATO and the Union on both an intangible and a practical level. For instance, the majority of memberstates in NATO also belong to the Union. Furthermore, the EU gives a political voice to those European states that do not belong to NATO, such as the traditionally neutral states of Austria, Finland and Sweden.[64] Even though these states belong to the EAPC and PfP, the EU provides the nation with a greater political role in the decision-making process which is dominated by NAC in NATO. In addition, there is broad support among the Allies, including the United States, for an increased security role for the Union. This support is manifested in the political and diplomatic efforts undertaken in order to champion the development of CFSP and specific military assets such as the ERRF. Support is also manifested through NATO's adoption of measures including the DCI in order to ensure that the European states have the military capabilities to fulfill an enhanced security role in the transatlantic security regime.

Speaking on the EU initiative to expand its security role and the importance of close collaboration with NATO during this initiative, former Finnish President Martti Ahtisaari (one of the two main negotiators that developed the settlement following the air war in Kosovo) stated that:

> The European Union is taking steps to improve its own civilian and military crisis management capacity and the development of more effective policy mechanisms for crisis management and prevention. As the EU develops its capabilities, we must ensure that the developments within NATO and the EU remain mutually supportive. After all, we share

the same goal on both sides of the Atlantic: the enhancement of European capabilities in order to achieve a better balance in terms of US-Europe burdensharing. The presence of US troops continues to be an important element of European security overall. The Common European Security and Defense Policy, ESDP, is not about the EU developing a collective defense capability. The ESDP is about crisis management and about increased flexibility in addressing crisis situations. To be able to reach this goal we need a well-oiled EU-NATO link.[65]

Concurrently, the operations in the Balkans affirm the practical ability to cooperate during specific missions. The EU has even extended an invitation to Canada to participate in future EU-led crisis response operations.[66]

Although there were some political and military disputes and differences over the operations, particularly in regard to Kosovo, Lord Robertson offers this overview on the comparability of the two organizations in their joint operations in the Balkans:

> At the political level, there is already deep and effective practical cooperation between the organizations, civil and military, working to ensure security in Bosnia, Kosovo and FYROM [Former Yugoslav Republic of Macedonia]. Paradoxically, the EU and NATO cooperate together better in practice on the ground in Macedonia than they do in theory in Brussels. Continuing US involvement is essential to avoid repeating the mistakes of the UNPROFOR era. But we must encourage the NATO-EU relationship so that the Europeans can take a greater share of the political burden in building peace throughout the Balkan region.
>
> Militarily, the current picture on the ground is equally positive. The Americans are fully engaged, but the bulk of the forces in SFOR, KFOR and Task Force Fox in Macedonia are European. Civil assistance and financial support is also overwhelmingly European.[67]

The level of cooperation in the Balkans was replicated in the aftermath of the Al Qaeda attacks on the World Trade Center and the Pentagon. On 24 September 2001, political and security officials met with NAC. At the meeting, representatives from both organizations agreed on the importance of close cooperation and regular meetings between the two during the counter-terrorism campaign. This meeting was followed on 12 October, by a briefing by Lord Robertson before a session of the EU defense ministers. At the briefing, Lord Robertson detailed the steps that NATO had undertaken in support of the U.S.-led military campaign and those broader counter-terrorism measures adopted by the Alliance. The EU again discussed potential means to assist the American counter-terrorism efforts at a joint meeting of the EU and NATO foreign ministers on 6 December 2001.[68]

In terms of specific measures, the EU adopted a variety of actions designed to support the American-led coalition. When U.S. Secretary of State Powell met with the EU there were no less than 33 proposals accepted for consideration by the European Council.[69] These measures involved a wide range of EU officials and were subsequently translated into concrete actions by committees made up of the EU's transport ministers, foreign ministers, finance ministers and justice and interior ministers. As befits its political and social orientation, the overwhelming majority of these measures were non-military and fell into seven broad categories: "1) aviation and other transport security; 2) police and judicial cooperation, including extradition; 3) denial of financing of terrorism, including financial sanctions; 4) denial of other means of support; 5) export control and nonproliferation; 6) border control issues, including visa and document security issues; and 7) law enforcement access to information and exchange of electronic data."[70] Among the more significant actions taken by the EU were the development of an EU-wide arrest warrant and agreement on an expanded list of terrorist organizations to be subject to various forms of sanctions, including the freezing of assets.[71]

While the EU's actions in the civilian sector were robust its military support remained minimal because of continuing fiscal and political constraints which impair the development of autonomous security capabilities. For instance, an expansion of the EU's role in crisis management requires a renewed commitment on the part of Western European governments to devote the necessary resources to meet their obligations within NATO and to satisfy their new responsibilities to the EU. However, such a commitment is lacking at this point:

> The longer term picture is much less optimistic. For all the political energy expended in NATO to implement the Defense Capabilities Initiative, and in the EU to push ahead with the complementary Headline Goal process, the truth is that Europe remains a military pygmy.
>
> Orders of battle and headquarters wiring diagrams read impressively. Overall numbers of soldiers, tanks and aircraft give a similar impression of military power. But the reality is that we are hard pressed to maintain about 50,000 European troops in the Balkans. And that a new operation would oblige most European countries to slash their contingents in Bosnia, Kosovo and FYROM to produce usable forces in any numbers.
>
> American critics of Europe's military incapability are right. If we are to ensure that the US moves neither towards unilateralism nor isolationism, all European countries must show a new willingness to develop effective crisis management capabilities.[72]

Only limited progress has been made on the ERRF and the larger idea of an ESDP. Even within NATO itself, current and near-term European military spending will only allow the Alliance to meet 35 percent of its goals and only 11 of NATO's 19 members have increased military spending once inflation is factored in.[73]   Instead, total EU military spending on defense only amounts to about 60 percent of that of the United States.   The ambitious goals of expanding the capabilities of both the Alliance through the DCI and the Union through ESDP cannot be achieved without dramatic increases in defense expenditures.

NATO's Deputy Secretary General, Alessendro Minuto Rizzo stated that when he took over that post he had just three priorities: "capabilities, capabilities, capabilities" and that in the aftermath of the 11 September attacks "I know the global economy is in a precarious state, and I am aware that Government budgets are being squeezed everywhere . . . . But just as before September 11, preserving the security of our societies requires the right amount of spending–and spent in the right way, as part of the normal, balanced activity of any responsible government."[74] Without adjustments to defense expenditures, NATO-EU cooperation cannot be effectively managed as national governments in Europe will be faced with difficult choices over which priorities, DCI or ESDP, to fund, especially in an era of constrained fiscal budgets.   Furthermore, the political benefits of the NATO-EU ties may dissipate if the burdensharing dilemma between Europe and North America is not resolved in a more equitable fashion.[75]

NATO-Russian Cooperation

The fifth, and final, area of significant nonmilitary support of the United States by the Alliance has been the broad attempt to improve NATO-Russian relations. Although tensions between Russia and the Allies diminished significantly after the end of the Cold War, there were a number of areas of friction that arose between Russia and the Alliance.   For instance, the United States and most Western governments were highly critical of Russian efforts to suppress the rebellion in Chechnya.[76] Russia also indicated its strong opposition to further NATO expansion beyond the Czech Republic, Hungary and Poland.   Most significantly, Moscow opposed the NATO air campaign against Serbia and temporarily suspended meetings with NAC through the Permanent Joint Council (PJC) at the ministerial level.[77] However, Russia did cooperate in negotiating a resolution to the conflict and participated in KFOR.

The effort to improve relations with Russia has proceeded at an institutional level through NATO, even as the leaders of Russia and the United States have developed a close working relationship unmatched in U.S.–Russian relations since before the Russian Revolution in 1917.   The genesis of the close ties had its basis in the June 2001 summit between the two leaders in Brdo Castle, Slovenia.   At the Summit, Bush remarked that he wanted the United States and Russia to:

establish a new relationship beyond that of the Cold War mentality. . . . We have a unique opportunity to address the true threats of the 21st century–together. We have a great moment during our tenures to cast aside the suspicions and doubts that used to plague our nations. And I'm committed to do so.

I said in Poland, and I'll say it again, Russia is not the enemy of the United States. As a matter of fact, after our meeting today, I'm convinced it can be a strong partner and friend–more so than people could imagine.[78]

For his part, Putin characterized the meeting in the following manner:

We sat, talked about the past, about the present, about the future of our countries an about the development of the situation in the world for many years into the future. This was really a very interesting discussion. I think we found a good basis to start building on our cooperation. We're counting on a pragmatic relationship between Russia and the United States.

We compared our approaches in key areas. And, once again, we established our common ground. I want to return now to what the President said very recently–that Russia and the United States are not enemies, they do not threaten each other, and they could be fully good allies. And taking into account the fact that the United States and the Russian Federation, as no one else, as no other country of the world, have accumulated huge amounts of nuclear weapons, weapons of mass destruction, we bear a special responsibility for maintaining the common peace and security in the world., for building a new architecture of security in the world.[79]

This relationship was cemented at the November 2001 summit of the two leaders at President Bush's ranch in Crawford, Texas.[80] Meanwhile, Russia very early on signaled a strong degree of support for the United States in the aftermath of the 11 September attacks. Such support was manifested through official channels and through specific actions such as intelligence sharing, diplomatic efforts on behalf of the United States in Central Asia and even arms transfers to the anti-Taliban Northern Alliance forces.[81] When they met in Shanghai, China on 21 October 2001, Bush and Putin issued a joint statement in which they called for a:

sustained global coalition to defeat international terrorism. Nations must make use of diplomatic, political, law enforcement, financial, intelligence, and military means to root out terrorism and their sponsors and bring them to justice. . . . The leaders of the two countries view U.S.–Russian cooperation as critical element in the global effort against terrorism. They reaffirm their personal commitment and that of their two countries to fight this deadly challenge through active cooperation and coordination, both bilaterally and within the framework of international institutions.

> The Presidents note with satisfaction the fruitful cooperation between the United States and Russia in the United Nations and the UN Security Council, in the NATO-Russia Permanent Joint Council, and in the G-8. They also instruct their governments to reinforce bilateral cooperation throughout the U.S.–Russia Working Group on countering terrorist and other threats emanating from Afghanistan.[82]

The Bush Administration clearly signaled its NATO Allies its intention to use the 11 September attacks to foster increased cooperation with Russia both bilaterally and through the institutional framework of NATO.

NATO Initiatives

NAC and the leadership organs of NATO undertook a variety of both broad and specific measures to encourage Russian support and participation in the counter-terrorism campaign. Russian support was seen as particularly important in light of that nation's history in Afghanistan and its continuing influence in the region among the anti-Taliban Afghan groups and the governments of the Central Asian Republics.[83] Following the 11 September attacks, the Alliance included Russian Foreign Minister Sergei Ivanov in their informal discussions on counter-terrorism strategy.[84] NATO invited Russian officials to participate in all major Alliance meetings and briefings in "19 + 1" sessions.[85] Lord Robertson also met twice with the Russian President and with the Russian foreign and defense ministers to brief them on NATO actions and strategy.

In addition to intelligence sharing and diplomatic endeavors on behalf of the Alliance in Central Asia, Russia engaged in a series of cooperative measures with NATO. First, NATO and Russia have expanded their discussions on counter-proliferation efforts, including "developing missile defense to protect us from weapons that have already fallen into the wrong hands."[86] Second, NATO and Russia have also launched a dialogue on security reform proposals designed to increase the efficiency of military units and contain costs while preparing to undertake new missions such as counter-terrorism operations. Third, and finally, Russia has agreed to cooperate with the Alliance in formulating strategies to enhance collaboration "in civil emergency planning, including in dealing with the after-effects of terrorist acts and natural disasters."[87]

In exchange for its cooperation, Russia requested increased power and influence within the Alliance. In order to satisfy Russian concerns and to increase cooperation with the former superpower, Lord Robertson proposed the creation of a new special council which would expand interaction between Russia and the Allies and give the former Cold War enemy a "right of equality" within the Alliance.[88] Lord Robertson described his proposal as "a huge change, a sea change, in the way we do business."[89] Moscow enthusiastically accepted the initiative. The proposal was initially put forward by Blair who advocated the immediate establishment of the council and a commitment to undertake missions, such as peacekeeping operations, with Russia as a full partner.[90] However, there was opposition to some elements of the British proposal by the United States, France and the Netherlands, in addition to the three former Warsaw Pact members now in NATO–the Czech Republic, Hungary and Poland, so NAC agreed to establish the committee in May 2002 and not accept the suggestion for an expanded Russian role in new missions until further consideration.[91]

On 7 December 2001, the Alliance's foreign ministers did agree in principle to establish the new committee with the goal of "building on the Founding Act, new effective mechanism for consultation, cooperation, joint decision, and coordinated/joint action."[92] Among the areas that the proposed committee might undertake joint decision areas are: "anti-terrorism, crisis management, nuclear non-proliferation, arms control, theater missile defense, search and rescue at sea, and civil emergencies."[93]

Continued improvements in the relations between the United States and Russia on a bilateral level are paralleled by progress between NATO and Russia on a broad level. As a result, tensions have been reduced between the former Cold War adversaries on a range of issues including NMD and NATO expansion with the promise of further cooperation in the future. Such cooperation serves the national interests of Russia and the major Western powers, including the United States, and the institutional interests of organizations such as NATO and the Union. Lord Robertson suggested that there will continue to be differences between Russia and NATO:

> but what the leadership of the NATO countries and the President of the Russian Federation agree is that we are at the moment in an era of unprecedented cooperation, the closest cooperation between Russians and the West since the battle against fascism 60 years ago, and we need to build on that, we need to look at perhaps different but certainly better ways of cooperating on the common agenda that we face. In the past we were divided by walls and by fences and by ideology and by armies. Today the threats to the Russian people are very similar if not exactly the same as the threats to the people in the NATO countries and the West. The international terrorists have gone global.[94]

The challenge for Alliance leaders is to maintain and expand those areas of cooperation and collaboration between NATO and Russia while ensuring that areas of disagreement do not seriously or permanently impair relations. The deeper that Russia is brought into the broad security framework of the West, the more likely that the former superpower will internalize the norms, principles and values of the regime. Concurrently, NATO must allow Russia to draw upon the benefits of the transatlantic security regime by engaging in measures which address Russian security concerns in issue-areas such as Chechnya and continuing in disarmament policies, especially in the realm of nuclear, chemical and biological weapons, which have the impact of reducing Russian defense outlays.

Conclusion

NATO's military contributions to the American-led military campaign in Afghanistan represented only one level of the Alliance's support for the United States. In addition, the non-military measures adopted by NATO may have farther reaching consequences and a broader impact on the transatlantic security regime. Measures to expand the capability of the Alliance to conduct humanitarian and civil emergency response operations will reinforce the utility of NATO both to the specific operation in Afghanistan and to future peace support missions. Such capabilities also bolster the ability of individual states to participate in such operations and improve the ability of organizations such as the OSCE and the EU to work closely with NATO on a variety of issues, including efforts to counter the proliferation of WMDs as well as the ongoing campaign against international terrorist organizations on both the military level and in terms of civilian actions such as freezing assets.

In the post-11 September 2001 era, NATO has bolstered American political and security efforts by serving as a bridge to enhance Washington's relations with both the EU and Russia. Euro-American relations will continue to exist in the context of the consolidation of both the role and the influence of NATO and the EU in the Atlantic region. As such, the growing political power of the EU must be reconciled with the critical role that NATO plays in the transatlantic security regime, even as the Union endeavors to develop its own military capabilities. Improvements in Russo-American relations are also bolstered by deepening ties between Russia and the Alliance since such action continues to reduce friction between the Cold War adversaries and expand areas of cooperation. Thickening ties also open the door for the increased security stability provided by the Alliance to resume its march eastward in Central and Eastern Europe through the next round of expansion. Significantly, NATO serves as a mechanism to reconcile the growing power of the EU with the waning power of Russia in the context of the relative consistency of American power.

Notes

1. Lord Robertson, "The Transatlantic Link: Speech by the Secretary General to the Annual Conference of the Defense and Society," Salen, Sweden (21 January 2001).
2. Robert O. Keohane, "The Diplomacy of Structural Change: Multilateral Institutions and State Strategies," in Helga Haftendorn and Christian Tuschhoff, eds., *American and Europe in an Era of Change* (Boulder: Westview Press, 1993), 56.
3. See, for instance, Beatrice Heuser, *Transatlantic Relations: Sharing Ideal and Costs*, Chatham House Papers (London: Royal Institute of International Affairs, 1996).
4. On this theme, see David G. Haglund, *Alliance Within the Alliance: Franco-German Military Cooperation and the European Pillar of Defense* (Boulder: Westview Press, 1991); or Philip H. Gordon, *France, Germany and the Western and the Western Alliance* (Boulder: Westview Press, 1995).
5. Michael Curtis, *Western European Integration* (New York: Harper & Row, 1965), 75.
6. See NATO, *The Alliance's New Strategic Concept* (8 November 1991).
7. Michael Brenner, "The Multilateral Moment," in Brenner, 8.
8. Bennett, 6.
9. Nancy Snow, "United Nations Peacekeeping," in Wayne Lesperance and Tom Lansford, eds., *Teaching Old Dogs New Tricks: International Organizations in the 21st Century* (Needham Heights, MA.: Pearson, 2000), 101-105. A more formal definition of peacekeeping operations would be "non-combat military operations undertaken by impartial military forces with the consent of the parties to a conflict and designed to facilitate the implementation of an existing truce agreement. Peacekeeping operations are deployed following a decision by the UN Security Council or under a mandate given by the OSCE. They are based on three key principles: the consent of the parties, the impartiality of the peacekeepers and the non-use of force in most circumstances." Meanwhile, peace support operations "are political-military multi-layered operations in a context of crisis and/or conflict in order to carry out various types of activities such as conflict prevention, traditional peacekeeping, peace enforcement. Peace support operations are often carried out under the Chapter VII of the UN Charter, whereby the UN Security Council gives the Member States the authority to take all necessary measures to achieve a stand objective;" Switzerland, "Humanitarian Aspects of Peacekeeping: Discussion Paper Submitted by Switzerland at the EAPC PMSC Ad Hoc Group on Cooperation in Peacekeeping" (11 September 1998).
10. NATO describes such operations as "missions . . . conducted to relieve human suffering especially in circumstances where responsible authorities in the area are unable, or possibly unwilling, to provide adequate services and support to the population. This suffering among large numbers of people may be the result of natural or man-made disasters such as earthquake, flood, famine and radioactive or chemical contamination. It may also be a consequence of war or the flight from political, religious, or ethnic persecution. Alliance involvement in humanitarian missions will be determined through the same decision-making process within NATO as peacekeeping or conflict prevention missions. Humanitarian missions may be executed in the context of a peacekeeping or conflict prevention operation, or it may be a completely independent task;" NATO, *Logistics Handbook*.

11. Switzerland.
12. Switzerland.
13. A. M. Fitz-Gerald and F. A. Walthall, "An Integrated Approach to Complex Emergencies: The Kosovo Experience," *The Journal of Humanitarian Assistance* (16 August 2001), available online at http://www.jha.ac/articles/a071.htm.
14. Switzerland.
15. Javier Solana, "Lessons Learned From Bosnia: Speech by Dr. Javier Solana, NATO Secretary General," Instituto De Defesa Nacional, Portugal (12 March 1999).
16. Charles W. Kegley, Jr., and Gregory A. Raymond, *From War to Peace: Fateful Decisions in International Politics* (New York: Bedford/St. Martin's, 2002), 229.
17. Ibid.
18. Boutros Boutros-Ghali, *An Agenda for Peace: Preventative Diplomacy, Peacemaking and Peacekeeping* (New York: UN, 1992), 11-13.
19. While still Secretary General of the Alliance, Solana stated that flexibility meant that "our [NATO's] force, our headquarters and our logistics have to be geared towards deploying rapidly into a crisis area, and then potentially staying in theater for extended periods. . . . a peacekeeping operation can quickly deteriorate into something more dangerous. Or we may be called upon to conduct humanitarian operations where the needs of civilians must be met, even if a peace agreement has not been fully achieved. We must therefore be ready and able to conduct a wide range of peace support operations. We are adapting our forces and procedures to deal with such challenges. Today's NATO forces are lighter, more flexible, more mobile, and more versatile than ever before;" Solana, Portugal Speech.
20. The success of both large, military-intensive operations in the Balkans and smaller preventive missions led by the OSCE demonstrate the utility of divergent approaches and the need for a case-by-case strategy. Past cases also demonstrate the importance of coordination between inter-governmental organizations, military structures, national governments and civilian agencies; Adrian Wood, Raymond Apthorpe and John Borton, "Introduction," in Adrian Wood, Raymond Apthorpe and John Borton, eds., *Evaluating International Humanitarian Action* (New York: Zed Books, 2001), 6-7.
21. Fitz-Gerald and Walthall.
22. Experiences with UN military command of the original Bosnia mission resulted in a perception that UN was slow to react and make decisions; see Steven J. Hoogland, *Peace Operations: Are We Getting Warm Yet?* (Carlisle Barracks, PA.: U.S. Army War College, 1997).
23. Daniel Byman, "Peacekeeping Forces Have a Long Afghan Haul Ahead of Them," *International Herald Tribune* (29 November 2001).
24. United Nations, General Assembly, "Implementation of the Recommendations of the Special Committee on Peacekeeping Operations and the Panel on United Nations Peace Operations: Report of the Secretary-General," A/56/732 (21 December 2001), 4.
25. Fitz-Gerald and Walthall.
26. Among these new tasks are humanitarian and peace-enforcement operations; NATO, "Jean-Pol Poncelet, Deputy Prime Minister, Minster for Defense: My Country and NATO, Belgium in the Heart of New Missions for the Alliance" (March 1999).
27. Italy, Ministry of Foreign Affairs, "Italy and NATO," available online at http://www.esteri.it/eng/index.htm.
28. Bennett, 7.

29. Ibid.
30. The exception to NATO and partner participation is the contribution of forces by New Zealand.
31. For instance, the American public supported military action in Afghanistan by an overwhelming margin (some 89 percent), however, only 40 percent supported a "large role" for American troops in any peacekeeping operations in the aftermath of the combat strikes; Richard Morton and Claudia Deane, "Most Americans Back U.S. Tactics: Poll Finds Little Worry Over Rights," *The Washington Post* (29 November 2001).
32. Even before the attacks on 11 September 2001, the Federal Bureau of Investigation (FBI) predicted an increase in the threat of the use of WMDs and the potential invocation of the threat of WMDs as a means to disrupt populations and cause chaos. For instance, in testimony before Congress in 1999, the FBI's Deputy Director for National Domestic Preparedness Office stated that: "Terrorist events such as the World Trade Center bombing [in 1993], the bombing of the Alfred P. Murrah Federal building in Oklahoma City, and the pipe bomb at the Olympic Games in Atlanta revealed the United States' increased susceptibility to terrorist assaults. These attacks, coupled with the March 1995 Tokyo subway attack, where the weapon was the chemical nerve agent Sarin, exposed the threat of use of WMD within the United States. The threat of WMD use in the United States is real, however, we must not inflate nor understate the actual threat. The United States is experiencing an increased number of hoaxes involving the use of chemical or biological agents perpetuated by individuals wishing to instill fear and disrupt communities. Yesterday's bomb threat has been replaced with a more exotic biological or chemical threat. While the FBI continues to investigate these hoaxes, other on-going investigations reveal that domestic extremists, as well as international terrorists with open anti-U.S. sentiments, are becoming more interested in the potential use of chemical and biological agents;" U.S., Congress, House of Representatives, Transportation and Infrastructure Committee, Subcommittee on Oversight, Investigation, and Emergency Management, "Barbara Y. Martinez, Deputy Director, National Domestic Preparedness Office Federal Bureau of Investigation: Preparedness for Terrorism Response" (9 June 1999), available online at www.fbi.gov/pressrm/congress99/comterr.htm.
33. U.S., Department of Defense, Office of the Secretary of Defense, *Proliferation–Threat and Response, January 2001* (Washington, D.C.: Department of Defense, January 2001).
34. Beyond chemical, biological and nuclear weapons, the attacks of 11 September 2001, demonstrated that non-military items, such as airplanes, trains or ships, could be utilized to inflict significant casualties or cause considerable damage to infrastructure. For an extremely thorough overview of the potential threats faced by the United States from both internal and external terrorist groups, including a comprehensive list and survey of such groups, see Anthony H. Cordesman, *Defending America: Terrorist Organizations and States and Weapons of Mass Destruction* (Washington, D.C.: Center for Strategic and International Studies, 24 September 2001).
35. NATO, NAC, *Alliance Policy Framework on Proliferation of Weapons of Mass Destruction*, Press Communique M-NAC-1(94)45 (9 June 1994).
36. Ibid.
37. Madeleine Albright, "Statement to the NAC," Brussels (8 December 1998).

38. NATO, *NATO Summit: Weapons of Mass Destruction Initiative*, Fact Sheet (24 April 1999).
39. Julianne Smith and Martin Butcher, eds., *A Risk Reduction Strategy for NATO*, BASIC Research Reports 99.1 (January 1999).
40. Such American efforts were viewed as part of the larger contemporary strategy of "dual containment" designed to prevent either Iraq or Iran from gaining regional hegemony in the Persian Gulf. Both states had WMD programs and extensive ballistic missile development efforts. For an overview of the tensions between the United States and its Allies (including Russia and Japan) over the dual containment strategy, see Anthony H. Cordesman and Ahmed S. Hashim, *Iran: Dilemmas of Dual Containment* (Boulder: Westview, 1997).
41. Wade Boese, "NATO Unveils 'Strategic Concept' at 50th Anniversary Summit," *Arms Control Today* (April/May 1999).
42. NATO, "Achievements of the Washington Summit: The NATO of the 21st Century Starts Today," NATO Fact Sheet (April 1999).
43. British American Security Information Council (BASIC), "NATO Assigns Counterproliferation Tasks to Military Forces," *BASIC-BITS*, Press Release (24 April 1999).
44. Baroness Ramsay of Cartvale, Written Answers: European Security and Defense Policy: NATO Access, *Hansard's Parliamentary Debates*, Lords, vol. 10319 (19 March 2001) col. WA 121.
45. See, NATO, Parliamentary Assembly, "Secretariat Report: Science & Technology Committee Sub-committee on the Proliferation of Military Technology," AT 189 STC/MT (00)5 (27 June 2000).
46. Bennett, 7.
47. Whiteside, 23.
48. Ibid.
49. Neill Wright, "Civil Military Cooperation in Peacekeeping and Humanitarian Operations," paper delivered at the *NATO/Croatian Seminar on Civil-Military Cooperation*, Florence, Italy (17 May 2000), 1.
50. Western European Union, "WEU Draft Concept on Civil -Military Cooperation (CIMIC)," WEU-DMS 99246 (Brussels: WEU 17 February 1999); see also Western European Union, "NATO Civil-Military Co-Operation (CIMC) Doctrine," AJP-09, Provisional Final Draft (2000).
51. Wright, 1-2.
52. For instance, NATO assisted Ukraine in 1995 after severe flooding by the Ouda and Donets Rivers contaminated the water supplies of some 2 million Ukrainians. The Alliance's Civil Emergency Planning Directorate served as the main international body to coordinate aid from the Alliance and PfP states. In 1998, the newly created Euro-Atlantic Disaster Response Coordination Center (EADRCC) undertook a similar mission in response to flooding. The EADRCC also provided assistance to Ukraine following storms which damaged power supplies in December 2000 and again in response to flooding in the Transcarpathian region in March 2001; *NATO Handbook, 50th Anniversary Edition*, Chapter 8. In January 2002, the Alliance undertook the latest in a series of exercises deigned to improve "crisis response capabilities" and the ability of NATO to coordinate activities with bodies such as the United Nations, the United Nations High Commissioner for Refugees and the International Red Cross; NATO, *Exercise Disciplined Warrior*, Press

Release (21 January 2001).

53. *NATO Handbook, 50th Anniversary Edition*, Chapter 10.

54. COMEDS is tasked with "improving and expanding arrangements between member countries for coordination, standardization and interoperability in the medical field; and improving the exchange of information relating to organizational, operational and procedural aspects of military medial services in NATO and Partner countries," and it works with a variety of the Alliance's other agencies, including the WMD Center; Ibid., Chapter 14.

55. Bennett, 7.

56. Raphael F. Perl, "Terrorism, the Future, and U.S. Foreign Policy," *CRS Issue Brief for Congress* IB95112 (17 December 2001), 6.

57. The U.N. also aided the American-led campaign in a variety of other fashions. For instance, U.N. Security Council Resolution 1333 (19 December 2001) called for the Taliban to surrender Bin Laden and close all terrorist training camps, even before the attacks. This provided an existing U.N. measure to justify American miltiary action. On 28 September 2001, the Security Council adopted the American-sponsored Resolution 1373 which called upon memberstates to freeze the assets of terrorist groups. Finally, U.N. involvement in the peace support mission further enhanced the mission's legitimacy.

58. Hans-Ulrich Seidt, "Lessons Learnt From the Crisis in the Balkans," *European Security* 5, no. 1 (Spring 1996): 70.

59. Miriam Sapiro, "The OSCE: An Essential Component of European Security," *Insight* 15 (March 1997), 2-3.

60. Organization for Security and Cooperation in Europe, *Chairman's Summary: Decisions of the Budapest Ministerial Council Meeting* (Vienna: OSCE, 1996), 2.

61. For an overview of the OSCE's efforts in Albania, see Marcella Favretto and Tasos Kokkinides, "Anarchy in Albania: Collapse of European Collective Security," *Basic Paper* 21 (June 1997).

62. NATO, "Euro-Atlantic Partnership Council (EAPC) Action Plan 2002-2004," Press Release M-2-EAPC(2001)165 (7 December 2001).

63. Lord Robertson commented that "both of them [the OSCE and the EU] have got capabilities in that area [peace operations], both of them are very interested and have a good success rate and clearly we'll give whatever help we can to any organization that is willing to take on that critical new role that is part of the development of a stable civic society;" NATO, "Transcript of the Press Point by NATO Secretary General, Lord Robertson and Wolfgang Petritsch, High Representative of the International Community for Bosnia and Herzegovina," Brussels (16 January 2002).

64. Austria, Finland and Sweden belong to the EAPC and the PfP, and have engaged in both military exercises with Alliance forces and operational missions in the Balkans as part of SFOR and KFOR. In the IFOR/SFOR mission, Austria deployed a transport company that was reduced to platoon strength (50 troops) in SFOR, Finland contributed an engineer battalion that was later reduced to company strength (100 troops) while Sweden supplied a mechanized infantry battalion that was also reduced to platoon strength (50 troops) in SFOR; Steven R. Bowman, "Bosnia: U.S. Military Operations," *CRS Issue Brief for Congress* IB93056 (8 January 2002), 9-10. In KFOR, Austria contributed a support

battalion (480 troops), Finland supplied a motorized infantry battalion (795 troops), and Sweden deployed a mechanized battalion (750 troops); Steve Bowman, "Kosovo and Macedonia: U.S. and Allied Military Operations," *CRS Issue Brief for Congress* IB10027 (8 January 2002), 11-12.

65. Maarti Ahtisaari, "Partnership: The Foundation of Euro-Atlantic Security," Speech at the EAPC Conference on Ten Years of Partnership and Cooperation, Brussels (26 October 2001).

66. NATO, "Meeting of the North Atlantic Council in Defense Ministers Session Held in Brussels on December 18, 2001: Final Communique," Press Communique PR/CP (2001)171 (18 December 2001).

67. Lord Robertson, Speech at Salen.

68. Bennett, 7.

69. EU, "Press Conference–U.S. Secretary of State Colin Powell and Belgian Foreign Minister Louis Michel," EU–US Ministerial Meetings, Washington, D.C. (20 September 2001).

70. *Joint U.S.–EU Ministerial Statement on Combating Terrorism*, Washington, D.C. (20 September 2001).

71. EU, "Powell and Michel Press Conference."

72. Lord Robertson, Speech at Salen.

73. Gordon.

74. Alessandro Minuto Rizzo, "Speech by the Deputy Secretary General of NATO Ambassador Alessandro Minuto Rizzo to the Atlantic Treaty Association," Bled, Slovenia (4 October 2001).

75. Unilateralist tendencies in the United States may be reinforced, especially as domestic public perceptions of the utility of European cooperation downplays the role of the Allies; see for instance, Vinocur,. "We'll Call You if We Need You;" or Daley, "NATO, Though Supportive."

76. The Chechen conflict resulted in a widespread terrorist campaign against Moscow which resulted in the deaths of some 300 Russian civilians. In addition, Moscow's military campaign in the break-away republic resulted in the loss of more than 10,000 troops (1999-2001). In response, the Russian military undertook a substantial bombing campaign against Chechnya which resulted in what many Western observers described as disproportionate" and "indiscriminate" civilian losses; Stuart D. Goldman, "Russia," *CRS Issue Brief for Congress*, IB92089 (12 December 2001), 3.

77. Thee contacts resumed with the PJC meeting in December 2000, NATO, "Russia-NATO Relations."

78. U.S., Department of State, "Bush, Putin Meet in Slovenia: Press Conference Following Meeting at Brdo Castle," Ljubljana, Slovenia (16 June 2001).

79. Ibid.

80. At the ranch, the two engaged in such activities as dancing the "Cotton-eyed Joe," and driving "pick-up trucks," however, the summit had a much more serious side and provided a forum for the two leaders to discuss a range of issues from NMD to the Afghan military campaign. While there were no dramatic diplomatic breakthroughs, the meeting reaffirmed the close relationship of the two; David J. Smith, "Presidents Get Just One Chance at the Cotton-Eyed Joe," *Janes.com* (19 November 2001), available online at http://www.Janes.com.

81. Russia agreed to transfer a variety of weapons that ranged from small arms and ammunition to tanks. Specifically, the Northern Alliance received 50 Russian tanks, including older T-55 and T-62 main battle tanks, and 80 infantry fighting vehicles and armored personnel carriers, including BMP-1s, BMP-2s and BTP-60s. In addition, the Northern Alliance received a range of artillery pieces and mortars (including 122mm D-30 howitzers and 120 mm 2B11 mortars and 122 mm 9K51 Grad multiple rocket launchers), as well as substantial numbers of small arms and ammunition. The American Department of Defense underwrote the cost of these weapons with between $40 and 45 million in cash payments to Russia; Bill Gertz, "Russia Supplies Tanks," *Washington Times* (25 October 2001); Kevin O'Flynn, "Russia in Multi-Million Arms Deal With Northern Alliance," *The Guardian* (23 October 2001); Veniamin Ginodman, "Russian Weaponry For Transfer to Afghanistan Northern Alliance Specified," *Moscow Vesti.ru* (14 October 2001).

82. U.S., White House, Office of the Press Secretary, "Joint Statement on Counterterrorism by the President of the United States and the President of Russia," Shanghai, China (21 October 2001).

83. The five central Asian republics, Turkmenistan, Uzbekistan, Kazakhstan, Kyrgyzstan and Tajikistan, were all former states within the Soviet Union. They were seen as critically important in any potential military campaign against the Taliban in Afghanistan. Three of the countries, Turkmenistan, Uzbekistan and Tajikistan bordered Afghanistan and therefore were potentially useful as military staging points. These nations also had sizable ethnic minorities within Afghanistan and these minority groups comprised the bulk of the anti-Taliban Northern Alliance forces. It was also recognized by the Bush Administration that the five states would be critically important in efforts to deliver humanitarian supplies and prevent the escape of fleeing Taliban and Al Qaeda fighters once military operations had commenced.

84. NATO, "Informal Meeting of the Defense Ministers," Press Release (2001) 132 (26 September 2001).

85. These sessions were significant in that before 11 September 2001, meetings of the PJC were constrained by an Alliance policy which mandated that all 19 memberstates be in agreement before initiating any discussions with Russia–a constraint that came to be known as "nineteen-minus-one" instead of "nineteen–plus–one" meetings. The Russians and several Alliance members perceived that this prevented any meaningful dialogue between the Cold War enemies since Moscow perceived that strategies or decisions were presented to it as a fait accompli; Willem Matser, "Towards a New Strategic Partnership," *NATO Review* vol. 49 (Winter 2001/2002), 20.

86. Lord Robertson, "A New Quality in the NATO-Russia Relationship: Secretary General's Speech in the Diplomatic Academy," Moscow (22 November 2001).

87. Ibid.

88. "NATO Sees Revolution in Russia Ties," *BBC News Online* (22 November 2001), available online at http://news.bbc.co.uk/low/english/world/europe.stm.

89. Ibid.

90. "NATO and Russia Seal New Ties," *BBC News Online* (7 December 2001), available online at http://news.bbc.co.uk/low/english/world/europe.stm.

91. In order to develop the new structure, NAC created a working group to overcome any differences in the Alliance. It was recognized that this was a historic opportunity to redefine relations between NATO and Russia; ibid.

92. NATO, Press Communique PR/CP(2000)171.

93. BBC, "NATO and Russia Seal New Ties."

94. NATO, "Press Conference With NATO Secretary General George Robertson: Izvestia Media Center," Moscow (22 November 2001).

Conclusion

NATO's Post-11 September Role

Introduction

During the American-led military campaign in Afghanistan, NATO provided both direct, albeit limited, military assistance, as well as non-direct military aid and support. The historic invocation of Article 5 cleared the way for the deployment of the collective military assets and resources of the Alliance, and NAC agreed to undertake a wide range of measures to assist the campaign ranging from intelligence sharing to efforts to enhance cooperation and collaboration with other international institutions. In developing its response to the 11 September attacks, NATO officials sought to formulate and implement strategies that would provide immediate measures against the Taliban and Al Qaeda and long-term capabilities to counter international terrorism and reinforce the centrality of the Alliance to transatlantic security.

Even as Lord Robertson endeavored to lead the Alliance into both a new century and a new range of missions, renewed criticism of and doubts about the Alliance emerged among those unilateralist factions in the United States and the Europeanist factions on the other side of the Atlantic. American critics questioned the utility of the Alliance in light of the limited military contributions of the Europeans to the campaign in Afghanistan while Europeans raised questions over the limited influence of the region in developing and implementing strategy. The challenge for NATO's leadership is to continue the institutional development of the Alliance by continuing to widen and deepen the organization.

Progress in deepening the Alliance is tied to two issues: 1) advancements in military capabilities; and 2) the evolution of NATO's command structure. NAC has agreed to expand the role of the Alliance in a variety of areas, including an increased role in counter-proliferation efforts and an enhanced counter-terrorism role. However, as NATO accepts new missions, as part of the deepening of the Alliance, the memberstates need to make progress on bolstering their capabilities. As such, one of the main areas that NATO must succeed in during the near future is the DCI. Concurrently, the continuing expansion of Europe's role in the decision-making procedures and in the overall structure of transatlantic security must become a greater priority for the Alliance if it is to ensure the importance of European security interests within NATO and in the broader context of international relations.

One component of this strategy must be American support for the development of European capabilities for use in EU-led operations.

Advancements in widening the Alliance are also tied to progress in two broad areas: 1) the expansion of the Alliance to include new members; 2) the development of structures to expand the institutional framework of the Alliance to those states that will not become formal members of NATO. The Alliance will expand again with the next wave of applicants set for approval in 2002. However, the next round of expansion cannot be the last for the Alliance. In addition, those states that cannot become full memberstates within NATO must be accommodated in ways that extend some of the benefits of membership and garner for the Alliance practical benefits in return.

The EAPC and the PfP currently serve as the main instruments for this level of engagement that is short of full membership and these structures must be enhanced while new means of engagement, such as the Mediterranean Dialogue, are also augmented. Only by continuing to deepen and widen the Alliance can the institution retain its prominence among the security structures that comprise the transatlantic security regime. This chapter examines the ongoing efforts to achieve the twin goals of strengthening the institutional capacity of NATO while expanding the Alliance.

Deepening NATO Through Increased Capabilities

In the aftermath of the Cold War, nations across the globe began to substantially reduce their defense expenditures in an effort to gain a "peace-dividend" which would allow them to transfer portions of their defense budgets to social spending. In the transatlantic region, all of the major powers, with the exception of Greece and Turkey substantially reduced military spending.[1] From 1994 to 1997, defense spending by the EU memberstates declined from $168 billion to $157 billion.[2] An EU study found that the eight nations of Europe that represent 80 percent of the EU's Gross Domestic Product (GDP) reduced their defense budgets from an average of 3.18 percent of GDP to 1.88 per cent during a ten-year period from 1985 to 1995.[3] On a global level, from 1987 to 1997, military expenditures declined at an average yearly rate of 4.5 percent. Worldwide military spending declined from its peak in 1987 of some $1 trillion to $668 billion in 1996 (at 1993 constant dollars).[4] This was an overall decline of one-third. It was not until 1997 that the first modest increases in global defense expenditures were noted (some 2 percent).[5] In 1999, military expenditures rose by a modest 2.1 percent.[6]

These reductions have constrained the ability of Western European states to develop or purchase new equipment and to maintain or undertake significant deployments of troops and assets. In fact, among the European states, the majority of the defense reductions came in the broad area of procurement of new equipment and new weapons systems. During the ten-year period from 1987 to 1997, there was an average decline of 10 percent in procurement among the West European Allies.[7] The most significant reductions were recorded by Germany which between 1991 and 2000 reduced defense spending on procurement by 80 percent.[8]

Cuts in procurement were often matched by corresponding or parallel reductions in spending on the research and development of new weapons. For instance, during a two-year period, from 1995 to 1997, the European Allies in NATO reduced their research and development budgets from $13.5 billion to $11.2 billion. Meanwhile, the non-NATO European memberstates of the EU also decreased their spending from $186 million to $172 million.[9] European spending on research and development is skewed toward the larger EU members and has resulted in a growing gap between the larger, more powerful states such as France, Germany and Great Britain, and smaller states including Belgium, the Netherlands and Norway.[10] Conversely, while the United States has also reduced defense expenditures, it continues to spend almost three times as much on the procurement of equipment and on the research and development of new weapons as do all of the NATO Allies combined.[11]

As a result of these trends in military spending and in the development and acquisition of new weapons, by the mid-1990s, there was an ever-widening gap between the capabilities of the United States and its NATO Allies. The Persian Gulf War, operations in the Balkans in Bosnia and regular training exercises confirmed the divergent capabilities of the Alliance. This problem was exacerbated by the political movement to develop autonomous military assets and resources for the Union. The effort to create these autonomous capabilities threatened to spread the limited military resources of the European allies even thinner since the nations would have to divide their assets between national forces, NATO and the new security structures of the Union.

NATO's Defense Capabilities Initiative (DCI)

Because of the increasing gap in military capabilities between the Allies, American defense officials began to advocate for the development of concrete goals to lessen the technological gap among the Allies. At a NATO conference in Norfolk, Virginia in November of 1998, then U.S. Secretary of Defense William Cohen initiated a proposal which called for increased cooperation among the Allies in the key areas of military logistics and the development of core strategic capabilities.[12] Specifically, Cohen called for the NATO Allies to "share technological innovations" in order to ensure continued interoperability in future operations.[13] In December 1998, the American proposal was accepted by the Alliance's defense ministers who, in turn, tasked NATO defense planners to develop a specific action program. The resultant plan was the DCI which was endorsed by NAC at the 1999 Washington Summit.

The main objective of DCI was "to ensure the effectiveness of future multinational operations across the full spectrum of Alliance missions in the present and foreseeable security environment with a special focus on improving interoperability among Alliance forces (and where applicable also between Alliance and Partner Forces)."[14] On a broader level, the purpose of DCI was to improve NATO's capabilities in five main areas:

1) 'mobility and deployability': i.e., the ability to deploy forces quickly to where they are needed, including areas outside Alliance territory;

2) 'sustainability': i.e., the ability to maintain and supply forces far from their home bases and to ensure that sufficient fresh forces area available for long-duration operations;

3) 'effective engagement': i.e., the ability to successfully engage an adversary in all types of operations, from high to low intensity;

4) 'survivability': i.e., the ability to protect forces and infrastructure against current and future threats, and;

5) 'interoperable communications': i.e., command, control and information systems which are compatible with each other, to enable forces from different countries to work effectively together.[15]

In order to achieve these five goals, the DCI listed 58 broad areas for cooperation and collaboration.[16] While many of the goals require long-range planning and the development of new weapons systems, others can be met quickly, although most will require increased defense expenditures.[17] To manage the implementation of DCI, NATO created a temporary, two-year body, the High Level Steering Group (HLSG). The HLSG was charged with monitoring progress toward DCI and undertaking action to correct or facilitate the initiative.

The momentum for DCI was tied to the increase in non-traditional missions undertaken by the Alliance. These operations, such as those in the Balkans, placed new strains on the ability of the Allies to deploy and maintain forces in the field and to establish the logistics infrastructure to support these missions. This is especially true in cases where NATO or Partner troops would be deployed in areas where these forces would not have access to NATO assets but would instead have to rely on resources delivered through strategic airlift.[18] In addition, Allies need to have the ability to operate with mobile or deployable command and control structures. Interoperability is also a major factor in DCI, especially as it relates to force cohesion: "in this context increased attention must be paid to human factors (such as common approaches to doctrine, training and operational procedures) and standardization, as well as to the challenges posed by the accelerating pace of technological change and the different speeds at which Allies introduce advanced capabilities."[19]

The air campaign in Kosovo dramatically reinforced the drive for both the DCI and for the development of autonomous European capabilities. The campaign demonstrated the vast "capability gap" between the European Allies and the United States in terms of sophisticated precision-guided weapons. Following the campaign in Kosovo, several key areas of military inequality were dramatically illustrated. Among the main areas that need to be addressed include the Allied need to acquire "more airlift and sealift", "precision-guided munitions" and improve their "glaring weaknesses in command, control, communications, computers and intelligence."[20] During the campaign in Kosovo, only the United States, Great Britain and France were able to utilize precision-guided weaponry and only the United States was able to make full use of Global Positioning Satellite (GPS) technology for targeting and attack.

The varying capability levels were exacerbated by the fact that defense spending by the European Allies continued to be constrained. Commenting on DCI and the impact of Kosovo, former U.S. Defense Secretary Cohen stated:

> Kosovo showed the need for progress. . . and there is a clear agreement at this conference that we have to move forward on all fronts.
>
> In some cases, countries will have to spend more money. But in many cases, we can achieve improvements by working together and spending our defense budgets more intelligently. For instance, Germany has proposed a European mobility command that promises to lead to greater coordination in the movement of troops and equipment.
>
> And there are other examples. The Alliance is studying ways to increase the use of commercial sea and airlift to improve military mobility. Italy and the United Kingdom are working together to create performance standards or benchmarks for measuring improvements in capabilities. NATO is developing a Multinational Joint Logistics Center to help the Alliance manage and deploy its assets more efficiently. NATO is developing a new architecture for a unified, modern communications capability. . . . I'd like to take this occasion to stress that the United States learned of shortfalls in its forces during Kosovo and we are working to correct them. For example, we are buying more C-17 transport planes and additional ships for carrying heavy equipment. We are developing new precision guided munitions and increasing supplies of others that are already in our inventory. We are looking at the increased use of commercial off the shelf technology to improve our ability to detect chemical and biological attacks.[21]

However, even as the United States continued its efforts to improve its capabilities, the majority of the Allies continued to fall further behind in many key areas. In order to facilitate measures to reduce the credibility gaps, officials in the Clinton Administration developed a broad initiative to ease American arms sales to its closest allies, including the NATO members, Japan and Australia. The new program was the Defense Trade Security Initiative (DTSI). Promulgated by former Secretary of State Albright on 24 May 2000, DTSI is designed to make U.S. technology and arms transfers less cumbersome and quicker. DTSI is intended to better delineate the needs and capabilities of the alliance partners for the future and thereby reduce redundancy and repetition of function and production.[22]

The Initiative is a 17-point program that mandates upgrades in the U.S. export licensing systems, expedited review for exports related to DCI, and increased export exemptions for the qualified nations.[23] It also allows for multiple destination licensing so that U.S. firms would be able to export certain types of weapons and technology to their European subsidiaries for re-export. As a result, DTSI would also benefit European firms with U.S. subsidiaries by streamlining the licensing process and allowing for increased joint projects between defense firms on both sides of the Atlantic. At the heart of the new rules would be bilateral International Trafficking in Arms (ITAR) treaties which would "streamline" the sharing of technology and increase interoperability.[24] According to the U.S. State Department, DTSI was developed because:

> several allies have encountered delays and difficulties in completing the purchase of U.S. equipment to fulfill DCI objectives. This impedes DCI progress and undercuts effective U.S. government leadership within the Alliance. In order to support the efforts identified by these governments to accomplish DCI activities, the U.S. government should expedite U.S. export licenses required to permit these efforts to move forward. Given State and DoD's [Department of Defense] joint interest in facilitating the DCI, the [DTSI] initiative . . . will facilitate allies' access to defense articles (including technical data) and defense services . . . exported or transferred in support of the NATO DCI.
>
> Building upon the commitments made by NATO governments during the NATO force planning processes and using the Javitis report, DoD will create an annual list of items that further DCI objectives. This list will be provided to State and DoD licensing officers and to NATO Allies. When license requests for a DCI-related project are received and confirmed, they will receive expedited treatment by State and DoD.[25]

Once in place, DTSI would shorten the regular review process by more than half.[26] Of course, DTSI is also designed to promote American defense exports and thereby aid the nation's defense industry. Concurrently, however, DTSI and DCI are both designed to benefit the European Union by clearly differentiating between the needs of the Union and of the Alliance. The American initiatives were also seen as a means to allow the Allies to better allocate resources by eliminating redundancy in equipment and capabilities and repetition of function. As such, the NATO actions also strengthen the Union's effort to meet its Headline and Capability Goals by separating the resources that may be utilized for operations in which the assets of the Alliance are not involved.[27] Informal meeting groups of officials from the Alliance and the Union have been meeting since the summer of 2000 to "define new forms of cooperation between the European Union and NATO, including mechanism to allow EU access to NATO collective assets and permanent arrangements for consultation between the two organizations."[28] The meetings also resulted in agreements that stressed that the objectives arising from DCI and the European Union's so-called "Headline Goal" are "mutually reinforcing and reaffirmed the importance of respecting the security interests of all Allies and the obligations which they have to each other."[29]

These programs reinforce the Union's drive for autonomous capabilities and "improve their [the Union's] capability to undertake EU-led operations . . . . and improve the ability of Allied and Partner forces to operate together in NATO-led crisis response operations."[30] Such improvements are linked to the broader Alliance goals designed to encourage greater capabilities among the European partners and thereby reduce the security burdens of the NATO.

The EU's Drive for Increased Capabilities

Alliance support for EU security initiatives reflected a newfound acceptance of the role of the Union within the transatlantic security regime. In the aftermath of the air campaign in Kosovo, the United States recognized the potential benefits of the EU in areas such as peace support operations. Furthermore, the attacks of 11 September 2001 reinforced the need for increased cooperation between the Union and the Alliance in a wide range of security issues (see Chapter 6). This increases the need for the EU to develop its own capabilities in specialized areas that do not conflict or overlap with NATO, but instead bolster the Alliance's abilities. The result is renewed support for the CFSP and ESDP. The Chief of Political and Academic Affairs of the European Commission's Washington Delegation, Cameron Fraser described American support for a greater security role in the following manner: "Our [the EU] efforts now are supported by the United States administration because they see the value of the Europeans taking on a greater share of the burden in dealing with European security issues . . . . It's a better rebalancing of the transatlantic relationship that we should see, not any threat to it."[31]

While American support for increased European security extends back to the immediate post-World War II era and the subsequent drive to develop the EDC, the effort to cultivate ESDI in the late 1980s culminated in the 1990s with specific steps to implement a CFSP. The 1993 Maastricht Treaty established the CFSP as a goal of the European Union. The main objectives of CFSP were:

1) to safeguard the common values, fundamental interests and independence of the Union;
2) to strengthen the security of the Union and its Member States in all ways;
3) to preserve peace and strengthen international security;
4) to promote and international cooperation; and
5) to develop and consolidate democracy and the rule of law, and respect for human rights and fundamental freedoms.[32]

The Maastricht Treaty was followed by the Amsterdam Treaty in 1997 which further delineated the tasks necessary to implement CFSP and ESDP.[33] Subsequent summits of the European Council at Cologne in June 1999 and at Helsinki in December of the same year further solidified the drive.[34] Furthermore, it was concluded that the WEU would play an "integral" role in the development of the security functions of the EU by providing the foundation for the planned expansion of functions. As a result, members of the EU were invited to join the WEU as full members and the non-EU European members of NATO were invited to become associate members of the WEU.[35] In June of 2001, the crisis management functions of the WEU were transferred to the EU and the WEU military staff ceased "operational activities."[36] ESDP remains an ongoing effort which Solana describes as:

an open, transparent process and good progress has been made in implementing the arrangements for cooperation with the non-EU European NATO members and EU accession candidates. In addition to the meetings of Ministers, PSC [Political and Security Committee] and Military Committee representatives with their counterparts from those countries, the non-European NATO members and other candidates for accession to the EU have as interlocutors to the PSC and points of contact to the EU military staff.[37]

On 15 December 2001, the European Council at Laeken announced that ESDP was operational and declared "the Union is now capable of conducting some crisis-management operations" and "is determined to finalize swiftly arrangements with NATO."[38] The only matter remaining for the Union was to actually develop the military components necessary to undertake missions under the auspices of ESDP.

Although both CFSP and ESDP have the support of the European Allies and the United States, significant questions remain over the capability of the EU to operationalize the structures necessary to implement the new initiatives. For example, the ability to develop autonomous assets is dependent on the ability of the

Europeans to develop closer defense-industrial collaboration. However, this would require national governments to allow the demise of inefficient industries and firms and accept difficult job losses. In a political demonstration of support for such measures, in August of 2000, the major West European defense powers signed a framework agreement to "facilitate the restructuring and operation of the European defense industry."[39] In addition, the nature and composition of both the non-military and military capabilities needed for ESDP remain a subject of contention.

RRF/ERRF

The EU Headline Goals were developed to expedite the formation of the ESDP. The Europeans have sought to develop both collective non-military and military assets. At the Union's Helsinki Summit in 1999, the leaders of the EU agreed to create a Rapid Reaction Facility (RRF). The RRF is envisioned as institutional mechanism to allow the deployment of civilian assets to "deal with natural disasters, conflict prevention, and crisis management."[40] The RRF is supposed to incorporate both governmental resources and those of NGOs, and to work with the military units of EU memberstates.[41] The ultimate goal of the initiative is to create a permanent standby force that could deploy up to 15,000 personnel specifically trained for "human rights monitoring, civil administration, policing, conflict resolution, election supervision, media monitoring and local languages."[42] Existing national civilian police forces would form the core of the RRF.

In addition to the proposed non-military organization, the core of the European ESDP proposal is the creation of a European Rapid Reaction Force (ERRF). At the 1999 Helsinki Conference, the EU agreed to develop a 50,000-60,000 member reaction force that could be deployed within 60 days and be maintained for a period of at least one year.[43] This decision was followed by calls from EU members for an even larger force of up to 100,000 troops.[44] The ERRF would be tasked to undertake various missions, such as peace operations, or other military actions that NATO would not or could not be involved in. This would grant the Union considerable autonomy to deploy forces in limited crisis operations.

In the effort to truly implement ESDP fiscal constraints continue to be one of the main impediments. For instance, on 30 January 2002, Germany announced that it could not guarantee that it would purchase 73 Airbus A400M transport aircraft, worth £5.1 billion.[45] The inability to meet the commitment endangers the prospects that the Europeans would collaborate on purchasing the aircraft and instead might turn to other aircraft such as the American C-17 in order to develop the strategic lift necessary to support operations by the RRF or the ERRF. Lord Robertson summarized these financial problems in the following fashion:

This is not purely an issue of finding new money for defence. It is about getting a good return on investment - literally "getting more bang for your buck." Today, the European Allies spend about 60% of what the United States spends on defence, but nobody would suggest that the European Allies have 60% of the capability. We need to improve that return on investment, through innovative management, defence industrial consolidation, setting of priorities, and courageous decisions.

We must spend more wisely and if that doesn't free up enough resources, there is nothing for it but to call for more resources. But let me be clear - I am committed to ensuring that DCI delivers - that the capability shortfalls will be addressed.

To the extent that European Allies are prepared to support DCI, and make faster progress in improving their capabilities, they will also fare better in fulfilling the EU's Headline Goal. Even at the relatively modest level of 60,000 rapid reaction troops set at Helsinki, it is clear that European nations have some serious gaps in capabilities, such as strategic lift, air-to-air refuelling and strategic intelligence. Hence, if Europe is not delivering as promised, we will have two gaps: a transatlantic capability gap, and a European credibility gap. This is hardly a recipe for a healthy 21st century Alliance. We must avoid such an outcome, and we must act now to avoid it.[46]

Events in the world, namely the terrorist attacks on the United States, have exacerbated the potential problems for the European Allies in meeting the manpower requirements necessary to overcome these credibility gaps.

European governments will have to develop the force structures to enable their militaries to continue the ongoing deployments in the Balkans, participate in any future anti-terrorist operations or support mission, such as the British-led peace support operation in Afghanistan, and maintain the assets for use in the ERRF. The capability to deploy forces in so many operations has not been needed since the end of the colonial era. In regards to the necessity of deployable forces, the president of the Assembly of the WEU noted that:

In the Balkans the situation has changed considerably since 11 September 2001 because the US may soon withdraw its troops and ask the Europeans to step in and replace them in the area. EU-countries already have about 40,000 soldiers operating in the area. This is not far off the 60,000 limit set by the Headline Goal. However, we will have to deploy more troops than we thought and probably much earlier than expected and we have to equip and train them.

With regard to the necessary capability improvements, there has been some progress since the Capabilities Commitment Conference last year.[47] However, this has mainly been limited to less pressing shortcomings and should not be presented as a major achievement. We still have not seen any progress on precision-guided missiles, anti-air defense or forces protection.[48]

Although the EU has certainly progressed on the political front in CFSP and ESDP, the above cited deficiencies continue to limit its operational viability. Thus far, the political will to commit to ESDP has not been matched by the political will necessary to undertake the difficult steps to successfully implement the objectives. A WEU report on the defense equipment of the EU that is supposed to be utilized for ESDP recommended that the Union initiate a number of steps to meet its goals:

a) devote a larger part of their national defense budgets to equipment procurement and research;

b) ensure that public opinion is aware of the importance of substantial defense budgets to cover European crisis-management tasks;

c) immediately to enter into practical cooperation on projects for equipment for crisis management, as a matter of priority, in areas where deficiencies have been found to be greatest;

d) envisage procurement of real-time intelligence capabilities, satellite guidance systems and capabilities in electronic jamming, command, control and communication, air-to-air refuelling, strategic air and sea lift, precision strike, anti-air defense penetration and damage assessment;

e) guarantee interoperability of all military equipment developed and/or purchased by the various European nations in all fields mentioned above;

f) facilitate, in so far as possible, joint use of military equipment;

g) acquire European command, control and communication systems, which can be projected to the theater of operations along with the Forces HQ;

h) undertake at the same time joint research projects, mainly through WEAO, so as to work together henceforward on the design of equipment for future decades;

i) take account of new terrorist threats, particularly from biological weapons, and set up a working group to study the capabilities and resources required for integrating the fight against terrorism into the Petersberg tasks framework, whilst also compiling a catalogue of measures to help neutralize any negative effects of such illegal action;

j) reflect, following the 11 September attacks, on the capabilities that urgently need developing so as to deal effectively with humanitarian aspects of the Petersberg tasks.[49]

Political support for ESDP among the memberstates of the Union is increasingly matched by rising levels of support on the opposite side of the Atlantic. One of the significant impacts of the 11 September 2001 attacks was a reversal of policy by the Bush Administration in regards to ESDP. For instance, initially upon assuming office, the Administration expressed concern over the proposal for the ERRF because of the potential that such a force would weaken the ability of the Allies to meet their commitments under DCI. While Washington has long supported the

Europeans assuming a greater share of their defense burden, many in the Bush Administration perceived that the ERRF might evolve into unwanted competition. Furthermore, Rumsfield publically articulated concerns that the ERRF would have a separate planning organization for operations.[50] Rumsfield asserted that this could cause conflict with NATO operations, especially since many of the forces pledged to the ERRF are "double-hatted" or committed to both NATO and the European force.[51]   Meanwhile, British opponents of the ERRF argued that "the creation of the ERRF will undermine NATO, discourage American involvement in European peacekeeping operations."[52] However, the attacks emphasized the need for the very capacities that the Union sought to develop.   European leadership of the peace support operation in Afghanistan reinforced the utility of the EU expanding its crisis reaction capabilities and bolstered the tepid support that the Bush Administration had previously demonstrated for the RRF and the ERRF.

Increased American support for greater European autonomy in security issues is based   on the assumption that the Alliance will remain the foundation for the expression of American security interests in the transatlantic region.   However, the Bush Administration has also indicated that it prefers the EU increase its role within the transatlantic security regime as a means to bolster the overall capabilities of the regime.   Part of the basis for the American reversal on ESDP is the belief that the initiative might finally serve as the basis for a more equitable division of labor in security issues.   The post-11 September actions of NATO also demonstrated the utility of the Alliance beyond the region.   The potential for an expansion of American-led military actions further underscores the need for increased European capabilities, especially if operations are undertaken in more than one theater simultaneously.

An expansion of operations to include action against possible targets in Iraq or Somalia would doubtless lead to further requests from the Bush Administration for increased assistance.   For instance, the potential for either a revival of Al-Qaeda operations in Somalia or the potential that Al-Qaeda operatives would seek refuge in that country, led the United States to bolster military assets in the area.   The State Department declared that the United States is "working to ensure that Somalia doesn't become a haven for terrorists."[53]   In support of the U.S. operations off the coast of Somalia, Germany dispatched a 7-ship naval flotilla and both France and Great Britain initiated surveillance flights over the country.[54]   Further expansion of operations against terrorist groups would require further use of European assets.

Even as the Bush Administration has sought to further bolster the capabilities of the Alliance by deepening the organization, it has further sought to widen NATO to include new members and stronger institutional relationships.   For the United States, enlargement of the Alliance extends the security guarantees of the regime and bolsters regional stability.   In addition, widening of the Alliance multiplies the capabilities of NATO by ensuring interoperability among an increasing number of national forces and equipment. Also, as the IFOR/SFOR and KFOR experiences indicate, widening NATO expands the number of troops and assets available for operations. As a result, an increasing number of Allies, besides the United States, support a substantial increase in membership in the next round of enlargement.

Widening NATO Through Expansion

Even before the terrorist attacks on the United States, Bush made clear his support of Alliance enlargement. In June 2001, Bush declared that "we [NATO] must extend our hand and open our hearts to new members to build security for all of Europe."[55] NATO enlargement remained a priority of the Bush Administration and the Alliance in the post-11 September era. At NATO's June 2001 Summit in Brussels, the Alliance agreed to admit one or more new members in the near future. At the Prague Summit in 2002, the Alliance will make decisions on the next round of expansion. Ten candidates are in line to join the Alliance. These states include the so-called "Vilinius 9," Albania, Bulgaria, Estonia, Latvia, Lithuania, Macedonia, Romania, Slovenia and Slovakia, in addition to Croatia.[56] The candidates have demonstrated a high degree of cohesion and have worked collectively to promote the notion that the 2002 round of enlargement should be as wide as possible.[57]

When NATO expanded in 1999 to include the Czech Republic, Hungary and Poland, there were concerns about the ability of these three former Warsaw states to achieve the levels of interoperability necessary to make meaningful contributions to the Alliance.[58] There were also concerns about the ability of NATO to achieve consensus at nineteen members and therefore maintain the cohesion of the Alliance. Finally, there was trepidation over the potential for Alliance expansion to damage relations with Russia. This was combined with concern among many over creating new lines of division between those nations that were admitted to NATO and those that remained on the "outside."[59]

In many ways, the opponents of both the expansion in 1999 and the next round of enlargement share "a blind spot, which is failing to see that NATO has changed dramatically since the end of the Cold War."[60] Opponents on the right, in both the United States and Europe, generally believe that expansion will undermine the security principles of the Alliance and dilute American leadership. Concurrently, opponents on the left, assert that expansion is propelled as much by the drive for new markets for arms manufacturers as for efforts to extend security and promote stability.[61]

The United States and Enlargement

The United States has assumed a leadership role in promoting the expansion of the Alliance. This is true of both the Clinton and Bush Administrations. The Clinton Administration asserted that NATO enlargement benefited the United States in four main ways. First, enlargement provided a means to improve transatlantic security by preventing potential conflict in Europe. As more states are brought into the institutional framework of NATO, the stability and patterns of cooperation of the Alliance are also expanded. Second, enlargement of the Alliance increased the capabilities of NATO. Expansion to the three Visegrad states added some 200,000 troops for use in future operations.[62] As such, the potential new members may be "security producers" instead of "security consumers."[63] Third, NATO expansion extends and strengthens democracy in Central and Eastern Europe. Among the conditions for Alliance membership are that candidates are expected:

a) to settle their international disputes by peaceful means;
b) to demonstrate commitment to the rule of law and human rights;
c) to settle ethnic disputes or external territorial disputes including irrendentist claims or internal jurisdictional disputes by peaceful means in accordance with OSCE principles and to pursue good neighborly relations;
d) to establish appropriate democratic and civilian control of their armed forces;
e) to refrain from the threat or use of force in any manner inconsistent with the purposes of the UN;
f) to contribute to the development of peaceful and friendly international relations by strengthening their free institutions and by promoting stability and well-being;
g) to continue fully to support and be engaged in the Euro-Atlantic Partnership Council and the Partnership for Peace;
h) to show a commitment to promoting stability and well-being by economic liberty, social justice and environmental responsibility.[64]

Fourth, and finally, counter to assertions that expansion creates new dividing lines in Europe, NATO enlargement actually provides a means to remove the artificial divisions established during the Cold War. NATO membership brings the states of the former Warsaw Pact into the institutional framework of Western Europe. Since expansion has been designated as an ongoing or "open door" process, all of the states of Central and Eastern Europe, including even Russia, can be potential members.[65] As a signal of American support, the House of Representatives passed a non-binding resolution (HR 3167) which called upon NATO to admit Bulgaria, Estonia, Latvia, Lithuania, Romania, Slovakia and Slovenia.[66]

European Preferences

American support for enlargement is not matched by the European Allies who tend to favor only limited expansion to include a small number of states. Furthermore, the Allies have different preferences over the viability of each nation's candidacy. For instance, many Allies support membership for Slovenia. One of the staunchest advocates on behalf of Slovenia is Hungary since that Ally is not at present contiguous with any of the other Alliance members and Slovenian membership would provide a bridge between Hungary and Italy.[67] Slovakia also has a number of supporters, however, there remain concerns about the political influence of the former Communist Party elites.[68] In addition, Allies including Denmark and Poland are staunch supporters of expansion to the three Baltic states, Estonia, Latvia and Lithuania.[69] Finally, France was a significant proponent for Romanian membership in the 1999 expansion round and continues to champion the inclusion of Romania in the Alliance.

Concurrently, the prospective new members have also employed a variety of strategies to enhance the likelihood that they will be in the next wave of enlargement. Following the Madrid Summit in 1999, in which the Czech Republic, Hungary and Poland were invited to join the Alliance, NAC published the "Membership Action Plan" (MAP) to provide guidelines for aspiring applicants. NAC announced that future expansion would be based on a "case-by-case basis" and declined to issue a concrete timetable for the next round of enlargement.[70] For instance, in an effort to enhance its potential, Romania has increased its defense budget by 35 percent. The Romanian government also invited NATO officials to visit the country and inspect its progress. The team concluded "that Bucharest had made real progress in the judicial, constitutional, political, economic, and security fields, but there were still areas that needed improvement."[71] In IFOR/SFOR, Romania contributed a 100-member engineering battalion.[72] Romania also cooperated closely with NATO during the Kosovo campaign and allowed the Alliance to use its airspace.[73]

The Baltic nations have also made a concerted effort to participate in NATO operations. All three states deployed troops in IFOR/SFOR and KFOR.[74] Estonia, Latvia and Lithuania each have received considerable aid and support from Denmark. For example, the Danes have sponsored Baltic participation in American operations in Afghanistan. Denmark will provide training and underwrite the costs of the deployment.[75] In addition, Estonia and Lithuania have agreed to increase their deployments in the Balkans in order to allow Alliance assets to be used elsewhere following the 11 September 2001 attacks.[76] Finally, the Baltic states have increased their defense budgets in order to bring them in line with spending levels among other Allies in NATO.[77]

Concurrent Enlargement

Enlargement of NATO provides an expansion of the transatlantic security regime while enlargement of the European Union solidifies the institutional framework of the region and extends the political and economic regime of Western Europe. As the Union increases its role in security matters, it becomes increasingly more important for close collaboration between NATO and the EU. Simon Serfaty writes that "convergence between NATO and the EU will demand–and, by implication, encourage–parallel decisions for the enlargement of both institutions."[78]   This is because enlargement of the Union brings with it the de facto security guarantees of NATO.   During the twentieth century this was because membership in the EU provided the opportunity for membership in the WEU, with its links to NATO, and the practical consideration that the United States could not allow the WEU to undertake military action to defend one of its members without also undertaking action. Concurrently, membership in NATO provided both tacit and overt forums for cooperation with the EU.

There are nations in NATO that are unlikely to ever join the EU.[79] For instance, the United States will not join the Union unless global circumstances change in some unimaginable fashion.   In addition, Norway has rejected membership in the EU for at least the near term.[80]   Concurrently, there are members of the Union for whom membership in NATO is highly improbable. This includes the Cold War neutral states of Austria, Sweden, Finland and Ireland. However, while NATO plans to announce enlargement plans in November of 2002, the EU is also set to declare another round of enlargement.   There are twelve candidates for EU membership: Bulgaria, Cyprus, the Czech Republic, Estonia, Latvia, Lithuania, Hungary, Poland, Romania, Slovakia, Slovenia and Turkey.   Hence, expansion by either organization draws on essentially the same candidate pool of prospective, or in the case of the EU, current members of the other institution.

Security cooperation between NATO and the EU has been a longstanding feature of the transatlantic region.   In the aftermath of the Cold War, this cooperation accelerated even amid repeated periods where the compatibility of the two organizations were questioned.   Nonetheless, close collaboration in missions in the Balkans and then again in the aftermath of the 11 September attacks reaffirmed the shared interests and commonality of purpose of the bodies. As NATO and the EU enlarge and admit new members, they will reinforce the capabilities of each. Significantly for the United States, the potential that enlargement of both bodies will improve the security capabilities of the transatlantic regime enhances the ability of the regime to develop a significant counter-terrorism role.

Conclusion

Following the end of World War II, the nations of Western Europe, Canada and the United States engaged in a broad and multifaceted series of efforts to develop institutions and to facilitate multilateral cooperation. The result was a wide variety of institutions and international organizations. NATO developed as the principle security body in the transatlantic region, while the EU emerged as the most powerful and intricate political and economic body in the world. Both organizations have developed a degree of integration previously unseen in international relations. As the EU has increased its security role, NATO has expanded its political role by accepting new missions, including peace support operations, and by providing a forum for political discussion in a range of areas such as Euro-Russian relations and defense industrial cooperation. The Alliance also serves as both a political and military mechanism for the integration of the nations of Central and Eastern Europe into the broad framework of the West.

The crises in the Balkans and the terrorist attacks on the United States reinforced the drive for a CFSP and ESDP among the Europeans. The French Defense Minister Alain Richard stated that:

> I believe the Europeans are ready to contribute seriously to the management of future security risks. We will not create the conditions for a decoupling in the transatlantic security relationship.
>
> At the same time, the Europeans have a newfound determination to take political responsibility for the management of crises that affect their security. This is a critical development. It has taken a long time–too long perhaps. But it is a direct response to a long standing US expectation of burden sharing and is based on a recognition of the role of effective capabilities, as well as on the political responsibility of the European Union, which is a political entity in development and no more a mere common market.[81]

The renewed determination of the EU to develop significant military capabilities may eventually pave the way for a truly equitable degree of burdensharing within the transatlantic security regime.

NATO began its existence as a hybrid organization that combined the essential features of a classic defensive alliance and the benefits of a collective security system. At the heart of the Alliance was the Article 5 guarantee which mandated that an attack on one Ally would be judged an attack on all of the Allies and prompt a collective response on the part of the Allies. The collective security functions of NATO allowed for the rearmament of World War II enemies and prevented the development of security dilemmas among the Allies by using the institutional mechanisms of the Alliance to promote transparency, cooperation and the collective action. With American leadership, the Alliance developed new missions and capabilities in the aftermath of the Cold War. NATO also inaugurated new agencies and bodies to accommodate the expanded tasks and to facilitate cooperation and collaboration with its former Cold War adversaries. NATO also engaged in its first combat operations and undertook one round of enlargement and make preparations for a second in 2002.

11 September 2001

For many of the critics and proponents of NATO, the organization's actions in response to the attacks on 11 September 2001 marked either the beginning of the demise of the body or the Alliance's finest hour. To the detractors of the Alliance, American domination of the military campaign in Afghanistan and the relegation of the Allies to conducting support missions for the U.S. seemed to demonstrate the fading utility of NATO. On the other hand, the invocation of Article 5 and the wide range of both military and non-military actions undertaken by the Alliance confirmed the continuing centrality of NATO to the supporters of the organization.

As with most issues, the overall assessment of the Alliance's contribution to the campaign against international terrorism falls somewhere in between the two perspectives. The Article 5 declaration marked the first invocation of the collective defense clause of the Washington Treaty in the history of the Alliance. This allowed NATO the option of mobilizing forces from among the Allies and implementing joint and combined operations against the Taliban and Al Qaeda in Afghanistan and around the world. Instead, the Bush Administration developed and undertook a military campaign in Afghanistan which relied primarily on American forces and assets and that was under the direction of an American command and control structure.

The nature of the campaign in Afghanistan did not necessitate the need for significant military resources. Instead, the United States was able to accomplish its military objectives with limited deployments. Nonetheless, the actions and strategies of the Alliance provided a variety of benefits for the United States and substantially aided the military campaign in Afghanistan. First, the invocation of Article 5 and the strong degree of Alliance diplomatic support provided moral and political benefits as the Bush Administration endeavored to develop its coalition of coalitions. Second, Alliance support facilitated deeper cooperation with the EU on security issues and other aspects of the anti-terrorist campaign, including increased police and financial cooperation and interaction. Third, NATO also provided an institutional forum to bolster collaboration with Russia and build on the personal relationship between Bush and Putin. This, in turn, expedited the ability of the United States to pursue its military objectives in the former Soviet republics of Central Asia (mainly receiving basing and overflight rights). Fourth, the Allies provided a variety of military assets, including special operations units, surveillance assets and supply and refueling resources, which did benefit the combat operations in Afghanistan. Fifth, the deployment of NATO AWACS to the United States, naval forces to the Mediterranean and various forces and assets to the ongoing missions in the Balkans, allowed the Bush Administration to shift or transfer resources to combat and other military operations. Sixth, British leadership and Allied participation in the peace operations in post-combat Afghanistan meant that American forces could be deployed in other missions thereby reducing the potential for casualties among the Europeans and decreasing the possibility for public resistance among domestic European audiences. Seventh, the Allies initiated a range of non-combat support initiatives including intelligence sharing, to develop means to counter future terrorist operations. Continued progress toward DCI will further enhance these efforts. Eighth, in light of the potential devastating impact of WMDs, the Alliance has accelerated its counter-proliferation programs and its strategies to develop response capabilities in the event of a WMD attack. Ninth, crisis management procedures have also been strengthened among the Allies and the Partners. This provides increased capabilities to respond to catastrophic terrorist attacks. Tenth, and finally, NATO enlargement further bolsters the capabilities of the Alliance by extending the region's security regime. Enlargement also draws in additional resources and bolsters collaborative responses to emerging threats.

In overall terms, NATO's contribution to the post-11 September 2001 campaign against global terrorism is demonstrative of the benefits provided by international institutions. These organizations bolster the capabilities of any individual state, even a powerful state with hegemonic tendencies such as the United States, by pooling the resources of a collective body. That the United States would turn to NATO for support in the aftermath of the terrorist attacks is indicative of the degree to which cooperation and collaboration has been institutionalized and internalized by the members of the Alliance. Upon entering office, the Bush Administration was initially criticized in many European capitals for actions that were perceived as unilateralist. However, its actions in regards to the Alliance demonstrate a renewed commitment to multilateralism in the context of NATO and the development of a series of counter-terrorism coalitions. This commitment is part of the longstanding American strategic preference for multilateralism and collective action through institutionalism. The evolution of the Alliance occurred concurrently with the broader development with the institutional framework that has characterized the transatlantic area and the region's security regime.

The transatlantic security regime that developed during the Cold War is the embodiment of the principles, norms and rules that have guided Alliance security policy since the end of World War II. NATO has proven itself able to reform and adapt to new missions and changing global circumstances. With the 11 September

2001 attacks on America and the historic invocation of Article 5, the Alliance again agreed to undertake new missions and expand its security role. The combined political and military assets of the institution constitutes the optimum means to operationalize both ongoing and future missions against international terrorism. NATO also continues to form the cornerstone of the transatlantic regime and the main means to coordinate the norms, principles and rules which underlie the regime.

Notes

1. While other nations were slashing defense outlays during the early and mid-1990s, Greek defense expenditures have increased by a average rate of 5.8 percent since 1990 while Turkish defense spending has increased by an average of 1.7 percent. However, Turkey has increased its procurement budget by 20 per cent, while cutting personnel costs by 15 percent; Stockholm International Peace Research Institute, *SIPRI Yearbook: Armaments, Disarmament and International Security, 1997* (London: Oxford, 1997), 165.
2. Institute Institute for Strategic Studies, *The Military Balance, 1996/97* (London: Oxford University Press, 1997), 34.
3. The eight nations included Denmark, Germany, Spain, France, Ireland, Italy, Portugal and the United Kingdom; European Union, *Eurostat*, no. 4298 (11 June 1998), 3.
4. See Bonn International Center for Conversion (BICC), *Conversion Survey 1998: Global Disarmament, Defense Industry Consolidation and Conversion* (Bonn: BICC, 1998), chapter 6, 2.
5. U.S., Department of State, *Fact Sheet: World Military Expenditures and Arms Transfers 1998* (Washington: GPO, 2000).
6. On the trends for increased expenditures, see Stockholm International Peace Research Institute, *SIPRI Yearbook: Armaments, Disarmament and International Security, 2000* (London: Oxford, 2000).
7. SIPRI, *SIPRI Yearbook, 1997*, 185-87.
8. Peter Wuerth: "Proceeding at a Crawl: Military Expenditure Has Been Declining for Years; Remains of Germany's Arms Industry Fighting for Survival," *Hamburg Die Woche* (23 June 2000), 17.
9. International Institute for Strategic Studies (IISS), *The Military Balance, 1997/98* (London: IISS, 1998), 34.
10. For example, in 1997, France spent $4.6 billion on R & D, while Germany spent $1.7 billion and the United Kingdom spent $3.5 billion. Taken together, the three nations routinely account for more than half the European defense outlays for R & D; ibid.
11. See SIPRI, *Yearbook, 1998* and *Yearbook 2000*; and IISS, *The Military Balance, 1997/98*.
12. See US, Department of Defense, "NATO Nations Hold Talks to Plan for 21st Century Security," Press Release, no. 593-98 (13 November 1998).
13. Linda D. Kozaryn, "Cohen: NATO Needs More Mobility, Better Commo," *DefenseLink* (19 November 1998).
14. NATO, "Defense Capabilities Initiative (DCI) December 1999: Overview," *NATO Fact Sheet* (2 December 1999).

15. NATO, *NATO Handbook: 50th Anniversary Edition*, Chapter 2.
16. The Alliance's 58 areas included a wide range of domains for improved cooperation and interoperability, including standoff detection of chemical and biological weapons, airborne ground surveillance, day and night all weather air weapon systems, interoperability through increases in standardization, and enhanced capabilities against modern sea mines and torpedoes.
17. For instance, all of the Allies possess air assets that can deliver precision-guided munitions. Therefore, to meet the objective of deploying these weapons types in greater number, states have to reprioritize these defense outlays so that they can purchase increased amounts of the sophisticated weapons; Linda D. Kozaryn, "NATO's Defense Capabilities Initiative Targets the Future," *DefenseLink* (23 September 1999), available online at http://www.defenselink.mil/news/Sep1999.html.
18. NATO, "Defense Capabilities Initiative," Press Release NAC-S(99)69 (25 April 1999).
19. Ibid.
20. Jim Garamone, "More Work Needed on Defense Capabilities Initiative," *Aerotech News and Review* (8 December 2000).
21. NATO, the U.S. Mission to NATO, "Transcript: Cohen and Shelton News Conference at NATO Ministers' Conference," Toronto, Canada (21 September 1999).
22. US, Department of Defense, "Background Briefing," *DefenseLink* (11 December 1998).
23. Madeleine Albright, *Statement at Ministerial Meeting of the North Atlantic Council*, Florence, Italy (24 May); U.S., Department of State, *Defense Trade Security Initiative Promotes Cooperation and Greater Technology Sharing With U.S. Coalition Partners* (26 May 2000).
24. U.S., Department of State, *New Export Exemption for Closest Ally to Promote Defense Security* (26 May 2000).
25. U.S., Department of State, Bureau of Political-Military Affairs, "Defense Trade Security Initiative: Expedited License Review Process for Defense Capabilities Initiative" (24 May 2000).
26. Ibid.
27. NAC, *Statement on the Defence Capabilities Initiative*, N-NAC-D-1(2000)64 (8 June 2000).
28. NATO, "Defense Ministers Look at Balkans, Capabilities and European Defense," NATO Newspages (7 December 2000).
29. Ibid.
30. NATO, "Statement on the Defense Capabilities Initiative Issued at the Meeting of the North Atlantic Council in Defense Ministers Session Held in Brussels on 8 June 2000," Press Release M-NAC-D-1(2000)64 (8 June 2000).
31. Cameron Fraser, "What They Said: Cameron Fraser on CFSP, ESDP & the Balkans," *Europe*, 397 (June 2000), 2.
32. NATO, *NATO Handbook, 50th Anniversary Edition*, Chapter 15.
33. The Treaty of Amsterdam "provides for the enhancement of the Common Foreign and Security Policy (CFSP), including the progressive framing of a common defense policy as provided in Article 17 of the TEU [Treaty on the European Union or the Maastricht Treaty]" and significantly, the agreement called for the WEU to be integrated into the EU

to serve as the core of the drive for operational military capabilities for the Union; EU, "Cologne European Council: Annex II of the Presidency Conclusions, Cologne European Council 3 and 4 June 1999" (4 June 1999).

34. For instance, the Helsinki Summit also "established collective capability goals in the fields of command and control intelligence and strategic transport; and envisaged a method of consultation by which the respective goals could be met and maintained including a regular review of progress;" NATO, NAA, "An International Secretariat Background Brief on the European Security and Defense Identity/Policy (ESDI/P)" (February 2000). Specifically, the Presidency Report from the Summit stated that "a common European headline goal will be adopted for readily deployable military capabilities and collective capability goals in the fields of command and control, intelligence and strategic transport will be developed rapidly, to be achieved through voluntary co-ordinated national and multinational efforts, for carrying out the full range of Petersberg tasks;" EU, "Helsinki European Council: Annex IV of the Presidency Conclusions Helsinki European Council, 10 and 11 December 1999" (11 December 1999). These goals were to be met by 2003.

35. NATO, *NATO Handbook, 50th Anniversary Edition*, Chapter 15.

36. WEU, "Address by Dr. Javier Solana, WEU Secretary-General: The First Part of the 47th Session of the WEU Assembly," Paris (18 June 2001).

37. Ibid.

38. EU, "Laeken European Council: Presidency Conclusions Laeken European Council, 14 and 15 December 2001" (15 December 2001).

39. These nations included France, Germany, Italy, Spain, Sweden, and the U.K; *Framework Agreement Between the French Republic, the Federal Republic of Germany, the Italian Republic, the Kingdom of Spain, the Kingdom of Sweden, and the United Kingdom of Great Britain and Northern Ireland Concerning Measures to Facilitate the Restructuring and Operation of the European Defence Industry* (27 July 2000).

40. BASIC, "EU Plan for Rapid Reaction Facility: A Small But Important First Step" (December 1999).

41. European Council, *Proposal for a Council Regulation Creating Rapid Reaction Facility* (11 December 1999).

42. BASIC, *ESDI: Right Debate, Wrong Conclusions* (2000).

43. EU Presidency, *Presidency Conclusions Helsinki European Council*, DN: Pres/99/3000 (20 December 1999).

44. "Meet Your New European Army," *The Economist* (25 November 2000), 55-58.

45. Toby Helm and Michael Smith, "Germany Likely to Pull Out of EU Airbus Deal," *London Daily Telegraph* (30 January 2002).

46. Robertson, Barcelona Speech.

47. The Capabilities Conference was held in November 2000 in Brussels. The meeting developed specific national commitments from EU members in order to achieve the goals outlined by the Helsinki Summit. Memberstates also agreed to specific national reforms in order to facilitate their ability to meet the needs of the ERRF.

48. WEU, Assembly of the WEU, "Statement by the President of the Assembly of the WEU on the ESDP Capabilities Enhancement Conference 19/20 November 2001 in Brussels," Press Release (20 November 2001).

49. WEU, Assembly of the WEU, "Defense Equipment for European Crisis Management–Reply to the Annual Report of the Council," WEU Document A/1760 (5 December 2001).
50. Richard Norton-Taylor, "Plans for EU Force are Confused, MPs Warn," *The Guardian* (11 April 2001).
51. The double-hatting arrangement was originally developed in order to give the WEU operational capabilities. Under this type of arrangement, units are pledged to more than one command or hat. For instance, NATO's Allied Rapid Reaction Corps (ARRC) which is made up of British and Dutch amphibious units is double-hatted as Forces Available WEU (FAWEU) which means that the troops could be used in WEU operations.
52. Derek Brown, "The European Rapid Reaction Force," *The Guardian* (20 November 2000).
53. Thomas E. Ricks, "Allies Step Up Somalia Watch; U.S. Aims to Keep Al Qaeda at Bay," *Washington Post* (4 January 2002).
54. Ibid.
55. "Bush Urges NATO Expansion," *The Guardian* (13 June 2001).
56. On 19 May 2000, the Vilnius 9 issued a combined statement expressing their candidacy for membership in advance of the June 2000 NATO Summit. Following the statement, Croatia also declared its candidacy.
57. In addition to the Vilnius meeting, the representatives of the candidates met in Tallinn on 2 July 2001 and in Sofia, Bulgaria and Bled, Slovenia in October of 2001. They also planned meetings in March of 2002 in Bucharest, Romania and in June 2002 in Riga, Latvia. At the Tallinn Summit, the Foreign Ministers of the ten candidates "expressed their conviction that NATO would adhere to the principle of widening the common zone of security and stability in Europe, regardless of geography and history, and would invite all qualified democracies to join the Alliance in 2002," and "pointed out that the Alliance is not in the process of expansion, but enlargement, based on a unity of values and the free expression of the will of the people of democratic nations, and that this process is in everyone's interest and not directed against any nation;" NATO, PfP, "Statement Adopted by the Ministers of Foreign Affairs of Albania, Croatia, Bulgaria, Estonia, Latvia, Lithuania, Macedonia, Romania, Slovakia and Slovenia," Tallinn (2 July 2001).
58. Much of the criticism centered around the costs associated with expansion. Estimates of the total costs to bring the Czech Republic, Hungary and Poland ranged as high as $125 billion over a 12-year period and that the new members of the Alliance would have to pay as much as $13 billion each; Ronald E. Powaski, "Joining the March of Folly," *The Bulletin of Atomic Scientists*, vol. 54, no. 1 (January/February 1998), available online at http://www.bullatomicsci.org/issues/1998/jf98/jf98powaski.html. However, as a Congressional Research Service report confirmed, "the issue of costs has now seemingly been put to rest because entry of Poland, the Czech Republic, and Hungary does not seem to have required extra U.S. funds. Most observers believe that the three countries have contributed to stability in Europe, and have made significant political contributions to the alliance in such matters as enhancing NATO's understanding of central and eastern Europe, Russia, and the Balkans, given the history of the new members' involvement with these regions;" Paul E. Gallis, "NATO Enlargement," *CRS Report for Congress*, RS21055 (9 November 2001), 2.

59. A BASIC report asserted that "it was not unreasonable to expect a backlash in Romania, Slovakia and Slovenia when the news of their exclusion from NATO becomes official in Madrid . . . NATO's policy of expansion could backfire. Future Partnership for Peace operations may suffer from a lack of the cohesion . . . after Madrid, central and eastern European countries that are excluded from NATO will be less enthusiastic about PfP operations with partners that make promises and deliver disappointment; Alistar Millar and Tasos Kokkinides, "NATO Expansion and the Excluded Countries: A New Division of Europe," *BASIC Notes* (July 1997), 3.

60. This includes a range of opponents from both the political left and right, including former American Secretary of State Henry Kissinger; Jane M. O. Sharp, "Spreading the Security Blanket," *Bulletin of the Atomic Scientists,*   vol. 54, no. 1 (January/February 1998), available online at http://www.bullatomicsci.org/issues/1998/jf98/jf98powaski.html.

61. Ibid.

62. For instance, during the missions in Balkans, all three of the new members contributed forces and support for the operations. In IFOR/SFOR, the Czech Republic contributed a mechanized infantry battalion and an engineer company which was later reduced to just the mechanized infantry battalion with some 400 soldiers; Hungary deployed a 200-troop engineer battalion; and Poland contributed an airborne infantry battalion of 200 soldiers; Bowman, "Bosnia," 9-10. In KFOR, the Czech Republic deployed a reconnaissance company, numbering 200; Hungary contributed a support battalion with 322 soldiers; and Poland supplied an airborne battalion with 750 troops; Bowman, "Kosovo and Macedonia," 11-12.

63. U.S., Department of State, Bureau of Public Affairs, *The Enlargement of NATO: Why Adding Poland, Hungary and the Czech Republic to NATO Strengthens American National Security*, no. 10533 (February 1998), 14.

64. NATO, NAC, "Membership Action Plan (MAP)," Press Release NAC-S(99)66 (24 April 1999).

65. U.S., State Department, *The Enlargement of NATO*.

66. "NATO Expansion," *The Washington Post* (22 November 2001).

67. Gallis, "NATO Expansion," 4.

68. For an overview of the strengths and weaknesses of each of the candidate states, see Steven Woehrel, Julie Kim and Carl Ek, "NATO Applicant States: A Status Report," *CRS Report for Congress*, RL30168 (2 February 2001).

69. This support is based on the degree of democratization of the Baltic states, their robust participation in peacekeeping operations and the tradition of close relations between some NATO allies and the states. Proponents also argue in favor of inclusion since the United States and most NATO Allies never recognized the Soviet annexation of the three countries; Gallis, "NATO Enlargement," 4.

70. NATO, NAC "Membership Action Plan." In the Alliance's Strategic Concept of 1999, NAC declared that "the Alliance remains open to new members under Article 10 of the Washington Treaty. It expects to extend further invitations in coming years to nations willing and able to assume the responsibilities and obligations of membership, and as NATO determines that the inclusion of these nations would serve the overall political and strategic interests of the Alliance, strengthen its effectiveness and cohesion, and enhance overall European security and stability. To this end, NATO has established a program of activities to assist aspiring countries in their preparations for possible future membership

in the context of its wider relationship with them. No European democratic country whose admission would fulfill the objectives of the Treaty will be excluded from consideration; NATO, NAC, "The Alliance's Strategic Concept."

71. Marian Chiriac, "Bucharest Steps Up NATO Bid," *Balkan Crisis Report*, no. 226 (14 March 2001).

72. Bowman, "Bosnia," 10.

73. Chiriac.

74. These deployments were relatively small. The Baltic states deployed 50 soldiers each in both SFOR and KFOR; Bowman, "Bosnia," 9-10 and Bowman, "Kosovo and Macedonia," 11-12.

75. "Latvian Soldiers to Serve in U.S.–led Force in Kyrgyzstan," *BNS* (31 January 2002).

76. "Lithuanian Peacekeepers to Replace Estonians in Bosnia," *BNS* (31 January 2002).

77. For instance, Estonia initiated plans to purchase new equipment and increased its defense expenditures from 1.8 percent of GDP to 2 percent; Toomas Hendrik lives, "Enlarging NATO: Views From Estonia and Austria," *Euro-Forum*, vol. 3, no. 5 (18 June 2001), available online at http://www.csis.org/europe/euroforum/v3n5.htm.

78. Simon Serfaty, *Stay the Course: European Unity and Atlantic Solidarity*, Washington Papers (Washington, D.C.: CSIS, 1997), 87.

79. The United States, Canada, Czech Republic, Hungary, Iceland, Norway, Poland and Turkey are members of NATO, but not the EU. In addition , Denmark has opted out of the military components of ESDP because of its traditionally pro-Atlanticist policies and its limited defense assets.

80. The Norwegian people have twice rejected membership in the EU during national referendums, in 1972 and then again in 1994.

81. Alain Richard, "Security in the XXI Century–A European Perspective: Statement by Minister of Defense Alain Richard," Washington, D.C. (9 July 2001), available online at http://www.csis.org/europe/sp01Richard.htm.

Bibliography

Documents and Official Sources

Amnesty International. *Crisis Report: Kosovo.* EUR70/48/98 (21 July 98).

Belgium. Ministry of Defense. *Who Are We? Organization of Our Navy.* Brussels: Ministry of Defense, 1997.

Blauuw, Jan Dirk. "WEU's Views on Theatre Missile Defence." Speech, Eilat (12 June 1997).

Commission on Security and Cooperation in Europe (CSCE). "Azerbaijan and Armenia." *Report on Armenia's Parliamentary Elections and Constitutional Referendum.* Washington, D.C.: CSCE, 1995.

EU. "Declaration by the Presidency on Behalf of the European Union: Massacres in Algeria." Press Release (5 January 1998).

_____. *Eurostat* (various editions).

_____. *Maastricht Treaty.* Single European Act. "Provisions on a Common Foreign and Security Policy." Title V, Article J.4 (1991).

_____. "Populations and Social Conditions: Migration Between the Mediterranean Basin and the EU in 1995." *Eurostat.* No. 3/98 (March 1998).

_____. "Step Forward in Euro-Mediterranean Statistical Cooperation." *Eurostat.* No. 397 (15 April 1997).

_____. "Unemployment in EU Regions." *Eurostat.* No. 7598 (24 September 1998).

EU. Commission of the European Communities (CEC). "EC Trade with Central and Eastern. Europe." *The European Economy.* Brussels: OOPEC, 1993.

_____. *European Economy: The European Community as a World Trade Partner, 1993.* Brussels: CEC, 1993.

_____. *Hungarian Foreign Trade. Statistics in Focus: External Trade.* No. 5. Brussels: OOPEC, 1997.

_____. *The Czech Republic's Foreign Trade. Statistics in Focus: External Trade.* No. 7. Brussels: OOPEC, 1997.

EU. European Commission. *Annual Report on Humanitarian Aid, 1995.* Brussels: European Commission, 1996.

_____. *1997 Annual Economic Report.* COM(97)27. Brussels: OOPEC, 1997.

_____. "KONVER (1993-1997)." *Guide to Community Initiatives.* Brussels: EC, 1998.

EU. European Council. "Corfu Summit." *Agence Europe.* NX 6260 (June 1994).

_____. *Declaration of the European Council on Strengthening the Common European Policy on Security and Defense.* NR 122/99 (6 March 1999).

_____. *Press Releases and Speeches* (various editions).

_____. *Proposal for a Council Regulation Creating Rapid Reaction Facility* (11 December 1999).

EU. Presidency. *Summit Conclusions* (various summits and conferences).

Federal Republic of Germany. Federal Press Office. "Eurocorps Will Strengthen European Pillar of NATO." Press release (22 July, 1992).

Federal Republic of Germany. *Government Declaration by the German Federal Chancellor, Dr. Konrad Adenauer, Before the German Bundestag on 20 October 1953.* Bonn: Press and Information Office, 1953.

Federal Republic of Germany. Ministry of Defense. *Fact Sheet: First German Netherlands Corps 1(GE/NE) Corps.* Munster: 1 (GE/NE) Corps, 1994.

Federal Republic of Germany. Office of Press and Information. Helmut Kohl and Jacques Chirac, letter to John Bruton. Dublin, 13 December 1996. Press Release no. 30487 (13 December 1996).

_____. Helmut Kohl, Speech Given on 3 November 1997 in Berlin. Press Release no. 19621 (3 November 1997).

France. Institut National de la Statisque et des Études Économiques (INSEE). *L'Économie française-édition 1998-1999.* Abridged English ed. Paris: INSEE, 1998.

France. Ministry of Defense. *White Paper on Defense, 1994.* Paris: SIRPA, 1994.

France. Ministry of Foreign Affairs. Press releases (various editions).

Hansard's Parliamentary Debates (various editions).

NATO. *The Alliance's New Strategic Concept* (8 November 1991).

_____. *The Alliance's Strategic Concept.* NAC-S(99)65 (24 April 1999).

_____. *Basic Document: The Study on Enlargement* (1995).

_____. *Basic Fact Sheets* (various editions).

_____. *Declaration of the Heads of State and Government Participating in the Meeting of the North Atlantic Council Held at NATO Headquarters.* Brussels (11 January 1994).

_____. *Founding Act on Mutual Relations, Cooperation and Security between the Russian Federation and the North Atlantic Treaty Organization.* Brussels (1997).

_____. *Membership Action Plan.* NAC-S(99)66 (24 April 1999).

_____. *NATO Handbook* (various editions).

_____. *The North Atlantic Treaty.* Washington, D.C. (4 April, 1949).

_____. Press releases and statements (various editions).

NATO. NAA. *Nuclear Proliferation.* AM 310 STC (95) 10 (October 1995).

_____. Sub-Committee on the Mediterranean Basin. *Frameworks For Cooperation in the Mediterranean.* AM 259 CC/MB (95) 7 (October 1995).

_____. Sub-Committee on the Mediterranean Basin. *Interim Report of the Sub-Committee on the Mediterranean Basin.* AM 87 CC/MB (95) 5 (May 1995).

_____. Sub-Committee on the Southern Region. *Draft Interim Report.* AM 295 PC/SR(95) 2 (October 1995).

NATO. NAC. *Alliance Policy Framework on Proliferation of Weapons of Mass Destruction.* M-NAC-1(94) 45 (9 June 1994).

_____. *Declaration of the Heads of State and Government Participating in the Meeting of the North Atlantic Council.* M-1(94)3 (11 January 1994).

_____. Final Communiques from various conferences and summits.

_____. *Partnership for Peace: Invitation Issued by the Heads of State and Government Participating in the Meeting of the North Atlantic Council.* M-1(94)2 (10 January 1994).

NATO. NACC. *Work Plan for Dialogue and Cooperation 1993 Issued at the Meeting of the North Atlantic Cooperation Council.* M-NACC-2(92)110 (18 December 1992).

NATO. Public Information Advisor. "Further Progress on Military Cooperation Between NATO and Russia." Press Release 10.98 (22 June 1998).

NATO. SACEUR. *Annual Report of the Supreme Allied Commander, Europe, 1953* (30 May, 1953).

_____. *First Annual Report.* Brussels: NATO, 1951.

Netherlands. Ministry of Defense. *Admiral Benelux.* Dan Helder: Dutch Ministry of Defense, 1997.

Organization for Security and Cooperation in Europe. *Chairman's Summary: Decisions of the Budapest Ministerial Council Meeting.* Vienna: OSCE, 1996.

_____. *Topic A: European Defense Identity.* Vienna: OSCE, 1996.

Perry, William J. Speech, Moscow (17 October 1996).

Robinson, Mary. *Statement by the United Nations High Commissioner for Human Rights On the Situation in Kosovo.* HR/98/14 (9 June 1998).

Russia, the United Kingdom, and the United States. *Joint Statement on Biological Weapons by the Governments of the United Kingdom, the United States and the Russian Federation.* Moscow (11 September, 1992).

Speeches (various authors) available online at http://www.nato.int.

Switzerland. "Humanitarian Aspects of Peacekeeping: Discussion Paper Submitted by Switzerland at the EAPC PMSC Ad Hoc Group on Cooperation and Peacekeeping" (11 September 1998).

Truman, Harry S. "Statement on June 27, 1950." U.S. Department of State Bulletin, no. 22 (July 3, 1950).

U.K. Ministry of Defense. *Defense Diversification: Getting the Most Out of Defence Technology* CM3861. London: HMSO, 1998.

_____. *Statement on the Defense Estimates* (various years).

UN. *Concluding Observations of the Committee on the Rights of the Child: Algeria.* CRC/C/15/Add 76 (18 June 1997).

_____. *Report of the Secretary-General of the United Nations.* S/1995/222/Corr. 1 (29 March 1995).

_____. "Secretary-General Deplores Continuing Loss of Life in Algeria." Press Release SG/SM/6434 (12 January 1998).

UN. UNSCOM. "UN Says All Iraqi Chemical Weapons Destroyed." Pol406/94062306 (23 June 1994).

U.S.–E.U. *Joint U.S.–E.U. Ministerial Statement on Combating Terrorism.* Washington, D.C. (20 September 2001).

U.S. Arms Control and Disarmament Agency. *Annual Report: 1998.* Washington, D.C.: GPO, 1997.

_____. *Annual Report to the President and Congress.* Washington, D.C.: GPO, 1996.

_____. *CTR Program: Accomplishments.* Washington, D.C.: GPO, 1998.

_____. *World Military Expenditures and Arms Transfers , 1997.* Washington, D.C.: GPO, 1998.

_____. *World Military Expenditures and Arms Transfers, 1995.* Washington, D.C.: GPO, 1996.

U.S. Committee for Refugees. *World Refugee Survey, 1997.* Washington, D.C.: Immigration and Refugees Services of America, 1997.

U.S. Congress. "For a Strong and Free World." *Quarterly Reports to Congress on the Mutual Security Act.* No. 1. Washington, D.C.: 1951.

U.S. Congress. Senate Committee on Governmental Affairs. William C. Potter. "Nuclear Leakage From the Post-Soviet States." Oral presentation before the Permanent Subcommittee on Investigations (13 March 1996).

U.S. Congressional Research Service (various reports and issue briefs).

U.S. Department of Commerce. *Historical Statistics of the United States: Colonial Times to 1970.* Washington, D.C.: GPO, 1975.

U.S. Department of Defense. *100 Companies Receiving the Largest Volume of Prime Contract Awards. Washington,* D.C.: GPO, 1995.

_____. *Arms Control: Status of U.S.-Russian Agreements and the Chemical Weapons Convention.* NSIAD-94-136. Washington, D.C.: GAO, 1994.

_____. *Defense Almanac* (various editions).

_____. *Fact Sheet: Biological Warfare Threat Analysis.* EUR 508 (20 February 1998).

_____. "Iraq's Weapons of Mass Destruction Programs." *U.S. Government White Paper, 3050.* EUR 205. Washington, D.C.: GPO, 1998.

_____. *ManTech: Program Funding Overview.* Washington, D.C.: GPO, 1998.

_____. *The 'New Look' in Defense Planning: Address by the Chairman of the Joint Chiefs of Staff Before the National Press Club.* Washington, D.C., December 14, 1953, Press Release 1163. Washington, D.C.: GPO, 1953.

_____. "NATO Nations Hold Talks to Plan for 21st Century Security" Press Release, no. 593-98 (13 November 1998).

_____. Press and news releases and statements (various editions).

_____. *Semiannual Report of the Secretary of Defense, 1950.* Washington, D.C.: GPO, 1950.

_____. *Weapons of Mass Destruction: DOD Report Accounting for Cooperative Threat Reduction Assistance Needs Improvement.* NSIAD-95-191. Washington, D.C.: GAO, 1995.

_____. *Weapons of Mass Destruction: Reducing the Threat From the Former Soviet Union.* NSIAD-95-7. Washington, D.C.: GAO, 1995.

_____. *Weapons of Mass Destruction: Reducing the Threat From the Former Soviet Union: An Update.* NSIAD-95-165. Washington, D.C.: GAO, 1995.

U.S. Department of Defense. Defense Science Board. *Achieving an Innovative Support Structure for 21st Century Military Superiority.* Washington, D.C.: GPO, 1996.

U.S. Department of Defense. Office of the Secretary of Defense. *Proliferation–Threat and Response, January 2001.* Washington, D.C.: Department of Defense, January 2001.

U.S. Department of Energy. Energy Information Agency. *International Petroleum Statistics Report: 1998.* Washington, D.C.: GPO 1998.

_____. Energy Information Agency. *International Energy Outlook: 1996, With Projections to the Year 2000.* Washington, D.C.: GPO, 1996.

_____. Energy Information Agency. *Persian Gulf Oil Export Fact Sheet* (February 1998).

192   *All for One*

U.S.   Department of State.   Bureau of Public Affairs.   *Background Notes: Libya.* Washington, D.C.: GPO, 1994.

_____. "Communique of the U.S., U.K. and French Foreign Ministers" (19 September 1950). *Department of State Bulletin,* no. 23 (2 October 1950).

_____. "Country Reports: Azerbaijan." In *Implementation of the Helsinki Final Act: The President's 35th OSCE Report to the Congress.* Washington, D.C.: GPO, 1997.

_____. "Country Reports: The Former Yugoslav Republic of Macedonia." *Implementation of the Helsinki Final Act: The President's 35th OSCE Report to the Congress.* Washington, D.C.: GPO, 1997.

_____. *Defense Trade Security Initiative Promotes Cooperation and Greater Technology Sharing With U.S. Coalition Partners* (26 May 2000).

_____. *Department of State Bulletin,* no. 25 (8 October 1951).

_____. *Documents on Germany, 1944-1985,* no. 9446. Washington, D.C.: Bureau of Public Affairs, 1986.

_____. *The Enlargement of NATO: Why Adding Poland, Hungary and the Czech Republic to NATO Strengthens American National Security.* No. 10533 (February 1998).

_____. *Facts Sheets, Bulletins and Press Releases* (various editions).

_____. "Mutual Defense Assistance Act." *Department of State Bulletin,* no. 22 (6 February, 1950).

_____. *New Export Exemption for Closest Ally to Promote Defense Security* (26 May 2000).

_____. "The New Framework for the Mutual Security Program: Report to Congress on the Mutual Security Program, August 17, 1953." *Report to Congress on the Mutual Security Program for the Six Months Ended June 30, 1953.* Washington, D.C.: Foreign Operations Administration, 1953.

_____. *Patterns of Global Terrorism: 1997.* No. 10535. Washington, D.C.: GPO, 1998.

_____. *Patterns of Global Terrorism: 1996.* No. 9525. Washington, D.C.: GPO, 1996.

_____. *Statement by the Secretary of State* (various editions).

U.S.   House of Representatives.   House International Relations Committee. "Developments in the Middle East." Statement by Robert H. Pelletreau, Assistant Secretary for Near Eastern Affairs (25 September 1996).

_____. C. Bruce Tarter, testimony. "Stemming the Proliferation of Nuclear Weapons and Other Weapons of Mass Destruction." *The Department of Energy's Budget Request for FY 1996: Hearing of the Subcommittee on Military Procurement.* Washington, D.C.: GPO, 1995.

_____. House Foreign Relations Committee. "Mutual Defense Assistance Act of 1949." Hearings on H.R. 5748 and H.R. 5895, 81st Congress. Washington: GPO, 1949.

_____. House International Relations Committee. "Containing Iran: Statement by Peter Tarnoff, Under Secretary of State for Political Affairs" (9 November, 1995).

U.S.   Office of the High Commissioner for Germany, Office of the Executive Secretary. *History of the Allied High Commission for Germany.* Washington, D.C.: GPO, 1951.

U.S.   Office of Technology Assessment.   *Defense Conversion: Redirecting   R & D.* Washington, D.C.: GPO, 1993.

U.S.   Senate.   Committee on Appropriations.   *Hearings, Department of Defense Appropriations for 1953* (Washington, D.C.: GPO, 1953).

U.S. Senate. Committee on Foreign Relations. *Start II Treaty: Report.* Washington, D.C.: GPO, 1995.

U.S. White House. *Arms Control and Nonproliferation: The Clinton Administration Record.* Press Release (20 May 1996).

_____. *Fissile Material Production Cutoff Treaty (FMCT) Negotiations.* Press Release (27 March 1997).

WEU. Assembly of the WEU. *Parliamentary Co-operation in the Mediterranean.* WEU Document 1485 (6 November 1995).

_____. *The State of Affairs in Disarmament (CFE, Nuclear Disarmament).* WEU 1590. Brussels: WEU, 1997.

_____. *WEAG: The Course to be Followed.* 1483 (6 November 1995).

WEU. Council of Ministers. *European Security: A Common Concept of the 27 WEU Countries.* Brussels: WEU, 1995.

_____. *Lisbon Declaration* (15 May 1995).

_____. *The Role of the Western European Union and its Relationship With the European Union* (10 December 1991).

_____. *Petersburg Declaration* (19 June 1992).

WEU. Defense Committee. *Draft Recommendation on European Armed Forces.* WEU Document 1468 (12 June 1995).

WEU. International Secretariat. *Structure and Functions: European Security and Defense Identity (ESDI) and Combined Joint Task Forces (CJTF)* (October 1995).

_____. *The Situation in the Former Yugoslavia.* WEU 1467. Brussels: WEU, 1995.

_____. *Transatlantic Cooperation on European Anti-Missile Defence, Part I.* WEU 1435 (4 November 1994).

_____. *Transatlantic Cooperation on European Anti-Missile Defence, Part II.* WEU 1435 (9 November 1994).

Newspapers and Serials

Aerotech News and Review (Available online). September 1998 - January 2002.

Arms Control Today (Available online). June 1996 - June 1998.

Associated Press (Available online). 6 September 1998 - 28 October 1998.

The Australian (Sydney). December 1998 - January 2002.

Balkan Crisis Report (Available online). January 1999 - January 2002.

Baltic News Service (BNS). January 2002.

BASIC Papers and Reports (various editions).

BBC News (Available online). December 1998 - January 2002.

Bulletin of the Atomic Scientists (Available online). January 1997 - January 2002.

CET On-Line (Available online). May 1996 - September 1996.

Christian Science Monitor. October 1999 - January 2002.

CNN Interactive (Available online). May 1998 - January 1999.

Daily Telegraph (London). August 1997 - January 2002.

Defence Systems Daily (Available online). June 1997 - January 2002.

Defense News (Available online). January 1996 - January 2002.

DefenseLink (Available online). June 1997 - January 2002.

The Economist (London). January 1995 - June 1996.

Euro-Forum (Available online). June 2001.

Europe (Brussels). June 2000 - June 2002.

FBIS: EEU (Washington). August 1996 - September 1998.

Financial Times (London). September 1996 - January 2002.

The Guardian (Available online). January 2000 - January 2002.

Hamburg Die Woche. (Hamburg). June 2000.

ICT News (Available online). January 1997 - January 1999.

International Herald Tribune (Chicago). September 1998 - January 2002.

Jane's Defence Contracts. June 1997.

Jane's Defence Weekly. June 1994 - January 1999.

Jane's Intelligence Review. September 1994 - June 1995.

Jane's International Defence Review. June 1994 - January 1999.

Jane's Military Exercise & Training Monitor. January 1996.

Jane's Strategic Weapons. May 1995 - September 1995.

La Monde (Paris). March 1997 - January 2002.

National Interest. Spring 2000 - Spring 2001.

NATO Review (various editions).

New York Times (New York). March 1997 - January 2002.

Reuters (Available online). January 2002.

Sydney Morning Herald (Sydney). May 1998 - January 2002.

Wall Street Journal (New York). 16 June 1987 - 21 January 1988; 6 June 1994 - 2 January 2002.

The Washington Post (Washington). September 1998 - January 2002.

The Washington Times (Washington). September 1994 - January 2002.

Monographs

Adenauer, Konrad. *Memoirs, 1945-1966.* Chicago: Henry Regnery, 1966.

Aron, Raymond. *Peace and War: A Theory of International Relations.* Malabar: Robert E. Krieger, 1966.

Avery, Graham, and Cameron Fraser. *The Enlargement of the European Union.* Sheffield: Sheffield Academic, 1998.

Axelrod, Robert. *The Emergence of Cooperation.* New York: Basic Books, 1984.

Bacon, Robert and James Brown Scott, *The Military and Colonial Policy of the United States, Addresses and Reports by Elihu Root.* Cambridge: Harvard, 1916.

Baldwin, David. *Economic Statecraft.* Princeton: Princeton University, 1985.

Baldwin, David, ed. *Neorealism and Neoliberalism: The Contemporary Debate.* New York: Columbia University, 1993.

Baylis, John. *Anglo-American Relations Since 1939: The Enduring Alliance.* New York: St. Martin's, 1997.

Berkeley Planning Associates. *Evaluation of Defense Conversion Adjustment Demonstration.* Oakland: Berkeley Planning Associates, 1995.

Bertram, Christoph. *Europe in the Balance: Securing the Peace Won in the Cold War.* Washington, D.C.: Carnegie Endowment, 1995.

Bloed, Arie, and Ramses A. Wessel, eds. *The Changing Functions of the Western European Union (WEU): Introduction and Basic Documents.* London: Martinus Nijhoff Publishers, 1994.

Bluth, Christoph, Emil Kirchner and James Sperling, eds. *The Future of European Security.* Dartmouth: Aldershot, 1995.

Bonkovsky, Frederick. *International Norms and National Policy.* Grand Rapids, MI.: Eerdmens, 1980.

Bonn International Center for Conversion (BICC). *Conversion Survey 1998: Global Disarmament, Defense Industry Consolidation and Conversion.* Bonn: BICC, 1998.

Boutros-Ghali, Boutros. *An Agenda for Peace: Preventative Diplomacy, Peacemaking and Peacekeeping.* New York: UN, 1992.

Bowers, Maria. *The Disposal of Surplus Chemical Weapons.* Bonn: Bonn International Center for Conversion, 1995.

Brenner, Michael, ed. *Multilateralism and Western Security.* New York: St. Martin's, 1995.

Bridge, F.R. and Roger Bullen. *The Great Powers and the European States System, 1815-1914.* New York: Longman, 1980.

Bronstone, Adam. *European Union–United States Security Relations: Transatlantic Tensions and the Theory of International Relations.* New York: St. Martin's, 1997.

Brown, Michael E. *European Security: The Defining Debates.* Cambridge: MIT, 1998.

Brown, Michael, Sean M. Lynn-Jones and Steven E. Miller, eds. *The Perils of Anarchy: Contemporary Realism and International Security.* Cambridge: MIT, 1995.

Bull, Hedley. *The Anarchical Society: A Study of Order in World Politics.* New York: Columbia University, 1977.

Burr, Robert N. *By Reason or Force: Chile and the Balancing of Power in South America, 1830-1905.* Berkeley: University of California, 1974.

Cahen, Alfred. *The Western European Union and NATO: Building a European Defense Identity Within the Context of Atlantic Solidarity.* London: Brassey's, 1989.

Calleo, David P. *The Atlantic Fantasy: The U.S., NATO, and Europe.* Baltimore: Johns Hopkins, 1970.

_____. *Beyond American Hegemony: The Future of the Western Alliance.* New York: Basic Books, 1987.

Camilleri, Joseph, and Jim Falk. *The End of Sovereignty?* Hants, U.K.: Edward Elgar, 1992.

Canadian Security Intelligence Service (CSIS). *Smuggling Special Nuclear Materials, Commentary.* No. 57. Ottawa: CSIS, 1995.

Carpenter, Ted Galen, and Barbara Conroy, eds. *NATO Enlargement: Illusions and Reality.* Washington, D.C.: CATO Institute, 1998..

Carr, E.H. *The Twenty Years' Crisis, 1919-1939: An Introduction to the Study of International Relations.* London: Macmillan, 1939. Reprint, London: MacMillan, 1946.

Chernoff, Fred. *After Bipolarity: The Vanishing Threat, Theories of Cooperation and the Future of the Atlantic Alliance.* Ann Arbor: University of Michigan, 1994.

Cipolla, Carlo M. *Before the Industrial Revolution: European Society and Economy, 1000-1700.* New York: W. W. Norton, 1994.

Clark, Wesley. *Waging Modern War: Bosnia, Kosovo, and the Future of Combat.* Washington, D.C.: PublicAffairs, 2001.

Cordesman, Anthony S. *Defending America: Terrorist Organizations and States and Weapons of Mass Destruction.* Washington, D.C.: CSIS, 24 September 2001.

Cordesman, Anthony S., and Ahmed S. Hashim. *Iran: Dilemmas of Dual Containment.* Boulder: Westview, 1997.

_____. *Iraq: Sanctions and Beyond.* Boulder: Westview, 1997.

Cornish, Paul, Peter van Ham, and Joachim Krause. *Europe and the Challenge of Proliferation.* Chaillot Papers, no. 24. Paris: Institute for Security Studies of the WEU, 1996.

Costigliola, Frank. *France and the United States: the Cold War Alliance Since World War II.* New York: Twayne, 1992.

Craig, Theodore. *Call for Fire: Sea Combat in the Falklands and the Gulf War.* London: John Murray, 1995.

Curtis, Michael. *Western European Integration.* New York: Harper & Row, 1965.

Dean, Jonathon. *Ending Europe's War's: The Continuing Search for Peace and Security.* New York: Priority, 1995.

DeGrasse, Jr., Robert. *Military Expansion, Economic Decline.* New York: M. E. Sharpe, 1983.

Downs, George W., ed. *Collective Security Beyond the Cold War.* Ann Arbor: University of Michigan, 1994.

Drumbell, John. *A Special Relationship: Anglo-American Relations in the Cold War and After.* London: Palgrave, 2000.

Duff, Andrew, John Pinder, and Roy Price, eds. *Maastricht and Beyond: Building the European Union.* New York: Routledge, 1994.

Duffield, John S. *Power Rules: The Evolution of NATO's Conventional Force Posture.* Stanford: Stanford University, 1995.

Duke, Simon. *The Burdensharing Debate: A Reassessment.* New York: St. Martin's, 1993.

_____. *The New European Security Disorder.* New York: St. Martin's, 1994.

Dunn, J., ed. *The Economic Limits to Modern Politics.* Cambridge: Cambridge University, 1990.

Eisenhower, Dwight D. *Mandate for Change: The White House Years 1953-1956.* New York: Doubleday, 1963.

Falk, Richard, Samuel S. Kim, and Saul Mendlovitz, eds. *Toward a Just World Order.* Boulder: Westview, 1982.

Feld, Werner J. *The Future of European Security and Defense Policy.* Boulder: Lynne Reiner, 1993.

Flynn, Gregory, ed. *Remaking the Hexagon: The New France in the New Europe.* Boulder: Westview 1995.

Friend, Julius. *The Linchpin: Franco-German Relations, 1950-1990.* New York: Praeger, 1991.

Fuller, Graham E., and Ian O. Lesser, *A Sense of Siege: The Geopolitics of Islam and the West.* Boulder: Westview, 1995.

Furdson, Edward. *The European Defense Community: A History.* London: MacMillan, 1980.

Gaddis, John Lewis. *The Long Peace: Inquiries into the History of the Cold War.* New York: Oxford University, 1989.
_____. *The United States and the End of the Cold War.* New York: Oxford University, 1992.
_____. *The United States and the Origins of the Cold War, 1941-1947.* New York: Columbia University, 1972.
_____. *We Now Know: Rethinking Cold War History.* New York: Oxford University, 1998.
Gardner, Hal. *Dangerous Crossroads: Europe, Russia, and the Future of NATO.* Westport: Greenwood, 1997.
Gedman, Jeffery, ed. *European Integration and American Interests: What the New Europe Really Means for the United States.* Washington, D.C.: American Enterprise Institute, 1997.
George, Alexander. *Forceful Persuasion: Coercive Diplomacy as an Alternative to War.* Washington, D.C.: United States Institute of Peace, 1991.
Gilpin, Robert. *War and Change in World Politics.* New York: Cambridge University, 1981.
Goodby, James. *Europe Undivided: The New Logic of Peace in U.S.-Russian Relations.* Washington, D.C.: U.S. Institute of Peace, 1998.
Gordon, Philip H. *A Certain Idea of France.* New York: St. Martin's, 1993.
_____. *France, Germany and the Western Alliance.* Boulder: Westview, 1995.
_____. *French Security Policy After the Cold War: Continuity, Change, and Implications for the United States.* Santa Monica: RAND, 1992.
Gowa, Joanne. *Allies, Adversaries and International Trade.* Princeton: Princeton University, 1994.
Grant, Robert P. *The Changing Franco-American Security Relationship: New Directions for NATO and European Defense Cooperation.* Arlington, VA: US-Crest, 1993.
Grapin, Jacqueline, ed. *Europe and the US: Partners in Defense.* Washington, D.C.: European Institute, 1998.
Grieco, Joseph M. *Cooperation Among Nations: Europe, America and Non-Tariff Barriers to Trade.* Ithaca: Cornell University, 1990.
Grilli, Enzo. *The European Community and the Developing Countries.* New York: Cambridge, 1993.
Grimmett, Richard. *Conventional Arms Transfers to Developing Nations, 1988-1995.* Washington, D.C.: CRS, 1996.
Guay, Terrence. *At Arm's Length: The European Union and Europe's Defence Industry.* New York: St. Martin's, 1997.
Gulick, Edward Vose. *Europe's Classical Balance of Power.* Washington, D.C.: AHA, 1955.
Haas, Ernst B. *Beyond the Nation-State: Functionalism and International Organization.* Stanford: Stanford University, 1964.
Haftendorn, Helga and Christian Tuschhoff, eds. *America and Europe in an Era of Change.* Boulder: Westview, 1993.

Haglund, David G. *Alliance Within the Alliance? Franco-German Military Cooperation and the European Pillar of Defense.* Boulder: Westview, 1991.

Haglund, David G., ed. *From Europhoria to Hysteria: Western European Security After the Cold War.* Boulder: Westview, 1993.

Haig, Simonian. *The Privileged Partnership: Franco-German Relations in the European Community, 1969-1984.* Oxford: Clarendon, 1985.

Hanrieder, Wolfram F. *Germany, America, Europe–Forty Years of German Foreign Policy.* New Haven: Yale University, 1989.

Harrison, Michael. *The Reluctant Ally: France and Atlantic Security.* Baltimore: Johns Hopkins, 1981.

Harrison, Michael M., and Mark G. McDonough. *Negotiations on the French Withdrawal From NATO: FPI Case Studies, No. 5.* Washington, D.C.: Johns Hopkins, 1987.

Herz, John. *Political Realism and Political Idealism.* Chicago: University of Chicago, 1951.

Heuser, Beatrice. *Transatlantic Relations: Sharing Ideals and Costs.* London: Royal Institute of International Affairs, 1996.

Hill, Christopher, ed. *The Actors in Europe's Foreign Policy.* New York: Routledge, 1996.

Hoffman, Stanley. *The State of War.* New York: Praeger, 1965.

Hogan, Michael J., ed. *The End of the Cold War: Its Meaning and Implications.* New York: Cambridge University, 1992.

Holmes, John W., ed. *Maelstrom: The United States, Southern Europe and the Challenges of the Mediterranean.* Cambridge: World Peace Foundation 1995.

Holsti, Ole, Randolph Siverson and Alexander L. George, eds. *Change in the International System.* Boulder: Westview, 1980.

Hoogland, Steven J. *Peace Operations; Are We Getting Warm Yet?* Carlisle Barracks, PA: U.S. Army War College, 1997.

Human Rights Watch. *Democracy Derailed: Violations in the May 26, 1996 Albanian Elections.* New York: Human Rights Watch, 1996.

International Institute for Strategic Studies (IISS). *The Military Balance* (various editions).

————. *Strategic Survey* (various editions).

Ireland, Timothy. *Creating the Atlantic Alliance: The Origins of the North Atlantic Treaty Organization.* Wesport: Greenwood, 1981.

Jackson, Robert, ed. *Europe in Transition: The Management of Security After the Cold War.* New York: Praeger, 1992.

Jervis, Robert. Perception and Misperception in International Politics. Princeton: Princeton University, 1976.

Joll, James. *The Origins of the First World War.* New York: Longmans 1984.

Jones, Peter. *America and the British Labour Party: The "Special Relationship" at Work.* New York: Taurus Academic Studies, 1997.

Kahler, Miles. *Regional Futures and Transatlantic Economic Relations.* New York: Council on Foreign Relations, 1995.

Kaplan, Lawrence. *A Community of Interests: NATO and the Military Assistance Program, 1948-1951.* Washington, D.C.: Office of the Secretary of Defense Historical Office, 1980.

Kaplan, Morton. *System and Process in International Politics.* New York: Wiles, 1957.

Karp, Regina, ed. *Security With Nuclear Weapons? Different Perspectives on National Security.* Boston: Boston Book, 1991.

Katzenstein, Peter J. *Small States and World Markets*. Ithaca: Cornell University, 1985.
_____, ed., *Between Power and Plenty: Foreign Economic Policy and Advanced Industrial States*. Madison: University of Wisconsin, 1978.
Kay, Sean. *NATO and the Future of European Security*. New York: Rowman & Littlefield, 1998.
Kelleher, Catherine McArdle. *The Future of European Security: An Interim Assessment*. Washington, D.C.: Brookings Institute, 1995.
Kemp, Geoffrey, and Robert E. Harkavy. *Strategic Geography and the Changing Middle East*. Washington, D.C.: Brookings Institute, 1997.
Kenen, Peter B. *Economic and Monetary Union in Europe: Moving Beyond Maastricht*. Cambridge: Cambridge University, 1995.
Kennedy, Paul. *The Rise and Fall of the Great Powers: Economic Change and Military Conflict From 1500 to 2000*. New York: Random House, 1987.
Keohane, Robert O. *After Hegemony: Cooperation and Discord in the World Political Economy*. Princeton: Princeton University, 1984.
Keohane, Robert O., ed. *International Institutions and State Power: Essays in International Relations Theory*. Boulder: Westview, 1989.
_____. *Neorealism and its Critics*. New York: Columbia University, 1986.
Keohane, Robert O., and Joseph S. Nye. *Power and Interdependence*. 2d. ed. New York: Harper Collins, 1989.
Keohane, Robert O., Joseph S. Nye and Stanley Hoffman, eds. *After the Cold War: International Institutions and State Strategies in Europe, 1989-1991*. Cambridge: Harvard University, 1993.
Keohane, Robert O., Peter Haas, and Marc Levy, eds. *Institutions for the Earth: Sources of Effective International Environmental Protection*. Cambridge: MIT, 1993.
Kerry, Richard J. *The Star-Spangled Mirror: America's Image of Itself and the World*. Savage, MD: Rowman & Littlefield, 1990.
Khalilzad, Zalmay, Ian O. Lesser and F. Stephen Larrabee. *The Future of Turkish-Western Relations: Toward a Strategic Plan*. Santa Monica: RAND, 2000.
Kingsley, Jonathon and John Mawson. *British Regionalism and Devolution: The Challenges of State Reform and European Integration*. London: Kingsley, 1997.
Kramer, Steven P. *Does France Still Count?: The Role of France in the New Europe*. Westport: Praeger, 1994.
Krasner, Stephen, ed. *International Regimes*. Ithaca: Cornell University, 1983.
Krippendorf, Ekkehart and Volker Rittberger, eds. *The Foreign Policy of West Germany: Formation and Contents*. London: Sage, 1980.
Kurz, Heinz, ed. *United Germany and the New Europe*. Brookfield, VT: Edwards Elger, 1993.
Laird, Robbin. *The Europeanization of the Alliance*. Boulder: Westview, 1991.
_____. *French Security Policy in Transition: Dynamics of Continuity and Change*. Washington, D.C.: National Defense University, 1995.
Laird, Robbin, ed. *French Security Policy: From Independence to Interdependence*. Boulder: Westview, 1986.

Lansford, Tom. *Evolution and Devolution: The Dynamics of Sovereignty and Security in Post-Cold War Europe.* Aldershot: Ashgate, 2000.

Leffler, Melvyn, and David Painter, eds. *Origins of the Cold War: An International History.* New York: Routledge, 1994.

Lesperance, Wayne and Tom Lansford, ed. *Teaching Old Dogs New Tricks: International Organizations in the 21st Century.* Needham Heights, MA: Pearson, 2000.

Lesser, Ian O. *NATO Looks South: New Challenges and New Strategies in the Mediterranean.* Santa Monica: RAND, 2000.

_____. *Security in North Africa: Internal and External Challenges.* Santa Monica: RAND, 1993.

Lesser, Ian O., Jerrold D. Green, F. Stephen Larrabee and Michele Zanini. *The Future of NATO's Mediterranean Initiative: Evolution and Next Steps.* Santa Monica: RAND, 2000.

Levine, Robert A., ed. *Transition and Turmoil in the Atlantic Alliance.* New York: Crane Russak, 1992.

Maier, Charles S., ed. *The Cold War in Europe.* New York: Markus Wiener, 1991.

Mandlebaum, Michael. *The Dawn of Peace in Europe.* New York: Twentieth-Century Fund, 1996.

Marolda, Edward J., and Robert J. Schneller. *Shield and Sword: The United States Navy and the Persian Gulf War.* Washington, D.C.: Naval Institute Press, 1998.

Marsh, David. *Germany and Europe.* London: Heineman, 1994.

Mazzucelli, Collette. *France and Germany at Maastricht: Politics and Negotiations to Create the European Union.* New York: Garland, 1997.

McCarthy, Patrick, ed. *France-Germany, 1983-1993: The Struggle to Cooperate.* New York: St. Martin's, 1993.

McInnes, Colin, ed. *Security and Strategy in the New Europe.* New York: Routledge, 1992.

McKenzie, Mary M., and Peter H. Loedel. *The Promise and Reality of European Security Cooperation.* New York: Praeger, 1995.

Miall, Hugh, ed. *Redefining Europe: New Patterns of Conflict and Cooperation.* London: Royal Institute of International Affairs, 1994.

Miller, Linda B., and Michael Joseph Smith, eds. *Ideals and Ideals: Essays on Politics in Honor of Stanley Hoffman.* Boulder: Westview, 1992.

Milward, Alan. *The European Rescue of the Nation-State.* Berkeley: University of California, 1992.

Moens, Alexander, and Christopher Anstis, eds. *Disconcerted Europe: The Search for a New Security Architecture.* Boulder: Westview, 1994.

Montgomery, Bernard Law. *The Memoirs of Field-Marshall Montgomery.* New York: World Publishing, 1958.

Morgenthau, Hans J. *Politics Among Nations: The Struggle for Power and Peace.* New York: Knopf, 1948.

Muller, Harald, ed.. *A Survey of European Nuclear Policy, 1985-1987.* London: Macmillan, 1989.

Mushaben, Joyce M. *From Post-War to Post-Wall Generations: Changing Attitudes Towards the National Question and NATO in the Federal Republic of Germany.* Boulder: Westview, 1997.

Newman, Michael. *Democracy, Sovereignty and the European Union.* New York: St. Martin's, 1996.

Nincic, Miroslav, and Peter Wallensteen, eds. *Dilemmas of Economic Coercion: Sanctions in World Politics.* New York: Praeger, 1983.

North, Douglass C., and Robert Paul Thomas. *The Rise of the Western World–A New Economic History.* New York: Cambridge University, 1973.

Olson, Jr., Mancur. *The Logic of Collective Action: Public Goods and the Theory of Groups.* Cambridge: Harvard University, 1965.

Olson, William C., and A.J.R. Groom. *International Relations Then and Now: Origins and Trends in Interpretation.* London: Harper Collins, 1991.

Osgood, Robert. *NATO: The Entangling Alliance.* Chicago: University of Chicago, 1962.

Ovendale, Ritchie. *The English-Speaking Alliance: Britain, the United States, the Dominions, and the Cold War, 1945-1951.* London: G. Allen & Unwin, 1985.

Oye, Kenneth A., ed. *Cooperation Under Anarchy.* Princeton: Princeton University, 1986.

Quester, George. *Offense and Defense in the International System.* New York: John Wiley & Sons, 1977.

Rappaport, Anatol, and Albert Chammah. *Prisoner's Dilemma: A Study in Conflict and Cooperation.* Ann Arbor: University of Michigan, 1965.

Rees, Wyn. *The Western European Union at the Crossroads: Between Trans-Atlantic Solidarity and European Integration.* Boulder: Westport, 1998.

Rittberger, Volker, ed. Volker Rittberger, ed., *International Regimes in East-West Politics.* London: Pinter, 1990.

_____. *Regime Theory and International Relations.* New York: Oxford University, 1993.

Rock, Stephen R. *Why Peace Breaks Out: Great Power Rapprochement in Historical Perspective.* Chapel Hill: University of North Carolina, 1989.

Rosecrance, Richard. *Action and Reaction in World Politics: International Systems in Perspective.* Boston: Little Brown, 1963.

_____. *Cooperation in A World Without Enemies: Solving the Public Goods Problem.* Working Paper, no. 2. Berkeley: University of California, 1992.

_____. *The Rise of the Trading State: Commerce and Conquest in the Modern World.* New York: Basic Books, 1986.

Rosenau, James N., and Ernst-Otto Czempiel, eds. *Governance Without Government: Order and Change in World Politics.* Cambridge: Cambridge University, 1992.

Rotberg, Robert I., and Theodore K. Rabb, eds. *The Origin and Prevention of Major Wars.* Cambridge: Cambridge University, 1989.

Rothwell, Victor. *Britain and the Cold War, 1941-1947.* London: Cape Books, 1982.

Ruggie, John G., ed. *Multilateralism Matters: The Theory and Praxis of an Institutional Form.* New York: Columbia University, 1993.

_____. *Winning the Peace: America and World Order in the New Era.* New York: Columbia University, 1996.

Ruiz Palmer, Diego A. *French Strategic Options in the 1990s.* Adelphi Papers 260 (Summer 1991).

Russell, Greg. *Hans J. Morgenthau and the Ethics of American Statecraft.* Baton Rouge: Louisiana State University, 1990.

Schelling, Thomas C. *Arms and Influence.* New Haven: Yale University, 1966.

Schumpeter, Joseph. *The History of Economic Analysis.* New York: Oxford University, 1954.

Serfaty, Simon. *France, De Gaulle, and Europe: The Policy of the Fourth and Fifth Republics Toward the Continent.* Baltimore: Johns Hopkins, 1968.

_____. *Memories of Europe's Future: Farewell to Yesteryear.* Washington, D.C.: CSIS, 1999.

_____. *Stay the Course: European Unity and Atlantic Solidarity.* Washington, D.C.: CSIS, 1997.

Sick, Gary S., and Lawrence G. Potter, eds. *The Persian Gulf at the Millennium: Essays in Politics, Economy, Security, and Religion.* New York: St. Martin's, 1997.

Simon, Jeffrey. *NATO Enlargement.* New York: New York University, 1997.

Smith, Mark. *NATO Enlargement During the Cold War: Strategy and System in the Western Alliance.* London: Palgrave, 2000.

Smith, Michael, and Stephen Woolcock. *Redefining the U.S.-EC Relationship.* New York: Council on Foreign Affairs, 1993.

Snith, Tony. *America's Mission: The United States and the Worldwide Struggle for Democracy in the Twentieth Century* (Princeton: Princeton University, 1994).

Sperling, James, and Emil Kirchner. *Recasting the European Security Order: Security Architectures and Economic Cooperation (Europe in Change).* Manchester: Manchester University, 1997.

Spiezio, Kim Edward. *Beyond Containment: Reconstructing European Security.* Boulder: Lynne Reiner, 1995.

Stares, Paul. *The New Germany and the New Europe.* Washington, D.C.: Brookings Institute, 1992.

Stebbins, Richard P. *The United States in World Affairs, 1951.* New York: Council on Foreign Relations, 1952.

Stein, Arthur A. *Why Nations Cooperate: Circumstance and Choice in International Relations.* London: Cornell University, 1990.

Stockholm International Peace Research Institute (SIPRI). *SIPRI Yearbook: Armaments, Disarmament and International Security* (London: Oxford, various years).

Strayer, Joseph R. *On the Medieval Origins of the Modern State.* Princeton: Princeton University, 1970.

Stuart, Douglas T. and Stephen F. Szabo, eds. *Discord and Collaboration in a New Europe: Essays in Honor of Arnold Wolfers.* Washington, D.C.: Johns Hopkins, 1994.

Taylor, Trevor, ed. *Reshaping European Defence.* London: RIIA, 1995.

Tiersky, Ronald. *The Mitterrand Legacy and the Future of French Security Policy.* McNair Papers 43. Washington, D.C.: INSS, 1995.

Tilford, Roger, ed. *Ostpolitik and Political Change in West Germany.* Lexington: Lexington Books, 1975.

Treverton, Gregory. *America, Germany and the Future of Europe.* Princeton: Princeton University, 1992.

Truman, Harry S. *Memoirs: Years of Trial and Hope.* New York: Doubleday, 1956.

Van den Broek, Hans. *Transatlantic Relations in the 1990s: The Emergence of New Security Architectures*. London: Brassey's, 1992.

Van Ham, Peter. *Managing Non-Proliferation Regimes in the 1990s: Power, Politics and Policies*. New York: Council on Foreign Relations, 1994.

Van Heuvan, Marten H.A. *Russia, the United States, and NATO: The Outlook for European Security*. Atlantic Council Occasional Papers. Washington, D.C.: Atlantic Council, 1994.

Viotti, Paul and Mark Kauppi, eds. *International Relations Theory: Realism, Pluralism, Globalism*. New York: MacMillan, 1993.

Walker, R.B.J. *Inside/Outside: International Relations as Political Theory*. Cambridge: Cambridge University, 1993.

Wall, Irwin M. *The United States and the Making of Postwar France, 1945-1954*. New York: Cambridge, 1991.

Walt, Stephen M. *The Origins of Alliances*. Ithaca: Cornell University, 1987.

Waltz, Kenneth N. *Man, the State and War: A Theoretical Analysis*. New York: Columbia University, 1959.

_____. *The Theory of International Politics*. Reading, MA: Addison Wesley, 1979.

Willis, F. Roy. *France, Germany and the New Europe: 1945-1963*. Stanford: Stanford University, 1965.

Wood, Adrian, Raymond Apthorpe and John Borton, eds. *Evaluating International Humanitarian Action*. New York: Zed Books, 2001.

Wood, Stephen. *Germany, Europe and the Persistence of Nations: Transformation, Interests and Identity, 1989-1996*. Aldershot: Ashgate, 1998.

Wyatt-Walker, Holly. *European Community and the Security Dilemma, 1972-92*. New York: St. Martin's, 1997.

Young, John W. *Britain and European Integration, 1945-1992*. New York: St. Martin's, 1993.

_____. *Britain, France and the Unity of Europe, 1945-1951*. Leicester: University of Leicester, 1984.

Young, Oran R. *International Governance: Protecting the Environment in a Stateless Society*. Ithaca: Cornell University, 1994.

Zahniser, Marvin R. *Uncertain Friendship: American-French Diplomatic Relations Through the Cold War*. New York: Wiley, 1975.

Articles

Ackerman, Alice, and Antonio Pala. "From Peacekeeping to Preventative Deployment: A Study of the United Nations in the Former Yugoslav Republic of Macedonia." *European Security* 5, no. 1 (Spring 1996): 83-97.

Adler, Emanuel. "Seeds of Peaceful Change: The OSCE as a Pluralistic Security-making Institution." Paper presented at the Carnegie Council on Ethics and International Affairs, Merrill House Program in New York City (December 1-2, 1995).

Anthony, Ian, Pieter D. Wezeman, and Siemon T. Wezeman. "The Volume of Transfers of Major Conventional Weapons, 1988-97." *SIPRI Arms Transfers Project Report* (17 July 1997).

Art, Robert J. "Why Western Europe Needs the United States and NATO." *Political Science Quarterly* 111, no. 1 (Spring 1996): 1-40.

Ashley, R. "The Poverty of Neorealism." *International Organization* 38 (1984): 225-286.

Atlantic Council. *Third Party Arms Transfers: Requirements for the 21st Century.* Atlantic Council Policy Paper (September 1998).

Augustine, Norman R. "Reengineering the Arsenal of Democracy." *Atlantic Council of the United States: Bulletin* 9, no. 6 (August 1998).

Axelrod, Robert, and Robert O. Keohane. "Achieving Cooperation Under Anarchy: Strategies and Institutions." *World Politics* 38, no. 1 (October 1985): 226-54.

Baker, Pauline H., and John A. Ausink. "State Collapse and Ethnic Violence: Toward a Predictive Model." *Parameters* 26, no. 1 (Spring 1996): 19-31.

Barkin, Samuel, and Bruce Cronin. "The State and the Nation: Changing Norms and Rules of Sovereignty in International Relations." *International Organization* 48 (Winter 1994): 107-30.

Bartelson, Jean. "The Trial of Judgement: A Note on Kant and the Paradoxes of Internationalism." *International Studies Quarterly* 39, no. 2 (June 1995): 255-80.

Bennett, D. Scott. "Security, Bargaining and the End of Interstate Rivalry." *International Studies Quarterly* 40, no. 2 (June 1996): 157-84.

Betts, Richard K. "Systems for Peace or Causes of War? Collective Security, Arms Control and the New Europe." *International Security* 17, no. 1 (Summer 1992): 5-43.

BICC. "US Conversion After the Cold War, 1990-1997: Lessons for Forging a New Conversion Policy." Brief 9. Bonn: BICC, 1997.

Bischak, Greg. *Defense Conversion.* National Commission for Economic Conversion and Defense (NCECD) Fact Sheet. Washington, D.C.: NCECD, 1997.

British American Security Information Council (BASIC). *NATO: Peacekeeping and the United Nations.* Report 94.1 (September 1994).

Bueno de Mesquita, Bruce. "Systemic Polarization and the Occurrence and Duration of War." *The Journal of Conflict Resolution* 22, no. 2 (June 1978): 241-68.

Cadnor, Michael. "Hanging Together: Interoperability Within the Alliance and With Coalition Partners in an Era of Technological Innovation." *NATO Fellowship.* Brussels: NATO (June 1999).

Chirac, Jacques. "Pour un modèle européen." *Libérération* (15 March 1996).

Christensen, Thomas J., and Jack Snyder. "Chain Gangs and Passed Bucks: Predicting Alliance Patterns in Multipolarity." *International Organization* 44, no. 3 (Spring 1990): 137-68.

Clarke, Jonathan G. "The Eurocorps: A Fresh Start in Europe." *Foreign Policy Briefing.* No. 21. Washington, D.C.: Cato Institute, 1992.

Cortell, Andrew P., and James W. Davis, Jr., "How Do International Institutions Matter? The Domestic Impact of International Rules and Norms." *International Studies Quarterly* 40, no. 4 (December 1996): 451-78.

Covault, Craig. "European Politics Burden Weapon Procurements." *Aviation Week & Space Technology* (13 March 1995): 57-61.

_____. "U.S. Export Push Challenges Europeans." *Aviation Week & Space Technology* (27 May 1996): 20-23.

Cragg, Anthony. "The Partnership for Peace Planning and Review Process." *NATO Review* 43, no. 6 (November 1995): 23-25.

Cutileiro, Jose. "WEU's Operational Development and Its relationship With NATO." *NATO Review* 43, no. 5 (September 1995): 8-11.

Deutch, John. "Transatlantic Armaments Cooperation: The United States' Point of View." *International Defense and Technology* (November 1994): 15.

Duffield, John S. "International Regimes and Alliance Behavior: Explaining NATO Counter Force Levels." *International Organization* 46 (Fall 1992): 819-56.

_____. "NATO's Functions After the Cold War." *Political Science Quarterly* 109, no. 5 (Winter 1994-95): 763-88.

Elrod, Richard B. "The Concert of Europe: A Fresh Look at an International System." *World Politics* 28 (January 1976): 159-74.

Ewing, Raymond C. "NATO and Mediterranean Security." *Atlantic Council of the United States, Bulletin 8*, no. 4 (March 1997).

Farkas, Andrew. "The Evolution of International Norms." *International Studies Quarterly* 40, no. 3 (September, 1996): 342-62.

Favretto, Marcella, and Tasos Kokkinides. "Anarchy in Albania: Collapse of European Collective Security." *Basic Paper* 21 (June 1997).

Fitz-Gerald, A. M., and F. A. Walthall. "An Integrated Approach to Complex Emergencies: The Kosovo Experience." *The Journal of Humanitarian Assistance* (16 August 2001): available online at http://www.jha.ac/articles/a071.htm.

Florini, Ann. "The Evolution of International Norms." *International Studies Quarterly* 40, no. 3 (September 1996): 363-90.

Forde, Steven. "International Realism and the Science of Politics: Thucydides, Machiavelli, and Neorealism." *International Studies Quarterly* 39, no. 2 (June 1995): 141-60.

Freedman, Lawrence. "Why the West Failed." *Foreign Policy* 97 (Winter 1994): 53-69.

Friedberg, Aaron. "The Changing Relationship Between Economics and Security." *Political Science Quarterly* 106 (Summer 1991): 265-276.

Gaddis, John Lewis. "International Relations Theory and the End of the Cold War." *International Studies* 17, no. 3 (Winter 1992): 233-62.

Gebicki, Wojiech, and Anna Marta Gebicka. "Central Europe: A Shift to the Left?" *Survival* 37, no. 3 (Autumn 1995): 126-38.

Gilpin, Robert. "Economic Evolution of National Systems." *International Studies Quarterly* 40, no, 3 (Spring 1996): 411-32.

Glaser, Charles L. "Realists as Optimists: Cooperation as Self-Help." *International Security* 19, no. 3 (Winter 1994): 50-90.

Goldgeier, John M. "Not Whether But When: Book Review." *Political Science Quarterly* 115, no. 2 (Summer 2000): 315.

Gordon, Philip H. "NATO After 11 September." *Survival* 43, no. 4 (Winter 2001-2002): available online http://www.brook.edu/views/articles/gordon/2002wintersurvival.htm.

Goulden, John. "The WEU's Role in the New Strategic Environment." *NATO Review* 44, no. 3 (May 1996): 21-24.

Grieco, Joseph M. "Anarchy and the Limits of Cooperation: A Realist Critique of the Newest Liberal Institutionalism." *International Organization* 42 (1988): 485-508.

Haas, Ernst B. "Why Collaborate?: Issue Linkages and International Regimes." *World Politics* 3 (1980): 357-405.

Hansenclever, Andreas, Peter Mayer, and Volker Rittberger. "Interests, Power, Knowledge: The Study of International Regimes." *Mershon International Studies Review* 40, no. 2 (October 1996): 177-228.

Harris, Ian. "Order and Justice in the 'Anarchical Society'." *International Affairs* 69, no. 4 (October 1993): 725-42.

Hechter, Michael. "Karl Polanyi's Social Theory: A Critique." *Politics and Society* 10, no. 4 (Fall 1981): 401- 25.

Held, David, and Anthony Mcgrew, "Globalization and the Liberal Democratic State." *Government and Opposition* 28, no. 2 (Spring 1993): 261-85.

Herz, John. "Idealist Internationalism and the Security Dilemma." *World Politics* 2 (1950): 145-57.

Hoffman, Stanley. "Obstinate or Obsolete? The Fate of the Nation-State and the Case of Western Europe." *Daedalus* (1966): 862-915.

Holt, Robert, Brian Job and Lawrence Markus. "Catastrophe Theory and the Study of War." *The Journal of Conflict Resolution* 22, no. 2 (June 1978): 171-208.

Howard, Michael. "1989: A Farewell to Arms?" *International Affairs* 65, no. 3 (Summer 1988): 407-14.

Hurrell, Andrew. "Explaining the Resurgence of Regionalism in World Politics." *Review of International Studies* 21, no. 4 (October 1995): 331-58.

Ikenberry, John G., and Charles A. Kupchan, "Socialization and Hegemonic Power." *International Organization* 44 (Summer 1990): 283-316.

James, Alan. "The Equity of States: Contemporary Manifestations of an Ancient Doctrine." *Review of International Studies* 18, no. 4 (October 1992): 377-92.

James, Patrick. "Structural Realism and the Causes of War." *Mershon International Studies Review* 39, no. 2 (October 1995): 183-99.

Jervis, Robert. "Cooperation Under the Security Dilemma." *World Politics* 30, no. 2 (January 1978): 167-214.

_____. "From Balance to Concert: A Study of International Security Cooperation." *World Politics* 38, no. 1 (October 1985): 58-79.

Joffe, Josef. "Collective Security and the Future of Europe." *Survival* 34, no. 1 (Spring 1992): 36-50.

Joseph, Robert. "Proliferation, Counter-Proliferation and NATO." *Survival* 38, no. 1 (Spring 1996): 111-30.

Kaufman, Stuart J. "The Fragmentation and Consolidation of the International System." *International Organization* 51, no. 2 (Spring 1997): 200.

Keohane, Robert O. "International Institutions: Two Approaches." *International Studies Quarterly* 32, no. 4 (December 1988): 379-96.

Kerbs, Ronald R. "Perverse Institutionalism: NATO and the Greco-Turkish Conflict." *International Organization* 53, no. 2 (Spring 1999): 351.

Kobrin, Stephen J. "Beyond Symmetry: State Sovereignty in a Networked Global Economy." *Carnegie Bosch Institute: Working Paper 95-8*. New York: Carnegie Bosch Institute, 1995.

Kokkinides, Tasos, Lucy Amis and Nino Lorenzini. "Diplomacy and Arms: West Sends Mixed Messages to Aegean Adversaries." *BASIC PAPERS*. No. 29 (August 1998).

Lake, David A. "Leadership, Hegemony, and the International Economy: Naked Emperor or Tattered Monarch With Potential?" *International Studies Quarterly* 37, no. 4 (December 1993): 459-89.

Lansford, Tom. "The Question of France: French Security Choices at Century's End." *European Security* 5, no. 1 (Spring 1996): 44-64.

Layne, Christopher. "The Unipolar Illusion: Why New Great Powers Will Arise." *International Security* 17, no. 4 (Spring 1993): 5-51.

Layne, Christopher, and Benjamin Schwartz. "American Hegemony Without an Enemy." *Foreign Policy* 92 (Fall 1993): 5-23.

Legge, Michael. "The Making of NATO's New Strategy." *NATO Review* 39, no. 6 (December 1991): 9-13.

Liberman, Peter. "The Spoils of Conquest." *International Security* 18, no. 2 (Fall 1993): 125-53.

Lieber, Robert J. "No Transatlantic Divorce in the Offing." *Orbis* 44, no. 4 (Fall 2000): 571-85.

Lievan, Anatol. "A New Iron Curtain." *The Atlantic Monthly* 277, no. 1 (January 1996): 20-25.

Mearsheimer, John J. "The False Promise of International Institutions." *International Security* 19, no. 3 (Winter 1994): 5-49.

Millar, Alistair, and Tasos Kokkinides. "NATO Expansion and the Excluded Countries: A New Division of Europe?" *BASIC Notes* (July 1997).

Miller, J. "Sovereignty as a Source of Vitality for the State." *Review of International Studies* 12 (April 1986): 79-90.

Milner, Helen. "International Theories of Cooperation Among Nations: Strengths and Weaknesses." *World Politics* 44, no. 3 (April 1992): 466-96.

Nardin, Terry. "International Ethics and International Law." *Review of International Studies* 18, no. 1 (January 1992): 19-30.

Papayoanou, Paul A. "Economic Interdependence and the Balance of Power." *International Studies Quarterly* 41, no. 1 (March 1997): 113-40.

Plesch, Daniel T. "Kosovo: A Symptom of NATO's Strategic Failure." *Basic* (7 April 1999).

Plesch, Daniel T., and Sam Fournier. "East Embraced in NATO's Arms." *The Nation* (December 25, 1995): 823-27.

Powell, Robert. "Anarchy in International Relations Theory: The Neorealist-Neoliberal Debate." *International Organization* 48 (1994): 313-344.

Pruneau, Renee. "WMD Proliferation From the Southern Tier of the Former Soviet Union." Paper presented at the International Security Studies Section of the International Studies Association Conference on October 31, 1996 in Atlanta, Georgia.

Pula, Gazmend. "Self-Determination: A Non-Confrontational Option for the Kosova Crisis." *Balkan Forum* 4, no. 3 (September 1996): 202-15.

Purver, Robert. "The Threat of Chemical and Biological Terrorism." *The Monitor: Nonproliferation, Demilitarization and Arms Control* 2, no. 4 (Fall 1996): 7.

Putnam, Robert. "Diplomacy and Domestic Politics: The Logic of Two-Level Games." *International Organization* 42 (Summer 1988): 427-61.

Rauf, Tariq. "Cleaning Up With a Bang." *Bulletin of the Atomic Scientists* 48, no. 1 (January 1992): 9.

Raymond, Gregory A. "Problems and Prospects in the Study of International Norms." *Mershon International Studies Review* 41, no. 2 (November 1997): 205-46.

Reinicke, Wolfgang H. "Global Public Policy." *Foreign Affairs* 76, no. 6 (November/December 1997): 127-39.

Richard, Alain. *L'Armement* (March 1998). Reprinted by FED- CREST (1 June 1998).

Rosecrance, Richard. "International Relations Theory Revisited." *International Organization* 35, no. 4 (Autumn 1981): 705-6.

_____. "The Rise of the Virtual State." *Foreign Affairs* 75, no. 4 (July/August 1996): 45-61.

_____. "The U.S.–Japan Trading Relationship and Its Effects." *Global Legal Studies Journal* 1, no. 1 (Fall 1993).

Rosecrance, Richard, and Chih-Cheng Lo. "Balancing, Stability, and War: The Mysterious Case of the Napoleonic International System." *International Studies Quarterly* 40, no. 4 (December 1996): 479-500.

Rosenblatt, Lionel A., and Larry Thompson. "Humanitarian Emergencies: Saving Lives and Resources." *SAIS Review* 15, no. 2 (Summer 1995): 91-110.

Ruggie, John Gerard. "Consolidating the European Pillar: The Key to NATO's Future." *The Washington Quarterly* 20, no. 1 (Winter 1997): 109-125.

_____. "Territoriality and Beyond: Problematizing Modernity in International Relations." *International Organization* 47 (Winter 1993): 139-74.

_____. "Third Try at World Order? America and Multilateralism After the Cold War." *Political Science Quarterly* 109 (Fall 1994): 553-70.

Rühe, Volker. "Europe and the Alliance: Key Factors for Peace and Stability." *NATO Review* 41 (June 1993): 12-15.

Samuelson, Paul A. "The Pure Theory of Public Expenditure." *Review of Economics and Statistics* 36 (1954): 375-97.

Sapiro, Miriam. "The OSCE: An Essential Component of European Security." *Insight* no. 15 (March 1997): 2-3.

Schlesinger, James. "Leadership in the New World Order: New Instabilities, New Priorities." *Foreign Policy* 85 (Winter 1992): 3-25.

Schulte, Gregory L. "Responding to Proliferation: NATO's Role." *NATO Review* 43, no. 4 (July 1995): 7-9.

Schumpeter, Joseph. "The Crisis of the Tax State." *International Economic Papers*. No. 4. London: Macmillan, 1954.

Schweller, Randall L. "Bandwagoning for Profit: Bringing the Revisionist State Back In." *International Security* 19, no. 1 (Summer 1994): 77-107.

_____. "Neorealism's Status-Quo Bias: What Security Dilemma?" *Security Studies*. Special Issue, Realism: Restatements and Renewal, 5, no. 3 (Spring 1996): 90-121.

Shevtsov, Leontiy P. "Russian-NATO Military Cooperation in Bosnia: A Basis for the Future?" *NATO Review* 45, no. 2 (March 1997): 12-15.

Seidt, Hans-Ulrich. "Lessons Learnt From the Crisis in the Balkans." *European Security* 5, no. 1 (Spring 1996): 65-70.

Snyder, Glenn H. "Alliance Theory: A Neorealist First Cut." *International Affairs* 44, no. 1 (Spring 1990): 103-24.

Solana, Javier. "Preparing for the Madrid Summit." *NATO Review* 45, no. 2 (March 1997): 3.

Sparaco, Pierre. "Europeans Advocate Unified Defense Market." *Aviation Week & Space Technology* (25 July 1994): 54.

Stefani, Andrea. "Gazeta Shqiptare." *Balkan Media and Policy Monitor* 3 (July 1997): 18.

Thomson, Janice E. "State Sovereignty in International Relations: Bridging the Gap Between Theory and Empirical Research." *International Studies Quarterly* 39, no. 2 (June 1995): 213-34.

Tripolskaya-Mitlyng, Viktoria. "Eastern Cheers, Russian Jeers, American Silence." *Bulletin of the Atomic Scientists* 53, no. 1 (January 1997): 5.

Ullmann-Margalit, Edna. "The Revision of Norms." *Ethics* 100 (July 1990): 756-67.

Underdal, Arild. "The Concept of 'Regime Effectiveness'." *Cooperation and Conflict* 27 (Fall 1992): 227-240.

Voisin, Gabriel, and Charles Voisin. "Breaking Taboos in European Defense Industry Consolidation." *TTU* (17 July 1997). Reprinted by FED-CREST (28 October 1997).

Von Moltke, Gebhardt. "NATO Moves Towards Enlargement." *NATO Review* 44, no. 1 (January 1996): 3-6.

Wagner, R. Harrison. "Deterrence and Bargaining." *The Journal of Conflict Resolution* 26, no. 2 (June 1982): 329-58.

Wallander, Celeste A. "Institutional Assets and Adaptability: NATO After the Cold War." *International Organization* 54, no. 4 (Autumn 2000): 705-36.

Walt, Stephen M. "Alliance Formation and the Balance of World Power." *International Security* 9, no. 4 (Spring 1985): 225-41.

Waltz, Kenneth. "The Emerging Structure of International Politics." *International Security* 18, no. 2 (Fall 1993): 44-79.

_____. "The Stability of a Bipolar World," *Daedalus* 93 (Summer 1964): 881-909.

Weber, Katja. "Hierarchy Amidst Anarchy: A Transaction Costs Approach to International Security Cooperation." *International Studies Quarterly* 41, no. 2 (June 1997): 321-40.

Weinberger, Casper. "The Helsinki Summit: Fact vs. Fiction." *Forbes* 159, no. 9 (5 May 1997): 37.

Williams, Nick. "Partnership for Peace: Permanent Fixture or Declining Asset?" *Survival* 38, no. 1 (Spring 1996): 98-110.

Wright, Neill. "Civil Military Cooperation in Peacekeeping and Humanitarian Operations." Paper delivered as the *NATO/Croatian Seminar on Civil-Military Cooperation* in Florence, Italy (17 May 2000).

Zelikow, Philip. "The Masque of Institutions." *Survival* 38, no. 1 (Spring 1996): 6-18.

Index

All for One

1915